Working World
Careers in International Education, Exchange, and Development

Sherry L. Mueller
Mark Overmann

Washington, D.C. / Georgetown University Press

Georgetown University Press, Washington, D.C.
www.press.georgetown.edu

Library of Congress Cataloging-in-Publication Data

Mueller, Sherry Lee, 1943-
    Working world : careers in international education, exchange, and development / Sherry L. Mueller and Mark Overmann.
        p. cm.
    Includes bibliographical references and index.
    ISBN-13: 978-1-58901-210-3 (alk. paper)
    1. Job hunting. 2. Employment in foreign countries—Vocational guidance. 3. International education—Vocational guidance.
    4. Globalization—Economic aspects. I. Overmann, Mark. II. Title.
    HF5382.7.M84 2008
    337.702--dc22

                                                        2007050931

∞ This book is printed on acid-free paper meeting the requirements of the American National Standard for Permanence in Paper for Printed Library Materials.

15 14 13 12 11 10 09 08   9 8 7 6 5 4 3 2
First printing

Printed in the United States of America

To the dedicated citizen diplomats throughout the United States who are part of the National Council for International Visitors. Your work turning strangers into friends is an immense contribution to your communities, our country, and our fragile planet.

• • • • •

To the memory of my loving parents, who always encouraged me to explore the world, count my blessings, and give back.
SHERRY L. MUELLER

To Mom and Dad, with love and gratitude, for always helping me— and allowing me—to find my way.
MARK OVERMANN

Everybody says, "Do what you love."
You'll know that you're doing what you love
when you realize that your work is not just a job,
but it's actually part of who you are.
—DAVID GREGORY,
NBC White House correspondent,
American University School of International
Service Commencement Address, May 13, 2007

Don't ask yourself what the world needs.
Ask yourself what makes you come alive,
and then go do that.
Because what the world needs is people who have come alive.
—HOWARD THURMAN,
American author, philosopher,
theologian, educator, and civil rights leader

I don't know what your destiny will be, but one thing I know:
The only ones among you who will be really happy are those who
will have sought and found how to serve.
—ALBERT SCHWEITZER

Contents

Preface

Working World: Careers in International Education, Exchange, and Development
is intended to be a resource and a useful tool for job seekers in international affairs, particularly those interested in international education, exchange, and development. It is designed to ease the burden of the initial
stages of career research and help you put your job search in broader perspective. The approaches and lessons shared throughout the book have
evolved over the course of a rewarding career.

About twenty-five years ago, as a new director at the Institute of
International Education (IIE), I was amazed by the many requests for
"informational interviews" I received each week from job hunters. In the
intervening years, the requests grew exponentially. Motivated originally
by a desire to save time and yet provide sufficient help, in 1982 I initiated what became known as Roundtables on Careers in International Education and Exchange. After several years of conducting monthly roundtables at IIE with Alex Patico, in 1986 Archer Brown and Lorenda
Schrader at NAFSA: Association of International Educators joined us by
hosting the roundtables on alternate months.

Individuals seeking career guidance were invited to the IIE or NAFSA
conference room on the third Thursday of each month. At the roundtable, each participant shared his or her educational and professional background and described the types of positions sought. Then the facilitators
and fellow participants offered suggestions and contributed ideas for the
job search. The roundtables proved much richer than one-on-one interviews because of the synergy that so many perspectives generated. A
group of people inevitably has more knowledge of relevant job openings
and successful job search tactics than one or two individuals do. Collectively, roundtable participants could recommend more resources to explore and offer contrasting analyses of trends in the field. In addition, the
participants did not feel so alone as they interacted with others going
through the solitary activity of a job search.

I gradually realized that the roundtables were much more than a time-saving device for a new manager. They were a particularly useful mechanism for recruiting new staff as well as a tremendous source of information about job seekers, the job search process, and job opportunities in the fields of international education, exchange, and development. The practical ideas, down-to-earth suggestions, and diverse resources offered in my first book on careers, published by NAFSA in 1998, were based on my experience working with hundreds of job seekers in our field for more than fifteen years.

Since that book was published I have given it to each intern at the National Council for International Visitors (NCIV) as a farewell gift and to other young people I wanted to encourage to enter these fields that I find so compelling. Years passed. My supply of books dwindled. Even before I gave the last of them away, I realized how outdated many of the resources had become. The need for a new edition was great not only because the Internet has greatly altered the job search process but also because the fields of international education, exchange, and development have expanded and evolved. In addition, there were other, more nuanced lessons about managing a career that I wanted to share.

This determination to write a new career book blossomed just as I was fortunate to have a young colleague on the NCIV staff who is an extraordinary writer. Mark has an agile mind, an ability to analyze his own experiences, and an engaging personality. Among other responsibilities at NCIV, he produced various publications and served as the editor of our newsletter. He was especially adept at keeping me on schedule writing my monthly column for the *NCIV Network News*. I was consistently impressed by his editorial suggestions.

I must confess that my initial motivation in inviting Mark to coauthor this book was to keep him at NCIV longer because he was so talented and he helped me be more productive. It was only later—after we started our active collaboration and ideas ricocheted between us—that I perceived the real value of juxtaposing my career veteran voice with that of his perspective as a young professional.

It was one of our spirited discussions that prompted our decision to include the profiles of outstanding professionals interspersed throughout part II. We realized that the book would be greatly enriched if we collected the views of others whose achievements we admired. We decided to include highlights of their careers, but we also asked them to distill lessons about networking, mentoring, and other topics that we discuss in part I of this book.

The book begins with some basic concepts to keep in mind as you launch a job search. The second part consists of selected resources that will prompt you to plan your next steps. In between, you will find the profiles of potential role models. You can learn much from their impressive cumulative experience and reflections. The book is designed to be a coherent whole with each chapter building on the preceding one. However, you can also pick and choose, as each chapter is written to stand alone.

Mark and I welcome your comments as well as your recommendations and suggestions for additional resources to be included in future editions. We hope this book will help you chart your course and shape your career in these growing and increasingly challenging fields.

Acknowledgments

We are most grateful to the interns and volunteers who helped compile and annotate the first edition of the selected resources in this book, which was initially assembled as a handout for career roundtable participants. We are deeply indebted to Chris Bassett for giving his time and considerable talents to help us finish the book. His meticulous editing and fact-checking, constructive questions and suggestions, and unfailingly cheerful attitude were invaluable.

We are grateful to Alexander Hunt for his thoughtfulness and guidance in plotting a direction for this book, for his detailed updates and edits, and for bringing his two-and-a-half-pound Yorkshire terrier, Oscar, to working sessions as a much-needed distraction. We also benefited from the research and editing skills of Joanne Tay, Melissa Whited, and other National Council for International Visitors (NCIV) staff members.

We extend a special thank you to Richard Brown, director of Georgetown University Press, for believing that this book would be a creative contribution to the fields and that we were the people to write it.

Mark: I am most grateful for the support that my former NCIV colleagues have shown Sherry and me on this book project as well as all that they have taught me about what it means to create a rewarding career in these exciting fields. My gratitude goes to Jim Stockton, former NCIV board chair, for recognizing that this project was one worth pursuing. I am indebted to Bo for his company and his insightful "editorial suggestions." My most sincere thanks must go to Sherry for inviting me to be a coauthor on this book—it has been a rich and rewarding experience. And last in this list but never least in my life, my love and thanks go to Katie for the unremitting encouragement she gives me and the unwavering confidence she always shows in me.

Sherry: Heartfelt thanks to my family and friends for their steady support and encouragement throughout the writing process—in particular Michael, Kathy, Jamey, and Chivalry. You are my anchors. I would also like to acknowledge my mentors, Bill Olson and Nancy Friedersdorf. Finally, I want to convey my gratitude to the NCIV board chairs I have been privileged to work with since joining the organization: Bruce Buckland, Sandy Madrid, Alan Kumamoto, Phyllis Layton Perry, Jim Stockton, and Larry Chastang. They have valued initiative and contributed in many ways to my professional growth and current view on what it means to embrace a cause.

Introduction
Idealists Preferred

For most of our adult lives, we spend more time at our workplaces than in our own homes. Pursuing a career means making a series of choices that determine what we do with most of our waking hours. Inevitably, each choice we make exacts a price. The key is to be as aware as we can possibly be—up front—of the trade-offs our choices generate.

Some people can be quite comfortable working within the large, elaborately structured bureaucracy of a government department or multinational organization. Others feel much more at home in a smaller, less-structured nonprofit organization. For some, with pressing student loans or a family to support, financial compensation is a primary concern. For others, salary and benefits are trumped by additional considerations. There are no right or wrong answers here—just the awareness that a job search requires engaging in serious reflection, knowing your preferences and predilections, and understanding the circumstances in which you do your best work.

The purpose of this book is to equip you to make good choices. Whether searching for that first entry-level job, making a midcareer change, or considering postretirement employment, it is vital that you make conscious choices and consider carefully the wide array of options within the fields of international education, exchange, and development.

PARAMETERS OF THE FIELDS

As the distinction between "domestic" and "international" becomes increasingly anachronistic, a precise definition of what constitutes a career in these fields is elusive. The fields are amorphous, constantly changing, resettling, then shifting again. The basic assumption of this book is that international education, exchange, and development involve moving

1

people, information, and sometimes supplies across national borders for educational or humanitarian purposes—to establish more effective communications, to tackle global problems, and to build the web of human connections so critical to survival in the twenty-first century. Each of these fields certainly has a unique space in which it operates. Each focuses on distinct goals. However, international education, exchange, and development naturally fit together not only because of the professional interactions that regularly occur across the fields, but also because the work done by many organizations, such as the Academy for Educational Development (AED), encompasses all three. In addition, and perhaps most important, the fields are all dedicated to improving the quality of life on our fragile planet. A Peace Corps volunteer in Paraguay, a U.S. historian teaching at the American School in Tangiers, a program manager for Save the Children in Sudan, a visiting Fulbright scholar from Odessa teaching at Indiana University, the president of the International Visitors Center of Philadelphia, a development consultant to a USAID contractor working regularly in West Africa, the manager of an IIE-administered project for teachers in Japan, and a cultural attaché at the U.S. Embassy in Bulgaria are all part of the mix.

Jobs in the fields are in every sector. An increasing number are in the nonprofit world—in nongovernmental organizations (NGOs), private voluntary organizations (PVOs), educational institutions, and other agencies. The overriding reality pertaining to most of these jobs is that the financial rewards are modest compared with those in the corporate sector. Most individuals aspiring to work in the fields of international education, exchange, and development are motivated more by a desire for psychological satisfaction than financial gain. They are genuinely idealistic, wanting to make a difference in the world and a contribution to a specific positive result. For example, we know a program officer at the Meridian International Center who is absolutely committed to helping the foreign leaders from the Middle East who are participating in the U.S. Department of State's International Visitor Leadership Program understand the United States and its democratic institutions. He is also determined to help U.S. citizens comprehend the complexity and historic circumstances that drive so many of the events in the Middle East. It is unlikely that his efforts will make him rich in monetary terms, but he is blessed with many psychological rewards as the impact of his work becomes apparent at home and abroad.

One example from Sherry's own career may help illustrate what we mean by psychological satisfaction. Sherry described this experience in her first book on careers:

> *Some years ago, before apartheid ended in South Africa, I was watching Ted Koppel's show* Nightline *on television. The format was a town meeting concerning South Africa. As I watched, I realized that I knew one of the men being interviewed. He was the current minister of education of South Africa and was arguing for the end of apartheid. I had served as his program officer at the Institute of International Education twelve years earlier when he was a participant in the U.S. Information Agency's International Visitor Program.[1] I remembered sending him to communities in Alabama and Oklahoma to study successful integration efforts in the United States. The realization that in some small way my work may have helped nudge a South African leader toward ending apartheid was powerful indeed. This experience was just one of many times I have known without a doubt that I chose the right career.*

A JOB VERSUS A CAREER

A job comprises a set of responsibilities that you accept at one point in time. A career is the trajectory of your cumulative efforts. It describes your accomplishments in a series of jobs—the impact you have made. As noted at the outset, charting your career is making a series of choices that determine what you do with most of your waking hours. These choices determine the context for your potential achievements. Each choice we make precludes others. We must emphasize again that it is essential to be knowledgeable about the trade-offs our choices involve.

The title of this introduction, "Idealists Preferred," reflects the basic assumption underlying this book: people drawn to careers in international education, exchange, and development want to have a positive impact. They envision their careers making a tangible difference in our turbulent world. "You are either part of the problem or part of the solution" is an often-quoted but relevant adage. People drawn to these fields want to be part of the solution.

"Idealists Preferred" was inspired by the original advertisement used to recruit Pony Express riders in 1860: "Wanted: Young, wiry, skinny fellows under the age of 18. Must be expert riders willing to risk death daily. Wages $25 per week. Orphans preferred." As the president of the National Council for International Visitors, Sherry presents speeches on citizen diplomacy and she often quotes the original advertisement. Then she recounts a revised version of this historic ad that she suggests her audience has already answered: "Wanted: Young at heart of all ages. Must be well-organized, eager to learn, and willing to risk breaking stereotypes daily. Wages—won't be discussed. Idealists preferred."

In fact, this ad is one that not only citizen diplomats but also most people drawn to careers in international education, exchange, and development have answered, at least on a subconscious level. They are idealists. They desire to make a positive difference. They are motivated by the notion of service. It is no surprise that one of the most popular job search websites for the fields is Idealist.org.

This book is designed to aid you in fashioning a career that allows your idealist inclinations to thrive. When structuring this volume, we kept in mind that your job search and career development can be a demanding, time-consuming process. Thus the book need not be read from front to back or cover to cover. Rather, it is divided into clearly marked and easily digestible parts and chapters, each of which can be read or skimmed alone. First there is the broad advice on career development offered in part I. We play on our differences in generation, experience, and viewpoint in these chapters to provide a nuanced perspective on several important facets of career development. Then there are the specific resources available in part II—lists of organizations and print and web resources designed to lead you to all manner of career possibilities in the fields of international education, exchange, and development. These resources are categorized much like a travel guide book so that you might easily skim the material and select those resources that catch your eye. And finally there are the profiles of professionals scattered throughout part II. These profiles can stand alone as intriguing portraits of how twelve people have shaped contrasting yet rewarding careers in these fields. However, taken together, they become a rich collection of anecdotes and advice for someone who feels drawn to similar career paths.

When using this book, it is important for you to determine what is best for you, and to pick and choose the resources that most closely fit with your career aspirations. Yet remember that just as creating a meaningful career is more than landing one job, your career exploration should include persistent research in more than one place. Take the time to investigate all that *Working World* has to offer, and in the end we hope that you will feel confident and prepared for the exciting opportunities that lie ahead.

Note

1. Since 1999 this U.S. government-sponsored program hs been administered once again by the U.S. Department of State. In 2004, it was renamed the International Visitor Leadership Program (IVLP).

Part I

Shaping Your Career Philosophy

Part I suggests a way of thinking about your career and leads you to consider a variety of activities that make up career development. While our focus in this book is primarily on the fields of international education, exchange, and development, the approaches discussed in part I can be useful to career seekers in many fields.

We first examine the need to identify your cause. Your cause is the underlying force that drives your career. We agree with journalist David Gregory's observation quoted at the start of the book: "You'll know that you're doing what you love when you realize that your work is not just a job, but it's actually part of who you are." As you work, if you are typically oblivious to time rather than constantly clock-watching, waiting for 5:00 p.m. to come, this is a good signal that you are doing what you love. Athletes call it "being in the zone." You are so caught up in what you are doing and derive so much satisfaction from it that you would keep that occupation even if you won the lottery. Identifying your cause will help you find a job that becomes a part of who you are.

We next turn to the frequently mentioned yet seldom analyzed art of networking. If the buildings in which we work caught fire, Sherry would grab her Rolodex and Mark would be sure he had his flash drive so our lists of contacts would not be lost. Whether the format is old-fashioned or electronic, the size and accessibility of the network of colleagues at your disposal is a key element in your job search and career development—and of real value to a potential employer. There are many methods and approaches to networking, several of which are discussed in this chapter. We also emphasize that the potential benefits of networking are not always clear when a new relationship begins.

In chapter 3 we encourage you to consider the value of having mentors, as well as the gratification of serving as a mentor. The kind of one-on-one tutoring a mentor provides and the example he or she sets are invaluable as you chart your career path. In addition, mentors often act as your best and most enthusiastic references. Some people have clearly defined mentors in their lives while others do not. Either way, most professionals have benefited from the wisdom and guidance of a friend or colleague at some juncture.

In the last chapter of part I we tackle the concept of professionalism. People are frequently admonished to "act like professionals," yet the exact meaning of this phrase can be elusive. We define what it means from each of our perspectives. We also explore the important notion that pursuing a career is a continuous journey, not simply something a person does intermittently while engaging in a job search.

COMBINED VOICES OF A CAREER VETERAN AND A YOUNG PROFESSIONAL

When American anthropologist Margaret Mead published the book *Culture and Commitment* in 1970, she conveyed her keen understanding of how modern culture has changed the way we learn and our sources of information. She reminded her readers that for centuries, young people looked to their elders as the font of knowledge. She also observed that this was quickly changing. People were finding many other sources of information. They were looking to their peers rather than to their parents. Think about how often in today's society the older person is dependent on the younger to help solve some pesky computer problem or resolve some other technical glitch. In some ways the traditional approach to knowledge acquisition described by Mead has made a U-turn. The trend she identified years ago has accelerated.

We acquire knowledge and access information in multiple ways. This idea suggested to us that the value of juxtaposing a career veteran voice with that of a promising young professional would produce a much richer experience for the reader than either author could alone. In the collaboration process, we discovered that our interaction helped each of us challenge our assumptions and develop our ideas with greater rigor. Discussing the generation gap between us helped us better understand the value of our respective approaches. We came to appreciate that, in a way, our collaboration process is just what has to happen in workplaces across the country as leaders work to tap the valuable institutional memory and experience of older employees and blend it with the fresh approach and technological dexterity of their younger colleagues. We hope that by guiding you to approach your job search with this realization in mind you will be better equipped to function in a workplace that requires constructive intergenerational cooperation.

Chapter 1
Identifying Your Cause

People often ask children, "What do you want to be when you grow up?" Children usually reply "a fireman, a doctor, an actor . . . ," perhaps echoing a recent movie or naming the profession of a relative they admire. They have yet to realize that they will be asked this question over and over again as the years pass. Hearing the question as children was just our first experience with identifying our cause.

Your cause is a major force that guides your career decisions. Whether clearly defined and structured, or perhaps hazy and still in need of refinement, your cause is, as Howard Thurman phrases it in the quotation at the beginning of this book, "what makes you come alive." In this first chapter we focus not on finding you a job with clearly defined steps up a structured career ladder but on helping you locate something much bigger—the force that will help illuminate your career path.

Sherry approaches the quest to identify a cause from the perspective of "your place in history": how your search for a cause is inevitably anchored in the trends and happenings of a particular period in history. How will you find your place in today's historical context? What will historians say about your cause and career when looking back on them many years from now? Or more important, what would you *want* those historians to say? In Sherry's view how you approach these questions will help you define your cause and develop your career.

Mark, on the other hand, approaches the issue of finding a cause from the postcollege question of "What am I going to do with my life?" For him, there is less focus on the bigger picture of finding a place in history and more attention to microlevel decision making, namely, figuring out what is good for you at this point and going from there. Even if you are unsure of your exact cause or how you will want historians to view your career choices, Mark urges you to go with what you *do* know. Pursue your interests, follow your feelings, and listen to your gut. If a certain path is attractive at this point in your life, it is probably a good direction in which to head, even if you're not sure of your ideal destination.

SHERRY
Your Place in History

There are certain forces at work—economic, political, military, and social factors—that make possible, or restrict, certain job options. Understanding these factors can help you approach your job search more realistically. Certainly the economic marketplace is vastly different for you than it was for your parents. In recent years I have often fielded the question, "How can I explain to my father why it is taking me so long to find full-time work when he found his first job right after graduation?"

Although one can certainly point to many bureaucratic organizations with multiple hierarchies, technological advances and current management practices now suggest that lean, downsized, and restructured organizations are the norm in both the for-profit and nonprofit worlds. In some cases the result has been the reduction of jobs in traditional institutions or an increase in one part of the world with a corresponding reduction in other geographic areas.

Paradoxically, there are fewer jobs at the top of many organizations (upper management), as well as fewer at the bottom (receptionists, secretaries, clerks). A job that represents a rung on the career ladder in the traditional sense is increasingly scarce; it will perhaps be outmoded in a few decades.

We tend to think of history as those events that occurred before we were born. In our schoolbooks, history seems to be a series of dramatic events, such as revolutions, wars, and social movements, all far in the past. We should bear in mind that some decades hence our time on earth also will be a "historical" period. Historians will assign labels and designations, analyze trends, and otherwise describe the context in which we now live. Your effort to find your place at this particular point in history may be more productive if you start by viewing your career in a more holistic way. Instead of focusing on finding a job with clearly defined next steps in the same organization, focus on identifying your cause.

As Mark and I were discussing this chapter, we reflected on the historic context in which I started my career compared with the backdrop that existed when he launched his. As a farm kid from northern Illinois, I chose to attend the School of International Service at American

University. I didn't even know what the Foreign Service was, but what I did know was that serving internationally was appealing. A child of the cold war, I graduated from college and attended graduate school in the late '60s. Despite the assassination of President John F. Kennedy, the stirring words of his inaugural address continued to motivate many of my generation as we began our career journeys: "Ask not what your country can do for you but what you can do for your country." The Alliance for Progress with Latin America and the newly minted Peace Corps were just two sources of job opportunities that beckoned at the time. There was a call to public service. We had not yet become as disillusioned with our major institutions or those in authority as we are today. Despite the hovering nuclear threat, it was in many ways an easier time.

In the cold war era the United States was the "good guy." The U.S. was universally (in some cases grudgingly) admired. There was not a lot of ambiguity. In fact, the superpower prism was a somewhat comforting, if overly simplistic, way to view the world. The book titled *The Ugly American* by Eugene Lederer and William Burdick, published in 1958, was instructive and, in retrospect, one of the key factors that inspired my own career in international education and exchange. Though it is a novel, it nonetheless makes trenchant observations about the need for cultural and political sensitivity, effective approaches to development, and behaviors that produce constructive international relations. These are still valid. The authors prompted me to identify my cause. I wanted a career that would help project a positive image of the United States abroad.

In the intervening years the Vietnam War and other events produced disillusionment, distrust of authority, and a much more variegated and complex global scene. As I often jokingly reply to colleagues and friends when asked about my cause: "I am still idealistic; I still want to save the world. Only now, I realize just how reluctant the world is to be saved!"

Mark and his contemporaries face this complexity and the crisis of credibility surrounding many institutions much earlier in their lives than I and many of my idealistic classmates did years ago. Ironically, given these conditions, the need for exceptionally able people in service-oriented fields, such as international education, exchange, and development, has never been greater.

What Do You Care about Passionately?
The "Magic Wand Test"

Ask yourself, "If I had a magic wand, what would I do to make a difference in the world?" Leading a Council for International Visitors, preventing or curing river blindness in Burkina Faso, advising international students at a university, managing a major development project to establish village health clinics, organizing short-term exchange programs for parliamentarians, librarians, and farmers—these are all potential answers. There are many more as well. Part of the challenge is comprehending the array of options. Whatever cause you might espouse, chances are there are various organizations working to make a difference in that area. Your cause is their mission.

The impetus to get a job, or to find a new one, comes from various sources. Almost always, the urge to fashion a career with an international focus stems from a particularly positive international experience, such as living with a host family on an exchange program, hosting an exchange student in your own home, participating in a short-term development project overseas, serving as a Peace Corps volunteer, or studying abroad. The intense learning experience generated by the face-to-face encounters, the conversations, and the dawning awareness of intriguing cultural differences and common human aspirations prompts us to want to replicate this wonder-filled experience for others, as well as for ourselves. The desire to help solve some global problem observed during the overseas experience may also inspire the determination to chart a career in international education, exchange, or development.

My own experience is a good example. At the urging of an American University professor, Alexander Trowbridge, I participated in an Experiment in International Living (EIL) program in 1963. That eye-opening summer experience included living with a German family and traveling in Germany, Austria, and Switzerland with a group of German and American students. My host family exposed me to so many new and exciting experiences. It was a time of intense learning and adventure. My worldview grew and became more nuanced. I came home determined to be an EIL leader and take my own group of students abroad, which I did in 1969—a memorable trip to the Soviet Union. After visits back and forth over the years, my "German sister" remains a dear friend. That kind of deep connection across time and culture continues to be an immense source of learning and satisfaction. My passion became finding jobs that enabled me to give others opportunities for similar, enduring relationships that transcend nationality and other differences.

I literally do keep a "magic wand" on my desk. I use it to remind job seekers (and myself) that it is important to suspend limitations and just reflect on what you would do if no obstacles existed. Your answer is an essential clue to identifying your cause. The rest of this book concerns the process of identifying those organizations whose mission you can embrace and learning how to present yourself to employers so they recognize that your cause and their mission are congruent.

Get Specific

Once you have identified your cause, it is critical to answer three sets of questions:

1. Where (in what geographic location) do you want to work?
The answer may indeed be "anywhere," but be sure that is your considered answer. There are many international jobs that do not require a perpetually peripatetic existence. Of course, others require worldwide availability, or the willingness to relocate to a specific project site or other destination determined by the nature of the work. For example, if you are working for the Red Cross as a specialist in humanitarian assistance, you may be required to go to wherever the latest crisis has struck. Hurricanes, earthquakes, and conflicts determine your worksites. Some job seekers know they want to be in a particular country; others must, at the moment, stay in a particular locale because of obligations to a family member or because they need to be rooted in a place for their own identity and effectiveness.

2. How do you want to spend your days? What kinds of tasks do you enjoy most? What news stories you read first, what subjects you enjoyed most in college, and what tasks you first tackle in your current job are valuable clues to your professional preferences and inclinations. What sorts of skills and talents do you offer? To what extent do you want to interact with international clients?
There are many international jobs where minimal contact with internationals is the norm. If you think you want to be a foreign

student adviser, which requires daily face-to-face contact with international students, then you may want to avoid a job where your only contact with internationals is by e-mail, fax, or telephone—unless, of course you see it as useful preparation for an aspiring foreign student adviser.

3. What type of organizational culture do you prefer? Do you thrive in a large, structured environment or do you shine in an environment where being a self-starter and having initiative is highly valued? What type of supervisor motivates you to do your best?

Many job seekers underestimate the role their boss plays until after they are ensconced in a job. To the extent possible, you want to work for people who care about your professional growth and development, even if you sacrifice a bit on the salary side of the ledger. When you are interviewing for a job, you are actually interviewing with someone who reflects and shapes the culture of a particular organization. This is the person who will give you assignments. And this is probably the person you will ask for a reference at some point. The value of having a supervisor you respect, admire, and learn from is tremendous. In fact, it supersedes many other considerations, such as job title and pay.

MARK

What Am I Going to Do with My Life?

While teaching English in the northeast part of China the year after college graduation, I found myself feeling pessimistic, as evidenced by journal entries like this one:

> *I don't know what the hell to do about grad school—or my life for that matter. People tell me I shouldn't worry so much about the future because "life is what happens when you're busy making other plans." That's all well and good for John Lennon— but apparently he never had his dad hounding him day after day about getting a job and figuring his life out. I'd really like someone to come along and just* tell *me where I need to be.*

If you have ever, at least for a minute, wondered what you should do with your life, you are not alone. At some point, everyone has had that feeling—that perplexing, sinking, fish-out-of-water feeling. You know you need to proceed into your future, but you have no inkling of which direction to go, or even where to take that first step. You are wondering, to paraphrase myself, "What the hell should I do with my life?"

I am not always so negative, however. Back when I was studying in France during my junior year of college, I was more optimistic about my search for a life and career course:

> *You never know where the wiry arms of the world are going to push you. . . . Many people saw my coming to France to study for a year as misguided and perhaps fundamentally against the purpose of my major, English. From time to time I still doubt my choices both to come to France and to pursue English as a major. But, in general, I believe they were both wise choices because they challenge me and, quite simply, because they feel right.*

Looking back on this, I am surprised to find that I was so comfortable with "going with what feels right," especially at a time when I was beginning to feel the growing pressure of making postgraduation plans. This sense of going with my gut stayed with me when I decided to go to China for a year, or as my dad characterized it, "put off the inevitable." Later, when figuring out what to do once I got back to the United States, I attempted to keep perspective:

> *What do I want to do? Where do I need to be? . . . In the movie* Forrest Gump, *Jenny asks Forrest, "Who do you want to be?" Forrest responds, "Aren't I going to be me?" And that hints at the*

key to it all. As I am going through all of this examination and self-discovery, making decisions about grad school and trying to answer those questions, I must remember to be true to myself. Shakespeare said it in Hamlet: "This above all: To thine own self be true!". John Wooden said it: "You must have the courage to be true to yourself!". Even Tom Hanks said it. Be true to yourself and you can't go wrong.

My career, short as it has been up to this point, has not been strategically planned. I have always been a person of many interests but without ideas about how to channel those interests into a coherent professional life. Yet one thing that I have always tried to do is go with what feels right. Often this mentality led to choices that seemed random to others, or not in line with the path I was seemingly headed down or that they wanted me to follow. Somehow, though, those choices felt right to me. I went with them. Studying abroad in France even though I was an English major; spending a year in China even though I had no experience with Asia or the Chinese language; interning at a regional newspaper, then a nonprofit organization, then the Embassy of France . . . I certainly have no regrets about these choices. They not only gave me an array of diverse learning experiences that have shaped me in positive ways but they also led to where I am now. Never doubt the inherent worth of variety in your experiences.

There is a certain element of optimism and whimsy that exists in the search for a cause and a career. That element should not be ignored. Ralph Waldo Emerson describes this with no small amount of literary elegance: "A man should learn to detect and watch that gleam of light that flashes across his mind from within, more than the luster of the firmament of bards and sages."[1] In more mundane terms, what Emerson conveys is this: Don't necessarily be swayed by what everyone else has to say—go with your gut. Surely there are many other considerations to take into account as your career unfolds, considerations that will be examined as this book progresses. Yet your gut instinct is often your best source of direction.

So if I've been as successful as I claim at following my gut and doing what feels right, then surely I can easily articulate my cause, right? The mission that has thus far driven my career choices must be at my fingertips, no? If only it were that easy.

What Do You Care about Passionately?
The "Million Dollar Question"

My close friend Karl Dedolph, a graduate school classmate at American University's School of International Service and now a consultant for Accenture in its National Security Services Division, once asked me what I would do if I had a million dollars. I immediately thought of the movie *Office Space.*

Anyone who has seen this film knows that it is perhaps a dubious one to reference in a book on career development because the main characters are stuck in dead-end jobs. Cubicles are portrayed as prison cells. The boss, Bill Lumbergh, is so infuriating and incompetent that he actually drives one of his employees to set the building on fire. During one scene in the movie, the main character, Peter, tells his coworkers that a high school guidance counselor once informed him that how a person answers the question "what would you do if you had a million dollars?" will say everything about the career path he or she should choose.

Each of Peter's coworkers has a chance to answer the question. A character named Michael Bolton (no relation to the pop singer) thinks it is a worthless question, inexplicably exclaiming, "If there were no janitors, then who would clean up shit all day?" Another character, Samir, interprets the question literally and describes how he would invest the money. Then it is Peter's turn to answer his own query. His response to this all-important, life-defining question? "Nothing. I would sit on my ass all day and do nothing."

When it was my own turn to answer the question, I hesitated. I had no immediate answer. Karl jumped in and said that he would go back to Togo, where he had served for two years as a Peace Corps volunteer, and build a school. He has a passion for West Africa and the idea of spending his days in that area of the world, constructing and establishing a well-functioning school that would provide a quality education for countless young people . . . that was a dream for him.

Sherry and I also reflected on the question when discussing this chapter. Again, when I tried to answer it, I stammered and could not provide a response. Sherry, on the other hand, knew her answer without a doubt. She would be doing exactly what she is doing now: leading NCIV. She wholeheartedly embraces NCIV's mission of promoting excellence in citizen diplomacy. If only we could all be as fortunate as Sherry to be in a position where our career and our passion correspond so unmistakably.

I became dismayed that I had no ready answer. As Sherry points out earlier in this chapter, your answer to the "Million Dollar Question" (or the "Magic Wand Test," as she phrases it) is an essential clue to identifying your cause. I feared that because I had no answer, I also had an inability to uncover my cause. Or worse yet, I had no cause at all and had simply been bouncing from job to job, experience to experience, going nowhere.

I forced myself to take a deep breath. I stepped back and thought about *why* I had made my career choices to date. Suddenly I began to feel better.

My love of writing and communications led me toward an English major, an international communications higher degree, and my current position as director of college communications at Georgetown University. My
love of travel, foreign languages, and cultures led me to study abroad in
France and to work in China. My love of international exchange programs
and citizen diplomacy led me to NCIV. In several cases a number of these
loves were combined in a given experience: my positions at both NCIV
and Georgetown have allowed me to work with both communications and
international exchange and education.

While closely examining my career choices, common elements began
to emerge. My choices, while not linear, were tied together by one thing:
my love for them. It occurred to me that maybe *these* are my cause. Could
it be so simple that the things I enjoy are directly related to my cause, or
even *are* my cause? It seemed too easy but was impossible to ignore. My
cause is still not clearly defined; this much is certain. Yet I realized that by
doing things that I enjoy and by following my gut, regardless of whether I
knew for sure the result of those choices, I was being led directly to a cause
and a rewarding career.

Get Specific

Within this realization, I also came to see that my career choices have not
only had mission-oriented elements to them but task-oriented ones too. In
other words, I was gravitating toward organizations whose missions I admire, as well as toward jobs that offer daily tasks I enjoy. Balance your
search for a cause with an honest and clear examination of what it is you
like to do. Sherry poses the question in this way: "How do you want to
spend your days?" In answering the "Million Dollar Question" or performing the "Magic Wand Test," you surely wouldn't wish upon yourself a job
that includes daily tasks that you despise.

If you're like me and you hate the idea of asking others for money, then
you don't want to take a position with an international development organization as a fundraising professional, no matter how closely that organization's mission matches your own cause. If organizational skills are not your
strong suit, then you won't want a job as an event planner, even if it is for
an international education organization that perfectly complements your
worldview. You may be able to convince yourself for a while that distaste
for daily tasks comes second to fulfilling the mission of the organization.
But sooner or later, enjoyment of your job will markedly diminish, and that
will be a product of disliking and not being effective in your daily tasks.

If this notion seems a touch selfish, that's because it is. But to a certain
degree, self-interest is necessary in your search for a cause and a career.

By being self-aware in this way, you will better serve your cause because you will do your job well. And you will do your job well because you will be happy to do the tasks involved. Look for jobs and career paths that will not only allow you to work for a cause that you support but also allow you to do tasks at which you are effective. This might seem like a silly point, but it is one that can easily be overlooked in the quest for a broad, all-encompassing mission.

Risk Yourself

As Sherry notes at the conclusion of her section in this chapter, career choices should be made with an eye to who your supervisor will be and the kind of environment in which you thrive. This is terribly important advice, yet for young professionals like me, sometimes the most difficult thing is bringing ourselves to make choices at all. With no clear career destination in sight and no way of knowing if our choices are good ones, it can be easy for those of us without the experience and knowledge of someone like Sherry to become paralyzed by fear. However, as James Baldwin writes in *The Fire Next Time,* "One can give nothing whatever without giving oneself—that is to say, risking oneself."[2] Follow your gut. Be true to yourself. Risk. Choose. For even if you are unsure of what the hell to do with your life, you *will* find your way.

Notes

1. Ralph Waldo Emerson, "Self-Reliance," in *The Norton Anthology of American Literature, Shorter Fourth Edition* (New York: W. W. Norton & Company, 1995), 492.

2. James Baldwin, *The Fire Next Time* (New York: Vintage International, 1993), 86.

Chapter 2
The Art of Networking

Most everyone agrees that we ought to network, but we rarely reflect on how to do it most effectively and with the most positive results. Is there a certain formula that equates to successful networking? A certain type of event we must attend or a certain kind of person we should engage? A certain number of business cards we should collect?

Furthermore, we seldom stop to consider the question of what networking *is* exactly anyway. All professionals know the term, but it is likely that almost everyone has a different answer for what it means to them. Is networking only about going to networking events? Or does it have other facets as well? Conducting an informational interview? Talking to someone on the subway or an airplane? Chatting with a friend of a friend at a happy hour? Networking could be any or all of these things. It need not be confined to any one of them.

For Sherry, going to networking events and putting yourself in contact with potential employers or other people knowledgeable about the fields of international education, exchange, and development is invaluable. Yet she also advises professionals to avoid viewing these structured networking events as the only times that they need to "be on." Rather, for Sherry, you are always networking, or forever at the crossroads. You are constantly being judged as a professional and you never know when a seemingly innocuous situation may help you—or haunt you—in the future.

Mark is less comfortable than Sherry with the idea of attending a multitude of networking events. He explores the question of how a professional might effectively network if he or she is uncomfortable with approaching new people at a networking event. While he does not advocate abandoning the idea of attending events altogether, Mark suggests that you must be strategic about the events you choose to attend.

Much like Sherry, however, Mark sees networking as more than just attending events or gathering as many business cards as you can; every day, "in your own skin," you are networking. He insists that you not ignore the value of building relationships or getting to know people, even if the professional value of that relationship is not immediately clear.

SHERRY
Encountering Potential Employers and References

There is no substitute for putting yourself in the company of potential employers or other individuals knowledgeable about employment opportunities in your field. A productive way to do this is to join the professional associations most related to the cause you have identified. I joined the International Studies Association (ISA) as a graduate student and have remained a member in the intervening decades. My membership in ISA and participation in national conferences, where I sometimes present papers, enables me to keep in touch with a wide array of respected colleagues and to develop and retain a better understanding of the evolving context in which I work. Chapter 6 is an annotated list of major professional associations and the benefits and costs of membership.

You also can attend conferences, lectures, and other program events related to your areas of interest. Sometimes you can convince organizations to waive registration fees at conferences or other professional development activities by volunteering your services for these events. Participation in such events will enable you to gain vital knowledge about the field that is the focus of the sponsoring organization. You will learn more about the history of the field and key issues currently commanding the attention of its leaders, and in some cases, you may acquire skills pertinent to your career in training seminars. You will develop a strong sense of the major players and a better understanding of the organizations offering employment. Those events provide useful opportunities to raise questions and to demonstrate your own grasp of various issues to colleagues.

I always encourage colleagues to have a first question ready at the beginning of the question-and-answer periods that are often part of such events. This should be a carefully phrased question that enables a speaker to elaborate on a concept presented. It is a chance to demonstrate that you were paying attention, want to learn more, and are articulate. It also is an opportunity to help the organizers keep the event moving—and organizers will notice you contributed in that way. On the other hand, I also caution colleagues not to display insensitivity to others who have questions by dominating the discussion or monopolizing a speaker's time when he or she is answering individual questions after the formal part of an event has concluded. Questions are a way to demonstrate your consideration for others, not merely a way to illustrate your grasp of the subject matter.

Once you have determined that the mission of a particular organization and your cause are congruent, you will want to participate in that organization's activities and programs. Again, most organizations look for volunteers to help. Once the leaders of an organization know you embrace their mission and are a competent and diligent worker, you will have a distinct advantage when a job opening does occur. It is no mystery why many of the people I have hired at the National Council for International Visitors (NCIV) are former interns, including Mark. We know the quality of their work. They are familiar with our membership, systems, and office culture. Therefore, they require less training than someone completely new to the organization. They are a known quantity. Hiring them is less risky for the organization. Hiring the wrong person is expensive—in terms of time, energy, and dollars. Managers are always looking for ways to minimize that risk. That is why direct experience with a potential hire or the unqualified recommendation of a trusted colleague is a remarkable advantage. Networking is the process of getting to know potential employers and potential references.

Who Are the Gatekeepers?

One error people often make is to assume that networking is done only with "important" people. Accept at the outset that anyone you encounter may be important to your career. If you are waiting to meet the director of a program at a major organization, it can be particularly useful to visit with the administrative assistant who may be stationed nearby. People lower in an organization's hierarchy are generally less guarded about the information they will share. As a consequence, you as the job seeker may get a more accurate picture of the organization's culture and staff from observing and talking to them than you do from the formal interview. Plus, this may be the person who decides whether your call to his boss next week will go through or not, or whose favorable comment may help generate a second interview.

For another illustration of conscientious networking, consider events held at embassies, where everyone generally vies for the attention of the ambassador. In fact, this networking opportunity can often be better used

seeking out the spouse of the ambassador or another diplomat, who is almost always just as knowledgeable and has time for more than a thirty-
second conversation. Again, it might be this person's favorable observation to the ambassador that produces the follow-up meeting you desire.

Start a Support Group

The idea of participating in a support group is an important and seldom
discussed aspect of networking. When I was conducting career roundtables at the Institute of International Education (IIE), I often urged like-
minded participants with similar goals to form a support group. When
we are working steadily at a job, we often take being part of the workplace community for granted. It is only during periods of unemployment
that we realize how much we have depended on the camaraderie of colleagues and the structure of the workday to give shape to our daily lives.
The solitary nature of the conventional job search can be one of the most
difficult aspects of hunting for a new position.

Support groups provide a context in which job seekers can help each
other search for the right position. These job seekers are generally at similar stages in their careers. They meet on a regular basis to exchange information, critique résumés, and conduct mock interviews. They provide
the support and encouragement so necessary to persevere with a job
search. In some cases, the support groups have endured long after the job
searches that initiated them are over. They serve as a confidential forum
to discuss career challenges or other professional and sometimes personal
dilemmas.

"The Bee Gees"

An illustration from my own experience will underscore the value of having a vibrant support group. Mine came into being without a deliberate
intention on my part to form a support group. It is a classic illustration
of the fact that your efforts to help others often result in unanticipated
blessings for you.

In 1992, when I was the director of the professional exchange program staff at IIE, some of the young women program assistants on staff
came to me and said they had few role models. I wanted to be helpful.

We decided to have a potluck supper at my home so they could meet some of my women friends and colleagues who had fashioned fascinating careers in international affairs. There was the top woman at the Boeing Company, the head of a Japanese foundation, a Finnish Foreign Service Officer serving as the cultural attaché in Washington, a Middle East expert, the wife of a U.S. Foreign Service officer who had to remake her career every time her husband was reassigned to a new location, and several others. I asked each to share with the younger women a thumbnail sketch of her career and two lessons she learned the hard way. It was a remarkably stimulating evening; I should have had a tape recorder. Everyone learned a lot, and several of the younger women on my staff were mentored by my more experienced colleagues. (The Chinese parable I refer to later was shared as a lesson learned by my friend who heads the Mitsubishi Foundation.)

An unexpected result of the gathering was that the resource people I had assembled were riveted by each other's stories. The woman who worked at Boeing invited all of us to dinner the following month, and a tradition was born. We morphed into a support group that continues to this day. We meet monthly for dinner. Everything is off the record. We have created a safe place to process major job transitions and personnel dilemmas. We have also helped one or more members cope with the death of a parent, divorce, illness, and surgery. We serve as sounding boards and professional references for each other. In sum, this support group, dubbed "the Bee Gees" by one of our members (a reference in this case not to the musical group but to the Big Girls), has become a highly valued source of stability and support for all of us.

Look for opportunities to collaborate with others in this way. A support group can be an enormously enriching part of your life.

You Are Always On

Another related admonition to remember is that you are always on. You are always in the presence of potential employers, even if they are currently members of your own staff. One of the secretaries I hired years ago worked in White House personnel some years later. Had I been seeking a presidential appointment, her earlier judgments about how I treated her and my professional abilities could have made the crucial difference in getting, or not getting, a job.

I remember the first time I was asked to serve as a reference for one of my former bosses. What a surprise! Back then I did not realize how quickly tables could turn. Someone you interview today may be called upon to judge your credentials for a position or a consultancy a few years down the road.

Forever at the Crossroads

We sometimes look back on a specific event—an interview or encounter—that resulted in a specific job offer. In our memory it is a kind of crossroads or pivotal moment when judgments are made and choices determined. In fact, we have many more of these crossroads moments than we realize. (Someday I want to write a book titled *Forever at the Crossroads*.) Let me use my own experience to illustrate this notion.

As I reflect on the process that resulted in the NCIV board of directors hiring me to lead NCIV, I was at a crossroads in my career, particularly on the day I was interviewed by the entire board. As I looked around the room, I realized that I had known or worked with at least half of the board members present. In fact, long before that day, they had most likely drawn their conclusions about my competence and fitness for this position that has meant so much to me. I was not aware of these crossroads when they occurred. Every time I interacted with one of these board members, each was making judgments about my skills and talents. Perhaps these judgments were subconscious, but they certainly played a role on the day of that fateful group interview.

This story is another way of illustrating the concept that you are always on and forever at the crossroads. It reminds us that plain good manners—treating everyone the way you would like to be treated—are a fundamental part of any job search. Every day, what you do at your job is either increasing someone's confidence in your abilities or eroding it. Later on, that someone may play a major role in determining your future.

The Science of Record Keeping

I only wish that years ago some well-meaning counselor had told me to begin and maintain a database of the most useful contacts made through networking activities, whether these contacts were encountered at events attended as a job seeker or as the incumbent of a particular position. If you assiduously follow this one piece of advice, it will be worth much more than the price you paid for this book. Each time you accept a business card from someone you find informative and interesting, or who is active in your field, you must find a way to record details of the connection and store them, with the contact information on the card, so they are easily retrievable.

For some, a carefully kept three-ring notebook of annotated business cards or a Rolodex is the answer. For others willing to sacrifice the memory the graphic design of the business card evokes, an electronic database or Excel spreadsheet may be a preferred way of maintaining a list of contacts. For either system to be useful, you must record on each card or in each entry the date, place, and occasion of your meeting, along with a brief phrase that will help you recall the conversation or other details of your encounter. Meeting a colleague and being able to recollect an idea she expressed is ten times more valuable than just knowing you met her. It facilitates follow-up contacts and demonstrates your own intelligence and ability to listen (a sometimes underrated communication skill that is nonetheless valued by employers).

I cannot emphasize enough the value of a carefully annotated record of contacts. Too often people collect business cards and toss them in a drawer, erroneously confident that their memories are more efficient than they later turn out to be. The quality and comprehensiveness of the contact information contained in your business card notebook, Rolodex, or database are amazingly reliable indicators of your usefulness to an employer.

MARK
Do I Really Need Business Cards?

Several years ago, at the orientation for my graduate program at American University's (AU) School of International Service, a faculty member gave us his best piece of advice: start networking and start networking now.

According to this faculty member, the most important first step for any student was to visit the nearest print shop and have business cards made. *Business cards?* I thought. *I'm here to further my education, not negotiate corporate deals or sell knives door-to-door. What possible need could I have for business cards?*

But the faculty member insisted.

"There are hundreds of events *every day* in Washington, D.C. Go to them. Learn from them. But most important, network at them," he asserted with authority. "Talk to those who are already in your field. Give them your business card. Follow up with them. Because when you have finished your studies and are determining the next phase of your career, it is these people you met through networking who will be your most valuable resource."

I could not deny the logic of his point. As the oft-repeated maxim states, "It's not what you know, it's who you know." Even though I had just started a two-year quest to learn more of the "what," I determined that I would also make an effort to get to know the "who." I would get those business cards.

But this feeling of resolve quickly changed to one of anxiety:

"Remember," he said, "you should try to attend a networking event every day. Only 25 percent of your graduate learning will come in the classroom; the other 75 percent will come from out there." He made a dramatic and expansive gesture, presumably indicating a place outside of the auditorium, a place that I had the growing feeling I had no idea how to find.

Could this professor's statement have been correct? Could I possibly be expected to attend one outside event *per day*? How was I to manage such a schedule along with a full graduate studies workload? How was I to identify one event per day that I wanted to attend? I left this orientation no longer resolved to have my business cards made. Instead I was wondering what to do next.

Know Yourself before Networking

Looking back, I think this confused feeling stemmed from a combination of two factors: exaggeration on the part of that faculty member as well as my newness to the art of networking. I have since learned that, while it is *possible* to attend one networking occasion per day (especially in an event-saturated city such as Washington), it is certainly not practical. Whether you are a graduate or undergraduate student, a working professional, or a full-time job hunter, the demands of your schedule will most likely make it difficult to attend such a multitude of events. Even if you can make it happen, stretching yourself so thin is not worth the toll on mind and body.

When I first moved to Washington I attended a good number of networking events, although I did not enjoy them. I handed out a few business cards from time to time, but I never followed up, and more often than not, I left without talking to anyone. I felt guilty about this. It made me question the purpose of networking and why I had even bothered to get business cards printed. Why didn't I get more out of these events? Why couldn't I muster the courage to talk to anyone who wasn't standing directly by the cheese tray? Should I feel guilty because walking into a room full of strangers and shaking hands is not my forte? How is networking best accomplished? What purpose does it truly serve, personally and professionally? Does one network simply to gain something? To secure an internship, a job, or a recommendation? Or are there other reasons to network? Is it an inherently selfish enterprise?

I realized that the answer to my first two questions—why I couldn't get more out of the events or talk to more people—is that I simply do not like networking events. Some professionals, Sherry being a prime example, thrive on these events. To some, networking comes naturally and is relatively effortless. These extroverts walk into a room full of strangers and happily anticipate whom they might meet and where newly minted connections might be made. "Press the flesh" enough and who knows what might come your way, such professionals think. And if not, then at least you got to meet some interesting people and learn something new.

For me and other professionals like me, however, networking events are a struggle. They require major effort. While I am a decidedly outgoing and social person, I simply do not enjoy approaching people I don't know and introducing myself. If I attend an event with a group of colleagues, I will talk only to them. If I am by myself, you will probably find me near the bar or the food or slowly circling the room in order to avoid the embarrassment of standing alone. For better or for worse, this is me. Once I realized this about myself, that this was a primary reason I wasn't getting much out of networking events, I stopped attending them altogether.

Yet, after a bit of time, I figured out that just because going to networking events and meeting people was not a favorite pastime, this didn't mean I should cease going to any and all events. Rather, I needed to be much more discerning about which events I attended.

I liken it to receiving an invitation to a party. If I know nothing about the person throwing the party, I'm unlikely to attend. However, if I know something about the host and have friends or interests in common with him, I'll probably stop by for a drink. The same holds true with networking events.

I hated going to those events where I didn't have a specific passion for or interest in the work of the host organization. But I did begin to get something out of events that held a particular personal and professional interest for me and at which I found people with similar interests and experiences. A specific example is the day I met Sherry.

I was in my first semester of grad school at AU, and Sherry, an alumna and former faculty member, came back to her alma mater to give a talk on international exchange and citizen diplomacy. I had recently discovered the work of the organization she heads, NCIV, and was interested in pursuing an internship there. I figured that by going to this event I could find out more about the internship. Perhaps I could learn something as well. I had a specific interest in Sherry and NCIV. I also had a goal. I found that these things made all the difference in how I networked at this event.

At Sherry's talk I was engaged. I took notes. I asked questions. After the talk was over, I was compelled not only to hand Sherry my business card but also to ask her in-depth questions and inquire more about the internship position at NCIV. None of this felt forced; it flowed very easily. When I eventually visited NCIV's offices for an internship interview, I again saw Sherry and talked with her even more. After my summer internship there, I kept in touch with Sherry, often e-mailing or calling her for various reasons: for help on research projects, to pass along interesting articles on international exchange, or for advice on my job search. Eventually, just after I had graduated from AU with my master's degree, Sherry called. She knew I was looking for a position, happened to have an open one at NCIV, and thought it might be a good fit. She asked if I would like to come in for an interview. Less than a week later, I began a rewarding two-year stint at NCIV.

It is true that my networking encounter with Sherry was uncommonly successful, in that it led to both an internship and a job. Most meetings do not yield such tangible results. Certainly other factors influenced my ability to secure these positions as well: education, experience, timing, luck. But the point here is this: When it comes to the art of networking, learn to recognize your own skills and comfort levels. If you are a person who enjoys working a room and introducing yourself to new people at the events of organizations you know little about, by all means, go to as many events as your schedule allows. However, if you are someone who does not enjoy or is not particularly skilled at schmoozing, do not feel guilty or despair that you will never find a job. Rather, choose the events you attend and the people you engage in conversation wisely and strategically. Be truly interested in that event, have something specific to ask that person, and suddenly you will find that networking is not so forbidding. You will be up for that event because you have an interest and because you have a goal. Your encounter may not result directly an internship or a job, but you will find that you are building your career knowledge and list of contacts all the same.

Every Day, in Your Own Skin, You Are Networking

In my discussion of networking, I have confined the concept largely to one activity—networking at events. The art of networking need not be confined, however, to this strict parameter. Networking is so much more than just participating in events. It can certainly be performed successfully by people like me who are not skilled in the art of small talk. In fact, in my mind, networking is something best accomplished by not thinking too much about it.

Networking becomes difficult when a person says to himself or herself, "I'm going to go out and *network* tonight. I'm going to come home with at least ten business cards and shake no fewer than fifteen hands." When networking is approached in this manner, it is no longer about learning something new or meeting interesting people who share your cause. Rather, it becomes a tedious chore. And nobody likes to do chores.

Networking is not, in and of itself, about meeting people for the purpose of getting a job. While a job, an internship, or some other career-shifting/propelling benefit may come out of networking (and indeed this is a benefit we often hope will be the result of knowing interesting and well-connected people), we must understand that networking is not a predictable phenomenon. It is not a lock-step process or a formula:

Going to this event + meeting that person
+ applying for a job
+ sending a thank-you note = **CAREER SECURITY**

Unfortunately, it just doesn't happen that way.

If we can view networking not as a grim necessity but rather as organically developing a web of human connections, then we can begin to grasp that we are networking all the time. Or, to quote Paul Binkley, director of career development services for the George Washington University School of Public Policy and Public Administration, "Every day you walk around in your own skin, you are networking." Every time we meet someone and a conversation ensues based on mutual interest, we are networking. Each time we sit down next to someone on a plane or a subway and strike up a conversation, we are networking. Every occasion we meet a friend of a friend and talk about our interests or jobs, we are networking. In those moments we are most likely not thinking that a job opportunity will arise or that this connection will lead to a career-defining moment. Yet we are still networking.

We are networking all the time. The more we can realize this fact, the less pressure we will put on ourselves and the more we will see that networking cannot and should not be forced. It does not have to be a chore.

To be sure, as Larry Bacow, president of Tufts University, advised us in our interview with him, you must take responsibility for your career, which includes being proactive and learning to "recognize opportunity when it walks up and hits you in the face." But as Dr. Bacow was also quick to point out, careers are often "a series of fortuitous accidents." You cannot possibly plan your entire career, nor can you plan whom you will meet in the course of networking and how those people will affect your career. So instead, let your network develop organically, naturally, with genuine interest and connection as guiding principles.

"Get to know people for who they are," Belinda Chiu, a doctoral student at Columbia University, told us. "Some people you meet shut down when they think that you don't do what they want to do or you can't help them now. You can tell when people turn off."

Malcolm Butler, former president and CEO of Partners of the Americas, put it another way in his profile interview: "There are a lot of relationships that are valuable to establish even if you don't know why at the moment. You don't have to have an agenda at any given point when establishing a relationship."

Allow yourself to be open to the unanticipated directions that networking encounters, whether at an event or on a subway, might lead. Looking back on that day I met Sherry, it seems like a crossroads—a pivotal moment that resulted in a specific opportunity, as Sherry describes it earlier in this chapter. It all seems quite clear in hindsight: I wanted to get involved with Sherry's organization, so I attended an event featuring her presentation and got to know her. I eventually got an internship and a job. I was now working with her, in her field. Mission accomplished; usefulness of networking resource exhausted.

Yet I never could have anticipated that getting to know Sherry would lead in some of the directions that it has—namely, in researching and coauthoring this book. I never could have known that Sherry would not only teach me so much about careers but also give me the opportunity to be a published author. As Sherry says, we are forever at the crossroads, forever in the position to take our careers in unexpected directions. It is essential to remain open to establishing the relationships that may take us in those directions, even if, at the moment, we have no way of knowing where we might be headed.

Chapter 3
The Value of Mentors

Several stories regarding the origins of the word *mentor* exist. The two most common have elements familiar to many people:

1. In Greek mythology, when Odysseus left to fight in the Trojan War, he entrusted his son, Telemachus, to his friend and adviser, Mentor. In looking after Telemachus in Odysseus' absence, Mentor's duties required that he be a role model, a father figure, an adviser, a guardian, a counselor, and an encourager; in other words, a "mentor."

2. In 1689 the French writer Francois Fénelon was appointed royal tutor to Louis XIV's grandson, the duke of Burgundy. In 1699 Fénelon wrote his most famous work, *Les Adventures de Telemaque,* which was both a continuation of the story of *The Odyssey* and a thinly veiled attack on the absolutism of Louis XIV. Using *Les Adventures de Telemaque,* with its main character named Mentor, as a primary text, Fénelon "mentored" his young pupil to grow up to become a just and fair ruler, unlike his grandfather.

A third tale regarding the origins of the word, perhaps more farfetched but certainly intriguing, also exists:

3. "*La Grotte de Niaux* is a prehistoric cave located high in the Pyrenees in southern France. After walking through silent and womb-like stillness, a visitor emerges into a large, domed space filled with paintings estimated to have been created somewhere between 12,000 and 9,000 BC. While most of the paintings depict horses and bison, there is one theme that is repeated in many places. These paintings show a group of men taking children to what, at that time, was considered the edge or end of their physical world. The men exhort the children to be brave and expand their reach beyond the

borders of the present world. Some believe that the origin of the term 'mentor' comes from what has been loosely translated in these ancient depictions as 'men' taking children on a 'tour.'"[1]

Regardless of the origins of the term, the concept of having a mentor to aid in successful career development has become quite widespread. Professionals of all ages can, and do, benefit from the guidance of a more experienced and often older colleague who can provide advice, contacts, and encouragement throughout a career's progression. The way in which mentors are identified, utilized, and generally thought about, however, can certainly differ from person to person, from culture to culture, and from generation to generation.

Sherry is explicit in her use of the term *mentor* and in her view of the mentor–protégé relationship. She speaks often and reverently of her mentor, illustrates how she openly and actively looks for opportunities to mentor her younger colleagues, and encourages professionals to seek out a colleague or another professional to serve as a mentor.

Mark, on the other hand, is far more reticent about the term *mentor* and its implied relationship. He has no one whom he calls his mentor, nor has he ever actively sought out a mentor. Yet he also realizes that, while he may not typically use the term or view the mentor–protégé relationship in the same manner Sherry perceives it, he has benefited a great deal throughout his career from friends and other professionals around him who have played this guiding role.

SHERRY
Identifying Your Mentor

Mentors appear in our lives in various guises and at various times. In some cases nurturing relationships are literally lifelong. For example, I learned so much from my loving, disciplined, and congenial parents who always insisted that I do my best. In other cases mentoring may be limited to a particular period or the duration of a project. Some of us are particularly blessed (and this has been true for me), as mentors seem to be a built-in part of our lives. The relationship may have evolved with no conscious effort on our part, and we may not realize how much we rely on this person's wise counsel, willingness to serve as a sounding board, and the lessons shared from his or her own career. Others consciously seek out mentors and deliberately tap into their expertise and guidance.

Whatever the case for you, having at least one mentor is critical to professional growth and development. Each of us needs a relationship with a respected, experienced colleague to help us spot pitfalls and encourage us to take on new challenges. A mentor is a person who believes in your talents and skills, who offers suggestions to strengthen them, and who has a way of helping you transform obstacles into opportunities. Your mentor must be someone with integrity, whose professional accomplishments and personal traits you admire and wish to emulate to some degree. Look around. Who fits that description for you? How can you become better acquainted with a potential mentor?

The following are a few examples from my own life thus far—although I still expect that I will find myself mentored by new people in the years ahead. Our need for encouragement, new perspectives, and wise counsel never goes away, no matter what our age or career stage.

Sometimes it is only in retrospect that we realize we have been mentored by someone and that we view that person as a significant role model. To illustrate, I point to Vi Wellik, who owned and ran the Flying-E Ranch for many years. My parents and I started vacationing at the Flying-E, a guest ranch in Wickenburg, Arizona, in 1964. Friends and I still spend a week there each March. For most of those years, each night at dinner, Vi would ask new guests to say a few words about themselves and bid farewell to those guests who were departing the next day. I was relatively young as I first watched her and admired her extraordinary ability to make each person feel special and connected to the ranch. It was only about ten years ago as I was hosting a National Council for International Visitors (NCIV) dinner at my home that I realized I had been modeling myself after Vi for years. I have a tradition at my home referred to as "The Circle." Early during a party I host in my professional role, I invite my guests to stand in a circle. After I offer a few words of welcome, each person identifies himself or herself and his or her connection to the NCIV network. This tradition has enabled my friends and associates to make unforeseen connections and never fails to enrich the evening's conversations.

Fortunately, I realized what a powerful role model Vi had been for me and was able to thank her, both in person and in writing, before she died in 2003. To be able to observe, learn from, and acknowledge a mentor's contribution to your own life is enormously rewarding.

My primary professional mentor is Dr. William C. Olson. I first met Bill in the late 1970s when he became the dean of the School of International Service at American University (SIS), my undergraduate alma mater. He wanted to start an alumni association for SIS, and I was one of the alumni he recruited to help. Ultimately I became the founding president of the association. In the process of working together, my relationship with Bill has evolved and continues to evolve, even though he has retired and I am no longer actively involved in managing the association, which has been ably led by younger alumni for many years.

I cannot remember exactly when I first referred to Bill as my mentor, but we have explicitly recognized our mentor–protégé relationship for decades. In fact, Bill has been a quintessential mentor to me, always encouraging me to stretch and grow, always providing significant opportunities to do so. He would pose questions that prompted and shaped my aspirations. One day he asked, "Would you like to be a member of the Cosmos Club?" Thanks to Bill's hard work in shepherding my nomination through the admissions committee, I was elected to membership in this revered Washington institution in 1991 and have enjoyed the benefits of membership ever since.

Another time, Bill said, "I'm putting out a new edition of my book. Would you like to have a chapter in it?" This allowed me to add another publication to my résumé, while broadening my experience and exposure. Some years later, he queried, "What boards would you like to be on?" My first choice was the World Learning board, because participating in an Experiment in International Living program (EIL)—a World Learning program—had changed my life. Thanks in large part to Bill's support, I was elected to that board in 1999 and have been pleased to serve in that capacity since then. It remains one of my favorite volunteer activities.

Over the years Bill has served as a reference, made editorial suggestions for publications I have written, and closely followed and encouraged me in my career. (He even contributes to NCIV and reads our newsletter.) I have asked him for advice on topics ranging from personnel problems to evaluating major professional opportunities. Always, I knew that I could count on his thoughtful analysis, broad knowledge, and carefully considered counsel. What an extraordinary gift!

In April 2007 the School of International Service presented me with their Alumna of the Year Award at a wonderful event held at the German Embassy in Washington. The venue was perfect because my first EIL program had included an extended home-stay in Bad Godesberg, Germany. Of all the words of congratulations offered that night, it was Bill Olson's tribute that meant the most to me. This was because he knew every dimension of my career—and had helped me through the inevitable rough spots.

Mentors are a valuable source of guidance and continuity. Over time, almost every career inevitably involves immense changes—sometimes sought after, and other times sudden and unexpected. The stability a good mentor provides is invaluable during these times of transition. Usually, mentoring relationships evolve out of shared interests or participation in a project, much as my relationship with Bill grew out of our efforts to establish an alumni association. Sometimes, though, individuals actively seek out mentors. You should not be shy about asking someone to be your mentor. At a minimum, you will be paying a compliment to an admired associate. When your request meets with an affirmative response, you will have gained valuable help in making informed career choices.

When asking someone to serve as your mentor, be sure to explain your expectations and leave your prospective mentor with a graceful way to decline, in case she feels unable to meet those expectations. You might ask, "Would you be willing to have coffee with me once a month? I'm in the midst of making a career change, and I want to make carefully considered decisions. I realize that you have a busy schedule and might not be able to do this right now, but I want you to know how much I would appreciate your advice at this point in my career. If you're interested, I'll be pleased to bring the latte."

Serving as a Mentor

Having been blessed with remarkable mentors and role models, I make an effort to be an active mentor to younger colleagues. I heartily concur with Larry Bacow, president of Tufts University, when he told us in his profile interview that the best way to pay back those who have mentored you is to "continue the tradition." At this stage in my career, it is a great joy to share some of the lessons I have learned the hard way, and to encourage and enable my colleagues to pursue their professional development.

In fact, I consider being a mentor to others a strong imperative. Whenever I attend events of any kind, I always ask if I can bring a guest. Then I make it a point to take a young person with me. I believe one of the reasons we attract such outstanding interns to NCIV is that we have a reputation for getting them out of the office and being truly concerned that they develop professionally under our tutelage. For example, recently I was invited to speak at the Foreign Service Institute. I immediately asked permission to bring our summer intern as an observer. Not only did she have the chance to visit the campus of the National Foreign Affairs Training Center and witness a training session, but we also had time on the way and returning to talk about her tasks at NCIV as well as broader issues. All of us who are lucky enough to hold senior positions have an obligation to nurture and help develop the next generation.

One of the reasons I invited Mark to coauthor this book is that I view it as a way in which I can mentor an extraordinarily promising young colleague. During our collaboration Mark has learned much from me, and I have learned an enormous amount from him as well. The best mentoring relationships result when both parties are innately curious and want to learn from each other's unique vantage point.

MARK
The Seinfeldian View of Mentors

There is an episode of *Seinfeld* from 1996 in which a woman whom Jerry is dating, Abby, talks constantly about her mentor: the impact her mentor has had on her life and career; the advice her mentor has given her; her mentor's favorite restaurants, movies, and books. Jerry's bald and neurotic friend, George Costanza, can't quite get his mind around this concept of a "mentor." Hilarity, as they say, ensues:

> George: *I still don't understand this. Abby has a mentor?*
> Jerry: *Yes. And the mentor advises the protégé.*
> George: *Is there any money involved?*
> Jerry: *No.*
> George: *So what's in it for the mentor?*
> Jerry: *Respect, admiration, prestige.*
> George: *Pssh. Would the protégé pick up stuff for the mentor?*
> Jerry: *I suppose if it was on the protégé's way to the mentor, they might.*
> George: *Laundry? Dry cleaning?*
> Jerry: *She's not a valet, she's a protégé.*[2]

Much like George, I've never quite known what to make of the concept of a mentor. True, it has become a common term, but it is not one that I grew up with, at least in a specific, personal sense. My parents never spoke of having mentors. I was never encouraged to seek out a mentor, nor have I ever done so. I have no one in my life that I have consciously referred to as a mentor.

Sherry, on the other hand, is extremely comfortable with the term. She speaks often of her mentor, Bill Olson, and she refers to herself as his protégé. They have been in a mentor–protégé relationship for more than twenty-five years. She openly searches for ways to be a mentor to young people around her.

So why the discrepancy? Where do our divergent perceptions of a fairly common term come from? Because I've never specifically looked for a mentor, does that mean I have none? Do I even need one? Or is it a concept that burned out before it reached my generation? Have mentors become irrelevant in a fast-paced, technology-dependent, and globalized world?

In attempting to answer these questions, I find it helpful to examine the characterization of my generation as, to borrow the term Arjun Desai used in his profile interview, the "on-demand generation." We have come of age in a world where everything is at our fingertips. News, information, communication—it all happens in an instant. This sense of the urgent, of instant gratification, has migrated to the professional arena. We want to do everything, and we want to do it now. We are confident and can-do. We are ready to perform the most demanding work possible, take on all challengers, and shoot straight to the top. This is not meant to imply that professionals of older generations do not want to perform challenging work or succeed in their careers; quite the contrary. While all generations may be striving for success, it is the on-demand generation who can't wait for it. Sure, we might realize that we have a few things to learn, but there's no reason to pause and learn these *before* jumping into a position. Forget about paying our dues; we want to do it here, we want to do it now, and anything we need to learn, we'll just figure it out along the way.

Because of this mentality, it seems that we are more inclined to view those older and more experienced than us simply as colleagues rather than as mentors. Perhaps admitting that we have much to learn somehow diminishes our proven abilities and hard work. It stunts our movement and growth, and the on-demand generation needs constant movement and growth. We are kinetic!

The irony of it all is twofold. First, my generation desperately needs mentors to rid us of the notion that we don't need mentors (got that?). That is, we need mentors to help us slow down and realize that, in fact, we *don't* know everything, we *do* have much to learn, and—you know what?—it's okay to take the time to learn it. In fact, it will help us achieve all that we want to achieve. Second, if there is one thing that mentors can do for their young colleagues, it is to help them create movement in their careers, help them grow. No matter how experienced, skilled, or confident a young student or professional may be, he or she will always benefit from the wisdom and experience of a colleague or friend.

So if I'm suggesting that the concept of mentors is *not* dead and that my generation has a clear need for them, then why the discrepancy? Why does Sherry have someone who has been her mentor for a quarter of a century while I've scarcely used the term? In the end I think the difference between Sherry's view of mentors and my own is both personal and generational. There is the issue of terminology. Something about the concept of a "the mentor taking the protégé under her wing" does not resonate with me. It comes across as dated. For some reason, it conjures images of a very formal relationship, filled with protocol, rules, and expectations. Yet Sherry is quite comfortable with this term and this image. While I may refer to those who have helped me along the way with monikers like "friend" or "favorite professor" or "great guy," Sherry prefers the term *mentor.* One is no more accurate than the other. It boils down to your preference, a preference determined by personality or generation or a little bit of both.

Just because I haven't approached things in the same manner as Sherry, however, doesn't mean that I haven't benefited from mentors in my life.

Upon reflection it is clear that I *have* benefited from the advice, guidance, and counsel of various mentors throughout my life, even though I have never consciously used that term. In fact, most young people have probably sought out a mentor or have mentors that are important in their lives. You may not call them mentors, but they are certainly there and play that role.

At my undergraduate university I became quite close to Paul McDowell, the director of my study abroad program in Angers, France. While I viewed P McD (as we called him) simply as a teacher and a friend, I now realize that he was also a mentor. He has helped me greatly with my postcollege decisions and direction and continues to provide guidance, counsel, and friendship. In graduate school I found myself repeatedly sitting in the office of my favorite professor, Christine Chin, whom, again, I viewed as a friend and colleague more than anything else. Typically, I had some class-related query each time I sought her out. More often than not, however, we ended up talking informally and frankly about my interests and possible postgraduation plans. While I would never have called her a mentor, in hindsight, she certainly was. I was looking for someone to talk to, someone who has much experience and insight, someone with whom I felt comfortable sharing on a personal level—some basic qualities of a mentor.

Sherry acted as an invaluable mentor to me during my time at NCIV and has continued to be one as I have progressed in my professional life. Not only did she teach me more on the job than I can possibly begin to relate, but she has also been extremely generous in recognizing my interests and abilities and providing me with opportunities to further them (see my presence as a coauthor of this book as example number one).

I realize that my father has always been a mentor to me throughout my entire life, especially as I have begun my professional career. In times of deep career contemplation, he has always been there to act as a sounding board, answer questions, and provide advice. True, his idea of advice can sometimes send me into fits of frustration—I point specifically to the times during my job search following graduate school when he asked me if I "had a résumé" and if I planned to "wear a suit" to an interview. But his experience, and more important his love and care for me, have always provided me with direction and stability that I sorely need and appreciate even more as time passes.

Mentors can come from all spheres of life: personal, professional, academic. A mentor can even be someone you've never met. In that same episode of *Seinfeld,* when first talking to Jerry about her mentor, Abby asks him if he has such a person in his own life:

> Abby: *My mentor suggested that I move into equities, the best move I ever made.*
> Jerry: *Mentor? You mean your boss.*

> Abby: Oh, no no no, Cynthia's just a successful
>   businesswoman who's taken me under her wing.
> Jerry: Hmm. So Cynthia's your mentor.
> Abby: And I'm her protégé. You must have someone like that.
>   You know, who guides you in your career path.
> Jerry: Well, I like Gabe Kaplan.

Jerry is certainly being tongue-in-cheek when he mentions his affinity for Kaplan, an American comedian successful in the 1970s. This is a professional whom Jerry admires from afar but probably does not know personally nor consider to be a mentor. But perhaps Kaplan *was* something of a mentor to Jerry as the latter developed his own career in comedy. While many people have mentors with whom they maintain a close and personal relationship, others, such as Charlie MacCormack, president and CEO of Save the Children, have found mentors in those they have admired but never met: "I think it is essential that we get help and support from others more experienced than we are, and I think we can get that through direct advice, as well as through watching from a distance," MacCormack told us. "I think there are, therefore, people you see at a long distance that become indirect mentors. Certainly in my formative years, President Kennedy was one, and Martin Luther King Jr. was another, and Nelson Mandela has taken on that kind of role in past decades."

To some, such people who have affected their lives, whether personally or from a distance, are called role models. Perhaps you might refer to them as "my colleague" or "my favorite professor" or "a great person" or "my friend." Regardless of their designation, they are still mentors and play a crucial role in your career development.

Serving as a Mentor

Sherry is conscious of being a mentor to the young professionals with whom she works. It is her way of "continuing the tradition," of giving back for all the help she received from her own mentors. As someone still early on in his career, I don't believe that I am at a stage in which I can be a mentor. I'm not sure at what age or point in my career the switch will flip and I will feel ready to mentor those around me, but I do know that my current need for mentorship outweighs my ability to provide it.

Yet I do feel that I can act, as Max Stewart characterized it for us in his profile interview, like something of an "older sibling" to my peers. Recently I have found that I have been able to help a peer handle a situation because I had recently experienced similar circumstances. While I never saw myself as advising or passing on wisdom, I do believe I was helpful by sharing my own trials and errors.

For example, a young woman named Michelline Granjean recently e-mailed me, asking for assistance with her job search. I did not know Michelline, nor she me, but she was finishing her master's degree at American University's (AU) School of International Service, as well as working for the same professor for whom I worked when I did my graduate work at AU. Because of these commonalities, and because Michelline was looking to start a career in international education/exchange, she thought I would be a good resource.

At first when she contacted me, I didn't know how I might help. I'm still a young professional myself—what do I know about helping other people get jobs? Getting one for myself had been hard enough. But then I realized that *this* was exactly how I could help her. I had been in Michelline's exact situation two years before. I began to reflect on the difficulties that I had run into in my job search, the strategies that I had found most successful, and the job search resources that I had used most effectively (all of which are included in part II). It was this information that I passed along to Michelline. When she began to apply for specific jobs, I used the contacts I had developed to try my best to get her résumé pushed to the top of the pile. It wasn't much, but as my peers had done the same for me, I figured it was the least I could do. I realized that even if I didn't see myself as mentoring just yet, at least I was continuing the tradition.

Notes

1. From the October 22, 2004, issue of *The Mentor News* (available at www.mentors.ca/thementornews13.html).

2. From *Seinfeld* episode no. 140, "The Fatigues"; original broadcast date October 31, 1996.

Chapter 4
The Continuous Journey

Like Alice, most of us think we want to go "somewhere," and it takes some experience to learn that, in life, there is no "somewhere." There is only the road to "somewhere," and we are always on the way.
—David Campbell, *If You Don't Know Where You're Going, You'll Probably End Up Somewhere Else*

Many of us have a tendency to think about career development in terms of conclusions—what we're going to do once we're finished. We consider our career paths, and our lives, in terms such as these: "Once I've finished my degree . . ." or "Once I've completed my overseas experience . . ." or "Once I've accumulated five (or ten or fifteen) years of experience. . . ." Yet we rarely reflect on the fact that we're never quite finished with anything. We may complete certain building blocks of our careers (such as a degree, an experience abroad, or a particular job), but, in a way, we never really make it. Our career journeys are never over. As Larry Bacow, president of Tufts University, phrased it for us, "The only time that you can *really* describe your career is on the day you retire. Up until then, you're just making plans." And even when you retire, the opportunities for a postretirement career are abundant. The road goes on and on.

We are often inclined to view a job search as a series of activities that cease once a job is found. On the contrary, it is just as important to devote time to these strategic job-search activities—defining your cause, networking, learning from mentors—once you have located a job. If you consider your career as a continuous journey of finding new and better ways to serve your cause, it is easier to understand why such activities must continue.

We have emphasized the importance of identifying your cause. But this is not a static activity. Causes do change. The first cause you identify—

46

easing the adaptation process to a U.S. university for international students as a foreign student adviser or conducting training on health system management in Uganda as a young development professional, for example— may later develop into a different but related mission, such as building the international dimension of a community college as its president or promoting best practices in health care as the publications manager at an international development organization. Whatever cause you embrace, and whatever accompanying aspirations are generated, a consistent way of thinking about your career will serve you well in your immediate job search and in your continuous journey.

In our respective sections in this chapter, we tackle the idea of the continuous journey in similar ways. Simply because a certain career activity has come to a close—because that building block has been laid and helped you to make your next career choice—does not mean that discernment can be suspended and you should stop thinking about your career path. Causes sometimes shift, and needs can change. Maintaining a consistent way of thinking about your career will help you to deal with these inevitable transitions.

We also deal with the issue of professionalism as a necessary virtue of the continuous journey. While our opinions about the details of "professional behavior" and what it means "to act professionally" often diverge— the issue of a professional dress code is one that we have had fun debating and come to no consensus—in the end, we both agree that consciously and consistently developing certain professional habits is not only essential to the advancement of your career but should remain an integral part of your continuous journey.

SHERRY
An Evolving Approach

It was in the midst of writing and compiling my first career book in the late 1990s when I realized that I had consciously developed a structured way of thinking about careers in the fields of international education, exchange, and development. Furthermore, it was actually a constructive approach one could readily apply to a career in most any field. After facilitating more than one hundred career roundtables, speaking on various career panels at NAFSA: Association of International Educators conferences and local universities, and interacting with hundreds of job seekers over the years, there were distinct patterns and consistencies in the career advice I shared. As Mark and I met regularly to discuss the book and engage in the stimulating process of collaboration—volleying ideas back and forth—I realized that this deliberate way of thinking about careers had evolved even more in the intervening years as I accumulated more experience as a manager.

In this chapter I share with you my approach to the continuous career journey. I do this not because I expect you to adopt it as your own but because I hope it will be catalytic and encourage you to consider your own career in a thoughtful, more philosophical way.

Career Choices as Building Blocks

I always encourage people to assume a building-block approach to their careers. This is the simple idea that early choices—interning with your member of Congress or serving as a resident adviser in a dorm when you are in college—are the foundation for later choices. Those early choices should be solid learning experiences that will not only be appealing to a wide range of potential employers but will also serve you well as your career takes shape. There are certain building blocks—serving as a Peace Corps volunteer, a Rotary ambassador, or an Experiment in International Living group leader, for example—that I like to see on résumés of job applicants. Experiences such as these, as well as others that are comparable, convey to a potential employer that you have survived a vigorous vetting process. They also suggest that you can handle a challenging assignment overseas and have well-developed cross-cultural communication skills and a willingness to accept responsibility. Consequently, I always ask job seekers to be sure to highlight the fundamental building blocks on their résumés. In interviews they should be prepared to articulate the lessons they learned from these basic experiences and be able to illustrate those lessons with concrete examples.

Taking Risks

"Why not go out on a limb? That's where the fruit is."

—Mark Twain

This quotation reminds us that risk-taking is an essential part of any successful career. Several of the professionals profiled in part II have made a point of emphasizing this fundamental fact, and Mark talks about the need for young professionals to take risks at the end of chapter 1. Careers in international affairs can, at times, put people into dangerous situations. Physical risks come in many guises. Other types of risks abound as well. Some might choose to accept a lower-paying job in tough conditions because they are truly impressed with those who will be their colleagues. Others may risk comfort because the chance to serve their cause is so compelling. Life is inherently risky. As those who opt for challenging assignments know so well, however, we humans are remarkably adaptable. We can get along quite well without many of the things we view as necessities in our home environment. In fact, the process of getting along without them and functioning well in a different country or cultural context builds our self-confidence and our ability to make considered judgments.

Lessons Learned

"That which hurts, instructs."

—Benjamin Franklin

Despite careful thought about the trade-offs involved in various career choices and decisions, we inevitably make mistakes, both large and small. I always tell my staff to try and avoid mistakes, but when they happen—

as they will despite the best of intentions—own up to them immediately. Together, we can work out a way to rectify promptly whatever problem was inadvertently caused. The key is to learn from mistakes of all types and realize that you are even more valuable as an employee because you can analyze your mistakes and apply that learning to the next comparable situation.

It is sobering to realize that I have learned the most—grown the most—from the job situations that seemed particularly problematic at the time. When things move along smoothly, we tend to take them for granted. Often it is only when we are coping with major difficulties that we consciously summon our problem-solving skills, engage in deep analysis, and use or combine our assets in new ways.

I remember one time when, as a relatively new manager, I hired a consultant to organize a seminar. I didn't know much then about monitoring a project and supervising a consultant. Thinking that she would handle her work the way I did mine, I blithely assumed she would be at the hotel to troubleshoot any problems that arose as the seminar participants checked in. It was only when I was called at home by irate seminar participants threatening to go back to their universities that I realized my mistake. Fortunately, before rushing to the hotel to salvage as much of the situation as I could, I had the presence of mind to notify the sponsor of the seminar and explain what had happened and what I was doing to remedy the situation. While I was on the edge of panic and envisioned being fired the next day, I certainly learned a lot from that episode. Never make assumptions and double-check everything. To this day, a manager—in fact, any employee—without a prioritized checklist makes me nervous. This is just one example from my own career where a tough situation was inarguably instructive. The lessons live indelibly in my memory.

Remember the Chinese Parable

At the outset of this book Mark and I described a career as a series of choices that determine what we do during the majority of our waking hours. The implication is that usually we make the choices and are generally in charge of our own destinies. Sometimes this is true, but not always. Occasionally the choices of others seem to determine our fate. Staffs are reduced in size, departments are restructured, new leadership may impose different requirements throughout an agency. Organizations are organic, after all, and subject to the same shifts, growth cycles, and metamorphoses as individuals. They, too, are buffeted by external forces. Sometimes our job search at a particular time is set in motion not by our own choices but by the decisions of others. Often this appears, at least at first, to be a tragic occurrence, but it need not turn out that way. As colleagues who were fired often attest, they were forced to grow and stretch, learn new skills, and found themselves in new jobs more satisfying than those they had assumed they wanted to keep.

The moral is that we cannot be sure if a particular career happening (or a personal one, for that matter) is in the longer term positive or negative. Remember the Chinese parable: There was a peasant family. One day their only horse and source of livelihood escaped—a "bad" thing. The next day the horse returned with another horse. Their herd doubled—a "good" thing. The next day when the eldest son was trying to ride the new horse, he fell off and broke his leg—a "bad" thing. The next day war broke out and the injured son was not required to fight—a "good" thing. You get the idea. The important thing is what we do when certain choices are made. We cannot judge immediately if an event is good or bad for the evolution of a career. The operative questions are "What lessons can I distill from this experience?" and "What do these lessons suggest for my job search?"

Professionalism

Frequently, people are designated professionals because they have attained certain academic qualifications. They have earned medical or engineering degrees, for instance. Often, it implies that they are equipped to and, in fact, do handle specific responsibilities. Lawyers defend clients in the courtroom. Professors of Russian must have a certain command of the language and levels of proficiency. Only professors with PhDs are considered qualified to teach higher-level courses. Nonetheless, in many offices employees are routinely admonished to "behave professionally" or "act like a professional." In that context, professionalism is an unwritten code of conduct one is expected to observe. What it means to be professional may vary considerably depending on the field and the internal culture of the organization in question.

Regardless of a person's role within an organization, it behooves her or him to behave professionally. Whether or not a particular manager can articulate just what being a professional means to that person, he or she has a notion of appropriate behavior against which the actions of employees are judged.

What follows is my own, admittedly parochial understanding of this elusive concept. I offer it not as the ultimate definition of professionalism but rather as a way to help you think about your behavior—as a job seeker and as an employee in a specific workplace.

Character Counts—Honesty and Dependability

For me, and I would venture to say for most managers, the first measure of professionalism is character. Above all I want people on my staff who are honest and have integrity. I need to know that I can count on that person. If my assistant says she will be there at 7:30 a.m. to check that the breakfast for a meeting we are hosting is indeed what we ordered, I can trust that she will arrive on time. If a colleague submits a receipt for a given amount, I know that is exactly the amount she paid for that taxi ride. If a colleague promised to complete a newsletter article or grant proposal by noon on Thursday, I have confidence that the article or proposal will be submitted on time. I no longer have to exert any mental energy considering those tasks. I can depend on these colleagues. They do precisely what they say they will do. They are professionals.

Ambassador Kenton Keith underscored this point in our interview with him: "No matter how good your excuse is, if at the end of the day you have not achieved what you're committed to achieving, that's what is going to be remembered."

If a mistake happens or a problem arises, a professional quickly informs a supervisor so a way to resolve the problem can be fashioned. In fact, a professional promptly passes along useful information to those who need to know. And in certain cases, you make sure you have done so in writing. The old paper trail concept may have morphed into an electronic record, but the fundamental principle is the same. Hone your judgment regarding who needs what information and when it is needed. In 1982 when I assumed my first managerial position, the comptroller of the Institute of International Education gave me one of the best pieces of ad-

vice I have ever received: "Remember, Sherry, never surprise anyone."
This has been a guiding principle for me ever since.

Doing Your Best

The second measure of professionalism for me is that I expect a member
of my staff to do his best at whatever task is assigned. Whether taking notes
at a hearing on Capitol Hill or defrosting the office refrigerator, I expect
a colleague to do these things to the best of his ability. I am a great fan
of the legendary former UCLA basketball coach John Wooden and his
philosophy of leadership.[1] His fundamental premise is that he coached
his players to work hard developing their skills, to do their absolute best
at every game, and the score would take care of itself. For Wooden, success is not defined as winning per se—it was produced from the synergy
of each person on the team giving his best effort each and every game.
Winning resulted, but it was not the primary goal.

Attention to Detail

Intertwined with doing your best is attention to detail. If I see a typo or
if poor grammar is used on a résumé, it immediately goes to the rejec-
tion pile. My reasoning is as follows—if a person cannot muster the discipline to review her own résumé for misspellings (the primary document
that projects her skills to a potential employer), how will she ever summon the discipline to produce error-free documents for our organization?
Good writing and editing skills, as well as the ability to review work and
catch mistakes (so I do not have to use my time to do it), are talents I
value a great deal.

Being a Team Player

Another dimension of professionalism is being a team player. In every organization there are crunch times. A major one at the National Council
of International Visitors (NCIV) is the month before our national conference. Everyone does what needs to be done to put on the best possible

conference. It doesn't matter if technically a task is in—or not in—your job description. The important thing is that our entire team is working together to produce the best possible event and experience for our conference participants.

When I overhear one of my colleagues offering to help another so his deadline can be met, I know that our office culture is evolving in a constructive way. This basic concept that collectively we are all responsible for our organization and its work (not just for our slice of it) is a key part of professionalism.

Curiosity—A Desire to Learn

A real professional always seeks opportunities to grow and learn. I try to help the staff at NCIV understand the overall context for our work. I counsel them to approach their work in two ways. The first is that we each play a role and do that to the best of our ability. Second, I always encourage colleagues to study organizational dynamics. It is important to be able to discern whether a reaction to your work is directed at you. Perhaps this reaction would be directed at anyone playing the role you are playing. This idea of wearing a certain hat within an organization, plus being a student of the process, can help you react to some situations more calmly. It is useful to try to treat every situation as an opportunity for learning—not only about the specifics of a particular project but about the bigger picture within which the project is managed.

Dress

Be conscious of what the way you dress says about you and your attitude toward your job. Please note that these comments are directed primarily toward those working in an office setting. Clearly, if you are managing the delivery of humanitarian supplies at a refugee camp, your attire will be dictated by tasks and climate.

Even in nonoffice settings, however, I would argue that professionals should opt for more conservative attire. Some of my colleagues will undoubtedly conclude I am hopelessly old fashioned when I say that sundresses (and similar garments), bare midriffs, short skirts, untucked shirttails, and flip-flops have no place in a modern office—even on casual Fridays. Yes, I will confess, that although when I started my first regular job at the Institute of International Education (IIE) I always wore skirts (sometimes with three-inch heels—what was I thinking?) and jackets, I have become an enthusiastic convert to casual Fridays. Each Friday I happily don my jeans and tennis shoes. Still, coming of age literally in another century, it seems to me that casual Fridays—in some offices at least—have gravitated to sloppy Fridays. One's dress should never be distracting to others. I expect my staff to be dressed neatly at all times. I try to convey this expectation during the interview process so no one can tell me later that he or she didn't know about my expectation and feels that his or her freedom of expression is unduly constrained.

The dress and image dimension of professionalism is especially important in international careers. Often we work with colleagues whose religious or other cultural beliefs mandate conservative dress. In my view, you should adapt to their norms rather than expect them to accept more casual standards. The office is not the beach, and professionals should dress accordingly. They are always aware that the image they project reflects not only on their own judgment but on their organization as well. Only you can decide what you believe is appropriate attire for you. Nonetheless, it is still prudent to be sure that your view meshes with that of the manager who hires you.

There is a useful way to think about dress, attention to detail, or any other aspect of professionalism I have outlined. Each action you take, as a job seeker or employee, will build or erode the confidence of others in your judgment and abilities. As you contemplate any action, be sure to consider what it conveys to your potential employer or supervisor. These managers are the people who will serve as your references, decide the amount of your next raise, and identify professional opportunities for you. They want to be reassured that you are worth the investment—that you are a true professional.

Don't Take It Personally

Such a glib, seemingly unfeeling phrase! It is easy to offer this advice as long as you are not the person who didn't get the second interview or the job that seemed like such a good fit. Yet this trite admonition has merit.

When I served as director of a relatively large staff at IIE and frequently hired new staff members, and now at NCIV, I have often passed over job applicants who were capable people with impressive qualifications. In my experience, for each job opening there are a number of candidates who can do the job. Managers building a team of people with complementary expertise look for someone who not only can do the job but also whose background builds the strength of the staff as a whole. Please keep this in mind as you cope with the inevitable rejections an extensive job search entails.

MARK
The Never-ending Job Story

A former member of NCIV's board of directors once told me that he looks for a job every day. Each morning, while drinking his coffee, he scans a list of available jobs in the fields of international education, exchange, and development, just to see what is out there. If he finds a particularly interesting opening, something that he thinks he would not only enjoy but that would also stretch him professionally, he applies for it.

"Why?" I remember asking. "Aren't you happy in your job?"

"I'm actually very happy in my job," he responded.

"Then why are you applying for jobs if you're not planning to leave your current one?" I wondered.

"I don't apply for jobs that would be a lateral move or a moderate step up or because I need a change of scenery," he explained. "I apply for jobs that are a stretch for me, that I may not quite be qualified for but, if given the opportunity, would work my butt off to succeed in. I'm always looking for the next way I can move on to bigger challenges."

For me, this story neatly illustrates the point that both Sherry and I stress in this chapter: Your job search never ceases. It is a consistent activity, a continuous journey that will constantly keep you on the lookout for ways in which to further challenge yourself and to better serve your cause.

Moving On Is Hard to Do

The time came when, as difficult as the decision was, I had to leave NCIV. I had previously viewed the attainment of my position at NCIV as the end of something: the end of a search, the end of a process, the end of wondering how I was going to pay my rent. Two years later, though, I learned that it was not the end of anything. Rather it was, as Sherry describes it earlier in this chapter, a building block of my career.

As I discuss in chapter 1, I had many experiences throughout college and graduate school that seemed random, that had no obvious pattern or path. Yet I was happy with these choices because they gave me varied, valued experiences and led me to where I am today. They were the foundation for my later choices. They were building blocks. It was easy to view them as such because they were impermanent, short-term opportunities. I knew from the start that, whether it was in three months, six months, or a year, I would be moving on.

But when I accepted my post at NCIV, I never thought about the position as a building block or a foundation for later choices. This job was full-time;

it was permanent. I was there to work. I had a job to do. Even though I knew that I wouldn't be at NCIV forever, I didn't much consider the fact that, at some point, I was going to have to make a difficult choice and take another step forward in my career.

One day, however, I realized with a start that it was time for me to move on. At first I felt guilty about this, as if I were betraying Sherry, NCIV, and the whole field of international exchange. Yet I came to realize that I wasn't experiencing a bout of disloyalty to my organization but rather a natural part of my career progression. This wasn't anything personal—I simply needed new challenges. Had NCIV been able to provide those for me, I would have considered staying and taking on a new role there. But because the organization is small—a staff of only eight—there was little room for me to advance.

I also came to see that not only was this need for a new challenge natural, it was also beneficial to both parties involved. A new position would satisfy my need for something fresh, as well as advance my career. This move would also be beneficial to NCIV and the cause of international exchange for, by staying in my job too long, I ran the risk of becoming complacent and allowing my daily performance to suffer, thus damaging the ability of the organization to serve its cause.

In searching for that next challenge for myself, it became apparent that my cause was shifting too. In chapter 1 I say that I had difficulty pinning down exactly what my cause is. In my search for a new job I found that while I wanted international exchange to remain a part of my career, I also yearned for a more communications-focused position. This shift led me to my current position as director of college communications at Georgetown College (the liberal arts school at Georgetown University), where my days are spent focusing on communications-related issues.

My position at Georgetown also allows me to remain involved with international education and study abroad, which is important to me because my cause still certainly includes these elements. But I also came to see, as I started my new job, that perhaps my cause was starting to grow. Part of the reason I was attracted to Georgetown College is because I studied in the liberal arts college at the University of Notre Dame, pursuing an English degree. I have always strongly believed that my liberal arts education has served me well. While my business major friends joked that I would have trouble finding a job that paid me to read books, I had the feeling that my choice of major was a good one, even though it did not point to an obvious career. Among other benefits, it honed my writing skills. I also believe that many more young people can be well served by a liberal arts education. It struck me that perhaps I had stumbled upon a burgeoning cause. While international exchange and communications still remain as two solid facets of my cause, perhaps encouraging young students to realize and pursue the benefits of a liberal arts education is becoming yet another guiding force as I make my career decisions.

Certainly there is no way of knowing how my cause(s) will evolve from this point forward or when I will be struck next with the realization that it is time to move on to another challenge. But I am confident that by utilizing the tools of discernment that Sherry and others have helped me to build, by continuing to go with my gut, and by risking myself when the occasions arise, I will succeed in crafting a meaningful and rewarding career.

Professionalism

Earlier in this chapter, Sherry points out that most managers hold a particular notion of what it means to "behave professionally" or "exhibit professionalism," even if they cannot articulate the sentiment. My career experiences thus far have illustrated that there seem to be commonly accepted modes of behavior when it comes to professional conduct. A professional should dress appropriately for his job, taking into account position responsibilities, location, and cultural context to determine what that appropriate dress should be. A professional should treat her colleagues and managers with respect and congeniality, being forceful when necessary, in order to create a productive working environment. A professional should give every project, proposal, newsletter, and e-mail that leaves his desk the required amount of diligence and detailed attention.

Yet, it is impossible to provide definitive guidelines on what *exactly* professional and appropriate dress is, or how one can best act in a congenial and respectful, yet sometimes forceful, manner, or what the proper level of attention should be for any given project. Not only do jobs in most fields operate in a particular cultural environment, but also every manager has a different idea of what professional conduct truly is. As she illustrates in her section of this chapter, Sherry can articulate the characteristics she believes a true professional should develop and exhibit. For me, however, pinning down those traits is not as easy. Rather than attempt to create an authoritative manual that can guide your actions no matter what position you hold, I instead recommend that you foster in yourself the trait that will allow you to cope with and thrive in any professional situation: adaptability.

Adaptability

You will find as you progress in your career that an important virtue is not necessarily how you *conform* to the opinions, expectations, and working styles of those around you but rather how you *adapt* to them. Kowtowing to varying needs and expectations is less important than learning to work comfortably and successfully within various organizational and cultural constructs. You must determine how you can work with colleagues of differing viewpoints and working styles in order to get the job done. You must determine how to incorporate compromise into your daily routine. If another party is resistant to compromise, you must decide how to maintain your composure to work around and through the situation.

For young professionals, this process of adaptation can be especially challenging. As I discuss in chapter 3, my generation has an acute sense of the urgent. We are the on-demand generation. Consequently, when we enter the workplace, we are eager immediately to bring our skills to bear on the tasks at hand. We don't necessarily stop to think about the need to adapt our performance and style to mesh with those around us, or look to our more experienced colleagues for guidance.

I learned the value of slowing down and adapting early on in two small but meaningful ways. The first example took place a mere three weeks into my job at NCIV when Sherry and I traveled to Denver for a board of directors meeting. A majority of the meeting was held on a Saturday, for which the board chair had determined dress would be casual. That morning in my hotel room, I put on a pair of neatly pressed khakis, a polo shirt, and black shoes—fairly dressed up for a dress-down day, at least by my standards. I even tucked in my shirt. I also decided to forgo shaving that morning.

The following Monday, back at the NCIV office in Washington, I got together with Sherry to discuss the outcomes of the board meeting. As I sat down in her office with a fresh cup of coffee, she remarked how she liked the particular tie I was wearing. She then made another observation about my appearance.

"You're looking nice and neat this morning, too," she said. "You looked awfully scruffy on Saturday."

I had no idea how to take this comment. Was it just a passing remark with no judgment intended? Or was it a comment meant to convey Sherry's displeasure with my hiatus from the razor and an admonition not to let it happen again? Our meeting concluded and Sherry never again remarked on my appearance, unless it was to comment on the fashionable tie I happened to be wearing (my mother supplies many of my ties—she has excellent taste!).

The second example occurred not long after that board meeting in Denver. Sherry requested that I compose an e-mail to the entire board to follow up on an issue that had been discussed at the meeting. Wanting to show my diligence as an employee, I immediately composed the e-mail and studiously checked and rechecked the facts and grammar. I also labored for some time over the wording and tone of the e-mail. I knew that it required a professional tone, but I had also just discovered that the board was a laid-back, personable group. I wanted to show that I too was laid-back and personable and would prove to be an excellent colleague. So I chose my words and tone accordingly. Pleased with the amiable yet professional nature of my e-mail, I copied Sherry and pressed the send button.

Later that afternoon Sherry came into my office and told me in a respectful way that she felt the tone of that e-mail was inappropriate. A business-related e-mail to the board of directors of our organization needed to be more *professional.* "The members of the board are my bosses," she remarked, "and I need everyone on staff to treat them as such."

Both of these events were significant learning experiences for me. While I had thought the tone of my e-mail was in fact quite professional, Sherry obviously had not. While I think there is nothing unprofessional about growing a bit of fashionable stubble from time to time, Sherry would tend to disagree. It is important for young professionals to determine their own ideas of professionalism or what it means to be professional. Yet it is equally important for us to learn from and adapt to, as necessary, the notions of professionalism held by our more experienced colleagues.

Adaptation to professional environments is not an attribute reserved for young professionals. Rather, you must possess it and hone it even as you progress deeper into your career. In fact, adaptation perhaps becomes even more important as you acquire additional responsibility in your job and come into positions of leadership. Not only do you have to deal with the irreverent young professionals like me who don't want to tuck their shirts in, but you are also required to be a leader for your organization. Leadership requires adaptation.

Sherry has constantly impressed me with her knack for adaptation. During my tenure at NCIV, we spent a large amount of time working with a coalition of other organizations in the fields of international exchange and education. While the mission and goals of this coalition were admirable, the working relationships between certain personalities in the group were sometimes strained. Competing interests stood in the way of progress. Programmatic expectations far surpassed what was feasible within our limited budget and staff support. As we attempted to plan a major event, the whole effort nearly collapsed under its own weight.

Sherry, however, showed remarkable adaptability during the entire process. She facilitated compromise between conflicting parties and ideas. She brought expectations back down to reality. She convinced coalition members to contribute not only to strategic direction but also to the grunt work. She even listened to my concerns about the direction of the coalition and took some of my ideas to the group for implementation. It is in part because of Sherry's leadership and ability to adapt to various situations and personalities that the coalition continues to move forward today.

"It's Just the Bottom Rung of Another Ladder"

In response to the questions asked of him in creating his profile, Fayezul Choudhury told Sherry and me a story that neatly summed up the main focus of this chapter:

On his wife's birthday in 1985, he worked for nearly twenty-four straight hours. At the time, Choudhury, now the controller and vice president of strategy and resource management at the World Bank, was working in London for a well-known international accounting and consulting firm. On that particular day in 1985, his wife dropped him off at the Underground station near their home at 3:30 a.m. and did not see him again until past 2:30 a.m. the next day. His wife was remarkably understanding and not upset at him for having to work on her birthday that year. Yet the experience unnerved Choudhury and spurred him to seriously consider if this job at this firm was the right place for him.

Not long after, Choudhury received a promotion and was made a partner in the firm. *Finally,* he thought. *This is proof that I've made it.* A senior partner called Choudhury into his office and followed up this news of the promotion with a simple, "Well done. Carry on." No congratulations or praise for the hard work Choudhury had put in to get where he was.

Excited about the promotion but equally frustrated by the lack of enthusiasm from the senior partner about his accomplishment, Choudhury turned to leave the office. Just as he reached the door, the senior partner stopped him. "Fayez," the senior partner called from his desk. Choudhury turned, an expectant look on his face. The senior partner finished: "Remember, you're not the only partner in this firm."

At that moment, Choudhury not only knew that it was time to move on, but he also came to realize a fundamental truth about careers: you've never really made it. The journey goes on and on. "A number of pieces just fell into place for me," he recounted. "You have this notion that if you're a partner, or if you've reached a certain point in your organization or your career, you've got it made. But really, it's just the bottom rung of another ladder."

Note

1. John Wooden and Steve Jamison, *Wooden On Leadership* (New York: McGraw-Hill, 2005).

Part II

Selected Resources

Part II is designed to help you map out the next steps on your career path and appreciate the many different routes that are available. Here you will find selected resources to aid you in your pursuit of a career in international education, exchange, and development. It is important to note that the resources contained in this section are indeed "selected." That is to say, our lists are not exhaustive; there is certainly much more information available on specific topics, fields, and organizations. However, the resources in this section are a kind of compass. We view them as the best tools available to point you in the right direction as you make your career choices.

Each chapter in this selected resources section is structured to best facilitate skimming, allowing you to readily locate the information that you will find most helpful. Chapters begin with introductions to their respective categories of resources. A list then follows this introduction, complete with contact information and short descriptions of various organizations or opportunities in that particular field. After these lists of sample organizations comes the real meat of the section—the print and web resources that are available for you to further research your interests.

Many of the resources in this section overlap—that is, they could be placed in any number of the various chapters or belong to several different categories. Thus, when arranging the organizations, publications, and web resources in this book, we attempted to place them in the category where we felt a reader would most likely and most logically look to find them, rather than the category that most strictly defines them.

There are instances in which we thought that the reader would benefit from having a particular resource referenced in several different places; in these cases, we have included a cross-reference. For example, InterAction is a coalition of more than 150 development organizations offering numerous resources and job opportunities for those interested in the development field. It first appears in chapter 6 because it is an association for development professionals. However, InterAction is also a leading nonprofit organization in the field of development; thus it is cross-referenced in chapter 9. Its members also offer substantial volunteer opportunities in international development, so it appears in chapter 8 as well. NAFSA: Association of International Educators, a large professional association representing international education, first appears as a resource in chapter 6. However, the job board hosted by NAFSA is an excellent resource for those looking for jobs or internships in international education, so a cross-reference to the organization is included in chapters 5 and 7. Not every conceivable cross-reference is included, however, as there are simply too many and the book would balloon beyond our space constraints.

Because any and all of the resources listed in part II may overlap across many topics, chapter 5 contains resources designed to help you begin with a more comprehensive job search. Websites such as Indeed.com, Simply Hired.com, and Weddles.com are meant to help you see what's out there. The chapters that follow are devoted to more topic-specific, niche job resources in the fields of international education, exchange, and development. Many of the organizations and associations included also host their own job banks and boards that pertain to their specific fields or areas of expertise; practically all organizations list internal job openings on their own websites.

As you use this resource section, it will be necessary to choose a starting point. If you are seeking volunteer opportunities abroad, you can certainly begin with that section. If a job in a multinational organization is your aim, start your reading there. But do not neglect the other sections and resources in the book, for you never know when a natural cross-reference will occur and lead you in a new and rewarding direction.

You will also find, interspersed between each of the resource chapters, profiles of accomplished colleagues. The considered advice from the professionals profiled is not presented as gospel, but rather as twelve examples of how people think about their careers in international affairs. These professionals represent each of the major focal points of the book—international education, exchange, and development—as well as some of the specific niches found within these fields. The colleagues profiled are at varying stages of their careers. We intentionally interviewed promising young professionals and several midcareer colleagues in addition to presidents, CEOs, and executive directors in order to present a richer collection of career advice that transcends generations.

Each professional was asked a common set of questions. In addition to providing information on his or her career, educational background, and interests, each person was asked to distill lessons learned and practical advice about building a career in international affairs. The subjects broached in the profiles are those also explored in part I: finding a cause, the importance of networking, and the value of mentors. In some instances, the advice offered by these professionals echoes the recommendations we share on these topics; yet, in other instances, their thoughts on careers do not mesh tidily with our own.

Thinking about the process of career development from various viewpoints is essential to sharpening our own skills of discernment. Making an informed choice comes not from hearing only one expert or from knowing only one way of tackling an issue but rather from examining the broadest range possible and interpreting for ourselves what is appropriate for us. Much like the career roundtables Sherry used to lead, the synergy generated by the multiple perspectives of the professionals profiled is much richer than one or two opinions could ever be.

Chapter 5
Your Job Search—A General Approach

Cast the net wide. Search broadly. See what's out there.

One of the greatest myths regarding the job search, international or otherwise, is that you should only be looking for open positions. It's true that the immediate goal of your job search is to land a job, and the position that you get at this time will have to be one that is currently available. In searching for those open positions, however, do not hesitate to explore the wide array of possibilities with an open mind. Check out jobs that you may not yet be qualified for but might someday be interested in. Dig deeper into organizations that do not have job openings at the moment but have missions that excite you and are doing work you would like to do.

The career resources noted in this chapter—specifically the job boards and search engines—can be great sources of information. This is not only because they supply the specific details of available positions but also because they give you a better idea of the enormous variety of jobs that exists. Many career websites give the option of researching jobs, companies, organizations, and industries and often provide articles and other advice for job seekers. The panoply of players on the international scene has expanded so much in recent decades that it is difficult for any one person to grasp the full range of possibilities. Using these tools to cast your net wide and discover what's out there will help immensely in this process.

This approach holds true not just for those who are in the market for a new job but also for those who, though they are currently in a stable job and have no immediate intention of leaving, might someday decide to seek change or greater challenges. According to the career and networking website Jibber Jobber (www.jibberjobber.com), *everyone* is a job seeker. Some are active job seekers—those looking to start a new job as soon as possible—while some are passive job seekers who are only exploring their options. Yet, according to Jibber Jobber, the average passive job seeker will become an active seeker every three to five years.

Regularly perusing job boards will aid you at that point when you do decide to begin an active job search; it will also assist you in thinking about your broader career development. To be fair, fifteen minutes spent one afternoon scrolling through a long list of job postings will not suddenly flip the switch and illuminate your lifelong career path. The cumulative effect of regularly gathering information and pondering your career, however, will better prepare you for that moment when it is time to make the next move.

WHAT IS YOUR GOAL?

It is important to keep in mind that *pursuing an international career* is not synonymous with *working abroad.* Just because a job enables you to travel does not necessarily mean it is the best opportunity to begin or continue your career in international education, exchange, or development. In the same way, even though a job does not have a travel component, it may still help to build your career in international relations in significant ways. While finding the job, whether part-time or full-time, temporary or permanent, that allows you to visit exotic locales can be an exciting and worthwhile goal, it is imperative to determine if this is *your* primary goal. What is more important to you? Traveling and working abroad, in and of itself? Or creating a substantive career in international education, exchange, or development? These two can certainly overlap, and they often do, but they are not one and the same. In fact, given family commitments and considerations, such as those described by Luby Ismail in her profile, the challenge may be to forge an international career in the field that requires minimal travel abroad.

A simple search on Amazon reveals the numerous books that offer advice on "working abroad": examples include *Work Worldwide, Work Abroad, The Big Guide to Living and Working Overseas, Work Your Way Around the World,* and *Live & Work Abroad: A Guide for Modern Nomads.* A Google search will take you to numerous websites, such as GoAbroad.com, that offer similar guidance. If you are indeed a modern nomad and your goal is simply to find a mode of employment that will send you far and wide across the world, then these sources may be excellent guides for you. If you are focused not on travel per se, however, but on a career in international education, exchange, or development (of which travel may be a component), then searching for the easiest and quickest way to work abroad may not be the best approach.

What about those people who are looking to be modern nomads for a time, then transition into an international career? Your adventures abroad certainly will be beneficial, formative, and broaden your horizons. Depending on what you do, international experience is a requirement for an employer who values cross-cultural communication skills. For example, serving as a Peace Corps volunteer or an Experiment in International Living group leader indicates to a potential employer that you have valuable experience and know how to get things done in another cultural context. Nonetheless, it is essential to realize that the position you land upon returning from your nomadic exploits abroad most likely *won't* pay you to continue strapping on your backpack and exploring the country of your choice.

BE REALISTIC

Being realistic is key to distinguishing between simply working abroad and fashioning an international career. Finding a job that lets you travel extensively *and* work on substantive issues in the fields of international exchange, education, and development is not easy.

"Don't expect the moon just because you have a certain level of education or certain experiences," Paul Binkley, director of career development services for the George Washington University School of Public Policy and Public Administration, told us. "International development, exchange, and education jobs demand a vast amount of experience: experience abroad, languages skills, etc. . . . many students come to me wondering why they're having trouble landing that job they really want even though they have a master's degree or a certain level of education or have spent a year abroad. In this environment, these qualifications are not remarkable. They are expected."

This fact is not meant to deflate the hopes of all recent college graduates and suggest that only those with master's degrees, five years of experience, and multiple international experiences can get a job. (Remember the old paradox of job hunting? Those with the experience get the job, but how can you gain the experience if you can't get the job?) What this means, however, is that it is important to have realistic expectations and understand that your dream job—the one with substantive responsibilities, a respectable salary, and business-class international travel—might not come right away.

"Remember that the vast majority of internationally oriented positions are located domestically," Binkley remarked, "so don't dismiss them. Everybody wants to go abroad, but finding a position that allows you to do this often takes a while. It's important to look for positions that give you experience, even if they don't send you abroad."

THE JOB SEARCH IN THE ELECTRONIC AGE

The advent of the Internet has transformed the nature of the job search. Some of the greatest benefits the Internet can bring in your job search are online job postings and job search engines. These bring with them the ability to peruse what's available in real time. Print resources such as this book are beneficial in their own right: they provide a broader context for your job search and easy-to-reference guidelines and resources that you can access at any time. However, online sources are more dynamic. They are constantly (in most cases) updated and allow for job seekers and other professionals to gain the most current view of what changes are taking place within a given field, what organizations are experiencing turnover at that time, and what specific jobs are available at that moment.

Online postings and job search engines are certainly valuable when you are actively searching and applying for positions. Yet these online resources should also be used at other times, well before the moment you actually *need* that job. For example, you may be a student some time off from graduation and starting a new career. However, it can be instructive to scan job postings and perform random job searches, just to get a better idea about possibilities that might intrigue you. By doing this when you are not under pressure to actually find, apply for, and obtain a job, you give yourself an opportunity to see the kinds of positions for which organizations are recruiting (and the qualifications and skills they desire), to learn about new organizations, and to better reflect on and refine your own interests. The job search is an ongoing process of searching and discernment.

UNIVERSITY LISTSERVS AND CAREER CENTERS

In addition to career websites and job search engines, university e-mail lists, or Listservs, are a great source of information about international organizations and position openings. If you have not already subscribed to the listserv of your undergraduate or graduate institution, or both, register for them immediately. While a university-wide e-mail list may offer some useful job and career information, typically the e-mail list of the school, department, or college within the university that focuses on international relations will have the most targeted and beneficial job information for you.

For example, on the e-mail list of the School of International Service at American University (AU), our shared alma mater, students and staff alike post job and internship openings daily. In addition, several AU staff members working in student services scour many of the job boards listed in this section and others (such as Idealist.org, FPA.org, and InterAction.org) and circulate a weekly "job round-up" on the e-mail list—essentially doing job searches for you. Like many universities, AU has its own institutional subscriptions to job boards that charge fees, allowing them to circulate information free to students and alumni. (Mark first learned about the National Council for International Visitors and internship opportunities there on the AU School of International Service Listserv.) University career centers are also invaluable resources, not only for résumé critiques, interview practice, and career counseling but also for their online job boards and résumé submission services.

GOOGLE IT!

Google is another valuable tool of the job search in the electronic age. Some people we know have found success by running such searches as "international education" to see what kinds of international education organizations exist. Searches such as "international development + job openings" or "internships in foreign assistance agencies" may enable you to link directly to a development organization's job openings or internship program page.

E-MAIL IS NOT ALWAYS THE ANSWER

Despite the fact that we are both enthusiastic advocates for the myriad of web resources that will make your job and career search easier and more effective, we both caution that, in some instances, going electronic is not always the best way. More specifically, e-mail is not always the answer. Far too often, instead of considering our communication options, we simply head to the keyboard and fire off an e-mail. When it would be far more productive and downright easier to make a telephone call, we'll instead spend twenty minutes composing an e-mail requesting information that takes two minutes to explain orally.

E-mail is a great way to request specific information, inquire about job openings (especially if nothing is posted on an organization's website), and ask for clarifications. It is a quick and efficient method of sending out a large volume of generic requests for general information, much more efficient than calling every organization of interest individually. If an organization asks that you apply for a position by e-mail (as most do), then you should do so.

However, when you are in the later, less generic stages of the job search—following up on an application or an interview or trying to foster a personal contact at the organization that you hope will lead to a job—e-mail is not always the best solution. Not only does your e-mail run the risk of being lost among the avalanche of messages many professionals receive every day, but also the sometimes impersonal nature of an e-mail may have a negative effect. It is not only people of an older generation (those who did not grow up using e-mail) who may respond more favorably to a phone call or a handwritten thank-you note, especially after an interview. People of a younger generation (those who grew up using e-mail) respond to—and should be accustomed to using—these traditional modes of communication as well.

Regardless of the manner in which you choose to do it—e-mail, phone call, handwritten thank-you note—we cannot emphasize enough the importance of follow-up. Whether to a first meeting, a job application, or an interview, follow-up is essential. It is an opportunity to remind a potential employer of how well-suited you are for an organization, as well as another opportunity to demonstrate your writing skills. As the president of an organization who has a constantly packed schedule, Sherry can attest to the fact that follow-up will keep you on her radar screen and make it that much more likely that she will not only remember you but also want to involve you in her work in some way. (For her, phone calls and handwritten notes are the best way to get her attention.) Mark has learned from personal experience that following up on a job application can make all the difference. After assuming his current position as director of college communications at Georgetown College, he learned from his colleagues that his initial application was placed in the "maybe" pile. It was only after he sent a carefully crafted e-mail to the position search committee following up on his application that he was moved to the "interview" pile. The tone and professionalism of his e-mail prompted renewed interest in his application.

GET INVOLVED

The job search engines, networking sites, and other impersonal, electronic resources are wonderful resources but they also can't replace a more personal, basic job search activity: getting involved. It is still possible to get a job by sending in a blind application (that is, when you don't know anyone at the organization and no one there knows you). You should never hesitate to apply if you find a position that truly excites you. It is easy to dismiss your chances of getting that job when you are an unknown quantity to an organization. You might tell yourself, "There must be *hundreds* of people applying and the organization doesn't know who I am. How am *I* going to get the position?" Yet you never know what can happen, and it certainly won't happen unless you apply.

However, you vastly increase your chances of getting that job if you make yourself a known quantity. Volunteer at conferences and other events. Organizations will be impressed by the initiative and commitment you show by volunteering your time for their cause. This will be remembered when positions become available. Network. Go to events sponsored by organizations in the field. Set up informational interviews with those who might be able to provide you with information about organizations in which you are interested. By putting yourself in front of people already working in the fields of international education, exchange, and development, you are making it that much more likely that they will eventually lock their sights on you and draw you into the field as well. And, of course, intern. It is no secret that, when positions must be filled, organizations often think first of the outstanding interns that have already done excellent work in their offices.

BUT I DON'T LIVE IN WASHINGTON, D.C., OR IN NEW YORK!

You may also find, and perhaps become frustrated by the fact, that many of the organizations offering substantive jobs and internships in international education, exchange, and development are in large coastal cities such as Washington, D.C., New York, Seattle, and San Francisco. What, then, are those who live throughout the rest of the United States to do?

While it is true that cities such as Washington, D.C., and New York have more international opportunities than most, many cities throughout the United States have an international presence. States and large metropolitan areas have their own set of international connections. You could even argue that some large cities and states conduct their own foreign policy. There are jobs with an international dimension at world trade centers, in chambers of commerce, in governors' offices, and often in mayors' offices as well. The jobs in the state and district offices of members of Congress are, of course, often dominated by domestic concerns. However, they also deal with various issues that we tend to consider international. As the distinction between domestic and international becomes increasingly blurred, many jobs will inevitably have a tangible international component, whether located in Bozeman, Montana, or Des Moines, Iowa.

You will find that job boards such as Idealist.org and NAFSA.org *do* have international job and internship listings in many cities other than Washington, D.C., or New York. If you are interested in an organization located in Washington, D.C., or New York, but you are looking to intern in Denver or Cincinnati, contact those D.C. offices anyway. Many organizations, such as the National Council for International Visitors and the Institute of International Education, have regional offices or member organizations across the country. These organizations may have internship opportunities in their own offices, and if not, they are plugged into the international pipeline in their particular city and can steer you in the right direction. And of course, every pocket of the country has universities and colleges. As higher education becomes more internationalized by the hour, the number of international opportunities on campuses will continue to expand as well.

SELECTED RESOURCES

Print

Best Résumés and CVs for International Jobs: Your Passport to the Global Job Market
Ronald Krannich and Wendy S. Enelow
Impact Publications, 237 pages, 2002 (www.impactpublications.com)

This guide to résumés and CVs includes more than one hundred examples of professionally produced international résumés and CVs for a variety of occupations and experience levels.

Building Bridges: A Manual on Including People with Disabilities in International Exchange Programs
Susan Sygall and Cindy Lewis, eds.
Mobility International USA/National Clearinghouse on Disability and Exchange, 262 pages, 2006 (www.miusa.org)

This comprehensive manual features suggestions and ideas for including, recruiting, and accommodating people with disabilities in international exchange programs. *Building Bridges* also addresses cross-cultural issues and international service projects and includes an extensive resource section for further research.

Careers in International Affairs, Eighth Edition
Maria Carland and Candace Faber, eds.
Georgetown University Press, 2008 (www.press.georgetown.edu)

Published in cooperation with Georgetown University's School of Foreign Service, this book—now in its eighth edition—provides a wealth of insight and information on global career networking. Particularly helpful is the addition of a chapter on Internet job searches. The publication further includes a list of organizations and businesses with brief descriptions and information about application processes. The editors review the challenges, possibilities, and realities of global careers. The guide features chapter introductions by professionals in the public, private, and nonprofit fields. It contains nearly 350 profiles of international organizations, multinationals and banks, government agencies, and nonprofit organizations.

Careers in International Business
See chapter 12 in this volume.

The Chronicle of Higher Education
The Chronicle of Higher Education is a weekly newspaper, in print and on-line, that discusses issues and events concerning institutions and issues in higher learning. The bulletin section lists job openings and recruitment in various fields of higher education, including internationally oriented jobs at colleges and universities. Visit http://chronicle.com for subscription information.

Directory of Websites for International Jobs
Ronald and Caryl Krannich
Impact Publications, 160 pages, 2002 (www.impactpublications.com)
   This book reveals more than one thousand websites of special interest to anyone seeking an international job. The publication includes practical information on key steps in conducting an effective international job search.

Directory of Executive Recruiters
Kennedy Information, Inc., 1,200 pages, 2006
(www.kennedyinfo.com)
   Executive recruiters can provide a channel to relatively high-level jobs that are, in some cases, not advertised on mainstream job boards and search engines. This directory may aid your job search with its list of 16,500 recruiters at more than 5,700 search firms, complete with contact information to help you start networking with executive recruiters.

Encyclopedia of Associations: International Organizations and Associations
See chapter 6 in this volume.

Encyclopedia of Associations: National Organizations of the U.S. and Associations
See chapter 6 in this volume.

The Foundation Directory
See chapter 12 in this volume.

The Global Citizen: A Guide to Creating an International Life and Career
Elizabeth Kruempelmann
Ten Speed Press, 384 pages, 2002 (www.the-global-citizen.com)

Written by Monster.com's former international career mentor, this book is targeted at those who wish to experience the world through educational travel, academic learning, volunteering, or professional experience overseas. The book takes a "life-planning approach" to designing a "unique global existence." With tips for researching and funding your international venture, secrets to adjusting to life abroad, and hints for making the most of your experiences when you return home, this publication lays out an approach to creating an international life and career.

IIENetwork Membership Directory 2007: Directory of International Educators
Institute of International Education (IIE), 200 pages, 2007
(http://iienetwork.org)

The IIENetwork Membership Directory lists more than 3,500 professionals at higher education institutions (study abroad directors, international student advisers, university presidents, and many more) who are active participants in international educational exchange.

International Career Employment Weekly
www.internationaljobs.org

International Career Employment Weekly is a newspaper filled with current international jobs in the fields of international development, exchange, education, communication, health care, democracy building, governance, policy, environmental issues, and others. According to its website, this newspaper has been published since 1991, with more than twenty thousand readers in approximately 160 countries. A subscription is required to receive the most comprehensive and up-to-date listings, though a more limited list of "hot jobs" is accessible online for free. Subscription lengths vary from six weeks to two years, and reduced subscription rates are offered for individuals. The newspaper can be delivered via hard copy or e-mail, or it can be accessed directly on the International Jobs Center website.

International Exchange Locator: A Resource Directory for Educational and Cultural Exchange
Alliance for International Educational and Cultural Exchange, 371 pages, 2005 (www.alliance-exchange.org)

The *International Exchange Locator* offers detailed information about more than 250 exchange organizations, including mailing addresses, websites, e-mail addresses, phone/fax numbers, exchange program descriptions, and key staff members. Tables at the end of the book provide an overview of U.S. Department of State Exchange Visitor J designations, as well as organizations offering programs in specific geographical regions and countries, academic levels (K-12, scholar, teacher exchange, and more), and cultural and professional exchange programs.

International Job Finder: Where the Jobs Are Worldwide
Daniel Lauber, with Kraig Rice
Planning Communications, 348 pages, 2002
(www.planningcommunications.com)

This fourth volume in the "Job Finders Series" has the stated purpose of "gathering together in one place the broadest collection of effective online and offline resources for finding international jobs." The book lists more than 1,100 websites offering international job vacancies, including résumé databases that serve the international community and directories of international employers. *International Job Finder* also catalogs specialty and trade periodicals, job matching services, job hot lines, print directories, and salary surveys.

International Jobs: Where They Are and How to Get Them
Nina Segal and Eric Kocher
Perseus Books Group, 336 pages, 2003 (www.perseusbooksgroup.com)

This guide, now in its sixth edition, offers guidance on opportunities and techniques for those interested in launching an international career. From jobs teaching English abroad to jobs analyzing intelligence for the federal government, the information in this book covers a diverse array of job opportunities with an international focus.

Jobs and Careers Abroad
Guy Hobbs, ed.
Vacation-Work, 448 pages, 2006 (www.vacationwork.co.uk)

This guide to permanent career opportunities abroad, now in its thirteenth edition, includes a substantial chapter on Internet-based job searches, as well as detailed information on more than thirty-five different international careers. *Jobs and Careers Abroad* also provides insights regarding recruitment and job sources. Individual chapters present career opportunities in fifty countries, with information on immigration and residency, costs and standard of living, health care, welfare, and education and employment prospects.

Jobs for Travel Lovers: Opportunities at Home and Abroad
Ron and Caryl Krannich
Impact Publications, 320 pages, 2006 (www.impactpublications.com)

The fifth edition of this work/travel guide explores opportunities for those who want to add more travel—domestic and international—to their careers. Laying out and dispelling sixty myths, exploring key motivations, and outlining effective job search strategies, the book identifies hundreds of jobs and careers that enable individuals to travel both domestically and abroad.

Monday Developments
InterAction (www.interaction.org)

This monthly newsletter provides in-depth news and commentary on global trends that affect relief, refugee, and development work. It features the latest information on the work of InterAction members around the world and keeps readers up-to-date on legislative action in Congress that could affect U.S. foreign assistance. *Monday Developments* also describes new resources for relief and development workers, professional growth opportunities, and upcoming events, and includes an extensive list of international employment openings.

Transitions Abroad: The Guide to Learning, Living, Working, and Volunteering Overseas
www.transitionsabroad.com

Transitions Abroad is a bimonthly magazine that has been published since 1977. It contains practical information for independent-minded travelers. Each issue covers alternatives to large group tourism, including living, working, studying, and volunteering abroad, as well as vacationing directly with the people of the host country. The magazine's emphasis is on enriching, informed, affordable, and responsible travel.

Work Abroad: The Complete Guide to Finding Jobs Overseas
Clayton A. Hubbs, ed.
Transitions Abroad Publishing, Inc., 186 pages, 2002
(www.transitionsabroad.com)

Find opportunities for both short-term and long-term jobs abroad with this guide. It covers a wide range of positions available to those seeking an international career or experience, including short-term paid work, teaching English (ESL jobs), volunteer work, internships, and teaching jobs. The author discusses other issues such as obtaining work abroad permits and starting a business abroad.

Web

Most people can probably easily rattle off a number of popular job and career websites: Careerbuilder.com, Hotjobs.com, Jobster.com, and Monster.com. Watch an evening of television and you will no doubt see several advertisements for one or more of these sites (a CareerBuilder ad campaign featuring monkeys dressed in business suits is particularly popular). These sites are excellent in their own right for performing a broad job search—for seeing what is out there in the fields of international education, exchange, and development. In a similar way, the online job boards for major newspapers are also good resources for larger-scale searches for job possibilities and opportunities.

The following web resources are job search engines and boards that will either assist you with your general job search, or are specifically focused on the fields of international education, exchange, and development. They will allow you to perform effective searches for international jobs. Several of the sites also offer other assistance, such as articles on career development, industry and company guides, salary surveys and calculators, and blogs and message boards.

CEO Job Opportunities Update
www.ceoupdate.com

CEO Job Opportunities lists executive-level job openings in associations, professional societies, and nonprofit organizations throughout the

United States. It also provides recruiting services and includes articles outlining business trends, recruitment strategies, and global economic issues.

Developmentex

http://developmentex.com

The Development Executive Group is a membership organization working to bring efficiency to recruitment for international development recruitment through business intelligence and other services. The Developmentex website hosts a free job board with more than one thousand international development jobs posted and more than fifty thousand visitors each month.

Foreign Policy Association

www.fpa.org

The Foreign Policy Association job board is a free resource and contains job postings from international think tanks and foreign policy research organizations, nonprofit organizations in international exchange, education, development, and related fields, as well as a host of other policy, research, and internationally oriented fields. The board allows you to sign up for a free e-mail newsletter so that job opportunities are delivered directly to your inbox.

Go Abroad

www.goabroad.com

GoAbroad.com has the stated purpose of filling "an information void in the area of international student travel." The website was designed to provide a one-stop information center for students wishing to travel internationally and to link prospective travelers with organizations providing international opportunities. The site has an abundance of information regarding travel and living abroad, with details about traveler's insurance, phone cards, travel gear, and airfare, as well as links to connected sites with distinct URLs on topics such as:
- Studying abroad (www.studyabroad.com)
- Interning abroad (www.internabroad.com)
- Volunteering abroad (www.volunteerabroad.com)
- Working abroad (www.jobsabroad.com)

Idealist

See chapter 9 in this volume.

Indeed

www.indeed.com

With its clean, simple homepage and broad search range, Indeed.com mirrors the best aspects of the Internet's most popular search engine, Google. The purpose of Indeed is clear from the get-go: with no highlighted features on its homepage except a job search function (enter keyword and city/state, hit "Find Jobs"), it cuts through the clutter present on some other job websites and presents you with pages and pages of available positions.

Indeed.com searches thousands of major job boards, newspapers, associations, and company career pages—each search hit gives information as to where that job was originally posted and when. Patience is required, however, as the breadth of options that an Indeed search offers can be overwhelming. Much scanning and scrolling is required to find a job listing that suits your interests or needs. The option to sign up for daily e-mail alerts of new jobs that match your keyword and city/state criteria is also available.

International Jobs Center

www.internationaljobs.org

The main component of this website is its weekly publication, *International Career Employment Weekly* (see above in *Print Resources*). This newspaper, which can also be received via e-mail or viewed online, is filled with more than five hundred current international jobs in international development, exchange, education, communication, health care, democracy building, governance, policy, environmental issues, and many others. A paid subscription is required to receive the most comprehensive and up-to-date listings, though a more limited list of "hot jobs" is updated daily and accessible online for free, as are profiles of development and assistance professionals.

NAFSA: Association of International Educators

www.nafsa.org

NAFSA: Association of International Educators is a leading professional association promoting the exchange of students and scholars to and from the United States (see chapter 6). Its online career center has plenty of useful information for those interested in international education, and its free online job registry is the go-to resource for anyone looking for a job in this field, whether his interest lies in universities or nonprofits, in teaching or in student and scholar services.

Simply Hired
www.simplyhired.com

With a Google-like simplicity and robust searching prowess similar to Indeed, Simply Hired allows you to search by entering a keyword and a location. Searching thousands of job boards, newspaper classifieds, and other organizations and company pages, this website presents you with a vast amount of position openings that are closely, and often not so closely, related to your search requirements. This range allows you to see what is out there but can be frustrating due to the vast number of job listings you are required to dig through to find the one that might interest you. Simply Hired also offers a free online résumé-posting service, allowing you to post your CV on up to five major job boards (including Monster.com, CareerBuilder.com, and Job.com) at once.

Vault
www.vault.com

In addition to a searchable job board, Vault offers a variety of resources intended to aid your job search and career development. Information is available on specific industries and companies, as well as advanced degree programs (such as MBA and law degrees). Articles about various job and career-related subjects are on the site, covering such topics as interview advice, occupation surveys and profiles, career changes, and diversity. Salary surveys, calculators, and negotiation tips are also accessible. Membership in the site, which provides access to a number of further benefits, can be purchased at several different levels and prices.

Weddle's
www.weddles.com

Weddle's is a well-known name in the area of career development. This website offers not a job board or search engine but rather a variety of resources for job seekers, as well as recruiters and HR professionals. Perhaps most useful is Weddle's long list of career publications, including *Guide to Employment Websites, Fast Facts on Job Boards,* and *Guide to Association Websites.* Weddle's also offers such resources as an online association directory (see chapter 6), training programs for job seekers, and free, bimonthly online career newsletters.

Wet Feet
www.wetfeet.com

A career guidance website, Wet Feet's jobs search function (powered by Career Builder.com) is free, but access to its numerous other resources is available only to subscribers (one-month and six-month subscriptions are available). These resources include career, company, and industry profiles, salary data, and résumé and cover letter advice and services.

Online Networking Resources

While networking has been and remains an activity traditionally done face-to-face, online networking has emerged in recent years as an important asset in career development. Popular social networking sites such as Facebook and MySpace are already used by some for career networking, though these sites are not ideally suited for the purpose. (It should also be noted that these sites can actually work against a job seeker if he or she is not mindful of the type of information posted on a personal page. Stories abound of employers getting the wrong idea about or changing their opinion of a potential employee because of questionable content on a social networking page. It is easy to think that our personal and professional worlds are separate and strictly defined—however, because the Internet provides instant, always accessible information, this is no longer the case.)

Intrepid career professionals have combined the ideas and principles of social networking sites and traditional career networking practices, creating sites that are essentially "MySpaces for professionals." The following sites have followed that formula and have gained a healthy reputation in the burgeoning area of online networking.

Doostang
www.doostang.com

Doostang is an online career community that connects people through personal relationships and affiliations. Doostang's stated purpose is to help you "doo something great" and operates under the principle that "70% of jobs are filled through referrals." The site allows you to look for jobs through targeted searches, share job opportunities with your friends, and network with other Doostang members. Doostang provides its services free of charge, but in an attempt to streamline its operations and reflect "the realities of the job marketplace," membership is by invitation of a current member only.

Jibber Jobber
www.jibberjobber.com

Jibber Jobber is a job seeking, networking, and relationship management tool for job seekers. The site allows you to keep track of prospective employers and people in your professional network; other tools include a peer library, an interview preparation area, and a document manager. A free version is available, as is a premium version that provides additional features for a monthly fee.

LinkedIn
http://linkedin.com

LinkedIn is a free online network of more than ten million professionals from around the world, representing 150 industries. Users can create profiles that summarize professional accomplishments and goals and help them find and be found by former colleagues, clients, and partners. You can also add more networking connections by inviting trusted contacts to join LinkedIn.

PROFILE
Lawrence Bacow
President, Tufts University

Career Trajectory
President, Tufts University, Somerville, MA, 2001–present
Massachusetts Institute of Technology, Cambridge, Massachusetts
   Chancellor, 1998–2001
   Lee and Geraldine Martin Professor of Environmental Studies, Department
      of Urban Studies and Planning, 1997–2001
   Chairman, MIT Faculty, 1995–97
   Assistant, Associate, and Full Professor, Department of Urban Studies and
      Planning, 1977–97

Academic Background
MPP and PhD, Harvard University, Kennedy School of Government, 1976,
   1978
JD, Harvard University Law School, 1976
SB, Economics, Massachusetts Institute of Technology, 1972

What awards and honors have meant the most to you?
I'm very proud of the fact that I graduated Phi Beta Kappa from MIT—I
was in the first class that was inaugurated into this academic honor society at
MIT. That was very meaningful to me because I was the first kid from my high
school to go to my alma mater, and I went there with the hope that I
wouldn't flunk out. It was very meaningful to be recognized for having
excelled.

The next big award I received was as a junior faculty member at MIT when
I was granted a career development chair. This is an endowed chair for junior
faculty members, of which a small number are awarded to promising faculty.
It sent a strong signal at the time that the administration had confidence in what
I was doing and that I had a promising career as an academic. Another big
honor for me was being elected chairman of the MIT faculty. The opportunity to head such a distinguished faculty was very humbling.

Are you involved in community service?
Board Member, Jewish Community Housing for the Elderly
Board Member, Hebrew College
Board Member, Wheaton College
Board Member, Minuteman Council of the Boy Scouts of America
Board Member, Cummings Foundation

I think that all of us have an obligation to try to make the world a better place. I was raised with the values that you're supposed to get involved and help others. In the Jewish tradition there is a phrase from the Talmud—in Hebrew it is *tikun olam*—which literally translates as "repairing the world." That's the obligation and responsibility of each individual, to repair the world, the notion that the world is not perfect and while we may each have different conceptions of what is imperfect about it, everybody has a responsibility to try to make it better.

How do you define your cause?

Deep down, I'm a teacher. I discovered that pretty early in life. When I was in college, I spent my summers teaching sailing, not just because I loved sailing, but because I loved teaching and having an influence on the lives of young people. It's not surprising that I went into teaching as a career. And, while I'd like to think of myself as a scholar, I'm probably a teacher first and a scholar second. I have enjoyed my time in academic administration because it provides an opportunity to help shape institutions of higher education, which I think are terribly important to society.

I took my first sabbatical abroad in 1981. I was a visiting professor at Hebrew University in Jerusalem. One of the things I discovered during my first time living abroad is that you learn a lot about your own country when you live in another. It was a wonderful experience for me, my wife, and our young son.

As a result, I came back to MIT interested very much in international education—in the opportunities to learn from different cultures, different societies, and different countries. I started giving a series of lectures at universities in other countries. I spent a fair amount of time in Italy—I was a visiting professor at a polytechnic institute in Turin—and I spent time every summer giving a series of lectures at Gabriela Mistral University in Santiago, Chile. During my time at MIT, I spent a year abroad as a visiting professor at the University of Amsterdam and oversaw a large-scale project involving collaboration between MIT, the Swiss Federal Institute of Technology, and the University of Tokyo. When I was chancellor at MIT, I took great pride in having developed a major partnership between MIT and Cambridge University (UK), which, among other things, created opportunities for MIT students to study abroad in large numbers for the first time.

One of the things that attracted me to Tufts University is that this is an institution that has always been global in focus. It leads the nation in the number of Peace Corps volunteers; international relations is always one of our most popular majors, and 45 percent of our students study abroad.

We live in a society and an economy that are defined by globalization. For students growing up in the United States especially, there's a tendency towards ethnocentrism. We expect everyone to speak our language, play our music, watch our movies. I think it's important for students to go live somewhere else and realize that there are countries and cultures and societies that are very different from our own. In the process of learning about those cultures and societies and languages, it will change their perception of the world writ large, as well as their role and their country's role in the world.

What drew you to this cause and to your field?

Like most of our careers, mine has been a series of fortuitous accidents. I was going to be a lawyer—my father was a lawyer—and I went to MIT "knowing" that I wanted to go to law school. After completing law school and my PhD, I thought I was going to go work for the government, but I started receiving teaching offers instead—I was just in the right place at the right time. I took a job teaching at MIT for two years. My first appointment was a two-year, nontenure track, terminal appointment. I stayed for twenty-four years. Like I said, fortuitous accidents.

I don't think you should be completely passive about your career, but at the same time, I don't think you can plan it out. The only time that you can *really* describe your career is on the day you retire. Up until then, you're just making plans.

I always say to my students, when confronted with career opportunities, ask yourself three questions: First, is the job worth doing? Second, are you going to grow and learn in the job? And third, are you going to enjoy the people you work with? I don't believe you take a job because it's going to lead to something else. You take a job because it's worth doing, because it's going to stretch you, and because you're going to enjoy the people you're working with. You have to keep asking yourself those three questions even *after* you have a job.

Do you have a mentor? How has he or she affected your life and career?

Oh, I've had wonderful, wonderful mentors. I had a very special mentor in college, Bob Solow. I was an economics major, and as an undergraduate, I took a macroeconomics course from Bob. I went to ask a question about a footnote in one of the readings after class and he invited me back to his office to talk about it. He said, "This is an interesting question and an interesting topic. Why don't we do a reading course about it?" So, as a second-semester sophomore, I spent an hour a week with one of the world's great economists (Bob went on to win the Nobel Prize in 1987). He became a fabulous mentor. Bob was chairman of the editorial board of the MIT Press and was instrumental in getting my thesis published. Every time I turned around, Bob was the invisible hand helping me along.

I also had wonderful mentors in grad school—my thesis adviser, Mark Moore, and another member of my thesis committee, Dick Zekhauser. Another person who really helped me out in grad school, Tom Schelling, won the Nobel Prize in Economics in 2005.

Do you consider yourself a mentor to others?

I try to be. I try to be helpful. With my students, I try to do for them what Bob Solow did for me. When people come to work for me in various capacities, I try to advise them on their careers. Giving advice and suggesting opportunities and sending things their way, the same way Bob sent opportunities my way.

It took me a long time to figure out how I could really pay back those who had helped me along. I realized the best way to do it was to continue the tradition. And that's what I've tried to do.

What is your best advice for developing effective networking skills?

It's interesting to me that the people I went to school with are all doing such interesting things these days. You don't realize it at the time, but the people you go to school with are going to grow up to do *very* interesting things. I've stayed in touch with my friends, not because I thought that they could help me, but because they are interesting people and they are my friends.

What lessons have you learned as your career has evolved?

There are a lot of ways to make a living, but what's more important is to lead a meaningful life. Probably one of the best decisions I ever made was not to practice law. I realized I wasn't cut out for law, and I was willing to take a risk and say, "This isn't what I want to do. I'm not sure what I want to do, but I'll figure it out." And I did.

Take risks early in your career when you have very little to lose. Don't think of your career as linear, but rather think of it as a series of opportunities that will reveal themselves to you over time.

To use a little technical jargon, I think of a career as a dynamic programming problem. You have a set of preferences and a set of opportunities at any point in time. Based upon how you optimize over the opportunity space, both your opportunities and your preferences will change.

Any final advice?

Take responsibility for your own career. It's what *you* make of it. If you don't like what you're doing, do something else. Don't feel trapped. I'm astonished at the number of people over the years who say, "Gee, I wish I could have done *that*." And my response is, "What's stopping you?" You want to go do something different, so go do something different. If you want to do it badly enough, you'll figure out a way to do it. It requires certain sacrifices and changes in your life, but you can do it.

PROFILE

Seth Green

Consultant, McKinsey and Company

Career Trajectory

Consultant, McKinsey and Company, Stamford, Connecticut, 2007–present
Founder and President, Americans for Informed Democracy, New Haven,
     Connecticut, 2001–7
Intern, Brookings Institution, Washington, D.C., June 2001–September 2001
Summer Analyst, Lazard Frères, LLC, New York, New York, June–August 2000

Academic Background

JD, Yale University Law School, 2007
MA, Women's Studies, Oxford University, 2003
MA, Development Studies, London School of Economics, 2002
AB, Political Science (Certificate in Political Economy), Princeton University,
     2001

What awards and honors have meant the most to you?

In 2005 I received the Search for Common Ground Award. Other recipients that were honored that year included Muhammad Ali, Jack Kemp, and Henry Cisneros. I really believe that today, more than ever, we need to focus on our commonalities and not our differences. Search for Common Ground is an inspiring organization which does exactly that. So to be given an award by them is the greatest honor I could receive.

Are you involved in community service?

Member, National Youth Council, March of Dimes
President, LSE Amnesty International Society
Child Health Advocate, Florida
Member, Princeton Workers' Rights Organizing Committee

I think that community service really gives you a lot. A lot of people see it as something that they do for others, but it's been something that has changed my own life for the better. In terms of my own leadership, my community service experiences have convinced me that I can make a difference. If you look at anyone who's successful and you ask them, "Beneath it all, what's one of the secret ingredients?" the answer often is, "You have to really believe in yourself." And I think that when you see an area where you've made a positive impact, it gives you that sense of confidence and inspiration that moves you to take on bigger challenges and overcome them.

How do you define your cause?

I have been blessed with tremendous opportunities in my life, and I really feel a need to give back. I had a cleft palate, and I received great care because my parents paid out of pocket. Even though I had insurance, it did not cover some very necessary surgeries. So as I grew up, I started meeting people with cleft palates who also had insurance but, unlike me, didn't have parents with pockets that were as deep, so they didn't have comparable care.

Meeting these kids, it was just incredible that our country could let them down like this. They were born with a difference—which I think is clearly an act of chance—and we owe them the dignity of respecting their lives. As I became more involved as a child health care advocate, I went before the Florida House of Representatives' Health Services Committee to argue for comprehensive health care coverage for children in need of cleft lip and palate repair. We argued: "These are citizens of Florida; they have the right to be given full access to care, and we want you to pass a mandate that says, if you're going to provide health insurance in Florida, you have to cover these basics." Our work led to the bill we were advocating becoming a Florida statute.

I don't know that this experience specifically pushed me to Oxford or my current position at McKinsey or to any specific place in my life. But doing this type of work really gave me a sense of the power that I had and the importance of what I had to say. It helped me understand how I could play a very positive role. I got involved with Americans for Informed Democracy (AID) because I saw a problem when I was abroad and wanted to be a part of the solution.

There's always a balance you have to strike if you're going to be innovative and have an impact, which is between building the skills through the institutions and opportunities that exist, and then figuring out how you jump off from those opportunities and lead without a guide book. I think that's something that these experiences really taught me: to lead without a guide-book. You can't get this kind of experience in school.

What drew you to this cause and your field?

I was actually sitting in a dorm room at Princeton University, reminiscing with an old roommate, when the two jets hit the World Trade Center. I had gone back to Princeton to gain some perspective before leaving for a two-year postgraduate trip to England. But I left a few days later pretty shaken and confused.

When I arrived at my new home, an international student dorm in London, I was pretty overwhelmed by the diversity of my new surroundings. Against my better judgment, I guess, I found myself worrying about the feelings of my Palestinian and Egyptian neighbors regarding terrorism. But really,

I couldn't have found a more supportive and friendly environment. From the dining hall to the classroom, my new friends displayed constant sympathy. Several times, strangers in the streets of London heard my accent and stopped me to express their grief.

However, over the year that followed, that immense goodwill really seemed to vanish. Instead of being seen as a defensive ally protecting the world against terror, the United States was now viewed as the aggressor. At the same time, stereotypes of the United States really added a fuel to the anti-American furor. All Americans were seen as something like SUV-driving, unilateralist cowboys. This backlash was sometimes directed at ordinary Americans like me. I was actually spit at by kids yelling, "Don't attack Iraq," and harassed by a drunk who declared that he gladly would blow himself up to kill me.

These experiences caused me to become deeply concerned by America's diminishing image abroad and the consequences. I thought, "What can I do to combat this? How can I bring about some sort of change?" So it was in October 2002 that I joined with my fellow Oxford grad students David Tannenbaum and Jason Wasfy to establish AID. Our goal was to inform average Americans about foreign views of the United States by publishing op-eds in U.S. newspapers about rising anti-Americanism and organizing e-mail campaigns. We became established on university campuses. We sought to bring about some kind of change to this problem that so bothered us.

Do you have a mentor? How has he or she affected your life and career?

My father was deeply committed to social justice, participating actively in the civil rights movement, and I always looked up to him as a role model. He never encouraged me to succeed for success' sake, which I think is incredibly important. He always wanted me to do things that I believed in, to make a difference, and to define for myself what success is. He never let others define success for him. He did lots of volunteer work and never was interested in being a high-profile lawyer in our community or having a fancy car.

When you see someone who is as happy as my dad and "just getting by," you realize it is a pretty good way to live and tend to follow it. I've definitely done things pretty differently than my dad—maybe it's a generational thing; in my way of thinking about social change, I put on a suit far more than he would have liked to—but I think that he was driven by the idea that he could create change by finding his own path. That allowed me to grow in the ways that I wanted and made me feel that my choices were always my own.

Do you consider yourself a mentor to others?

I see myself as a mentor in being a little bit like my father, in trying to follow what I believe. I think that gives others a signal that they can do the same. I have a lot of passion and the things that I have been able to do as a young person are hopefully a sign of what others can do as well if they put their minds to it. People sometimes think that you need to be of a certain mold to create change, that you need to act in a certain way. I try to be a bit different than that, and hopefully that communicates to people that, by doing what you think is best and right, by having lots of energy and inspiration, you really can get somewhere.

It's very true that I did go to some elite schools, met many helpful people, and used "the system" in that way. Unfortunately, we live in a country where using the system is still a big part of creating stepping-stones to change. But that said, you don't have to do everything by the book to still make a difference.

I am also trying to be very accessible for those who have questions or need recommendations. I have written literally hundreds of recommendations for AID chapter members around the country since starting the organization. I hope that this helps to bring opportunities for young people across the board.

What is your best advice for developing effective networking skills?

The best networker is someone who really wants to learn. Asking people what their talents are, what their interests are, what is driving their organization . . . I think that is the best way to, one, raise awareness about your own organization or cause—as people are always more interested in you if you're interested in them—and, two, to get a sense of where you should be spending your energies and your time.

Sometimes people hear about an organization and think, "Yes, I want to be connected to that." But they don't *really* listen to what the leader of that organization thinks or where he or she wants to take the organization. If you *really* listen, you may develop a beneficial partnership or network with someone you hadn't thought to partner with in the first place.

But don't spend too much time networking—if you do, you're not going to have very much time to do programming. We're in an "over-networked" culture at the moment. There are a lot of people with *a lot* of business cards who don't really know what their strategy is. They're going to a cocktail party every night, and this approach has only created a kind of "networking gone wild" scenario. Networking in this way doesn't go very far in terms of impact.

What lessons have you learned as your career has evolved?

The biggest personal lesson I've learned is that achievement isn't all it's cracked up to be. During college, and even before college, there were a number of pressures to excel that I took too seriously. I was really interested in getting a Marshall or Rhodes scholarship. I got the Marshall scholarship and went over to Britain when the United States was about to enter the Iraq War. I thought a lot of things about U.S. foreign policy were just wrong at that time. But I also realized that I had very limited ways of trying to impact our country's role in the world. I had all of these "achievements," so to speak, but I had very few ways to exert real influence or to create change. Too much institutional achievement can be paralyzing in a certain way. Look at all these U.S. senators at the height of so-called achievement who didn't feel powerful enough to vote against a war they knew was wrong.

So I started trying to get involved and determine how I *could* create change, how I could gain the skills to stop our country from colossal mistakes in the future. I essentially told myself, "I don't even care about what I do next; I just really want to devote myself to this." This could have been totally counterproductive from a professional standpoint, but I think the decision to devote myself to creating change is one of the best I've ever made.

Any final advice?

If you're going to succeed, you need to be embarrassed at some point in your life. There are few people who make it very far without really risking it big. There's a tendency to keep stepping up the ladder, rather than jumping and possibly falling to the bottom. I think it's a great thing, especially when you're young, to jump. You have a real chance to change the system, but only if you're willing to jump off the standard course.

Chapter 6
Professional Associations

Becoming active in one or more professional associations will lead you to critically important avenues for networking and information gathering—two fundamental aspects of your job search. One visit to the Weddle's Association Directory at www.weddles.com illustrates that the range of professions, occupations, and industries that professional associations represent is vast and wide reaching. Professional association activities, publications, and websites keep you abreast of what is happening in your specific areas of interest, who the leaders are, and where new jobs may be found. Many association websites contain information on training opportunities, as well as job banks, résumé boards, and other employment-related services.

Professional associations are an efficient and dynamic way to gain knowledge, network, and keep on top of current news affecting your industry or area of interest. Membership in associations also demonstrates to potential employers a serious commitment to your career development. Most professional associations have membership opportunities available for students, often at reduced rates. Many allow job seekers to volunteer at conferences or regional meetings in exchange for waived registration fees. These conferences and other assemblies provide opportunities to present papers, participate in discussions, and raise questions. This is an ideal way to hone your communication skills, share your expertise, and interact with colleagues who share your specific professional interests.

In addition, the association field is the third largest employer in the Washington, D.C., area, after the federal government and the tourism industry. Thus, you may wish to look to associations not only as career and job resources but also as possible places of employment.

Below you will find a selected list of professional associations with a focus on international exchange, education, development, or a related—sometimes more specific—field. This list of associations is followed by a catalog of print and web resources that provide more information on associations, allowing you to search the field more broadly or find a specific professional association not listed here.

SAMPLE PROFESSIONAL ASSOCIATIONS

Alliance for International Educational and Cultural Exchange
1776 Massachusetts Avenue, NW, Suite 620
Washington, DC 20036
Telephone: 202-293-6141
Fax: 202-293-6144
Website: www.alliance-exchange.org

The Alliance for International Educational and Cultural Exchange is a nonprofit membership association dedicated to formulating and promoting public policies that support the growth and well-being of international exchange. Representing more than seventy-five U.S.-based exchange organizations, the Alliance acts as a leading policy voice for the U.S. exchange community. The organization hosts an annual advocacy day when it leads its members to Capitol Hill to lobby for sound policies and more resources for federally funded international exchange programs. Their *International Exchange Locator,* currently in its eighth edition, contains profiles of more than three hundred exchange-focused organizations and federal agencies (see chapter 5). The Alliance was established in 1992 through a merger of two predecessor organizations: the Liaison Group, which represented academic and professional exchanges, and the International Exchange Association, a coalition of citizen and youth exchange groups.

Membership: The Alliance's full and associate membership programs are designed for international exchange organizations in the United States. Individuals can become affiliates (if affiliated with a full Alliance member) or subscribers (if not affiliated with a full Alliance member) for $325 per year. Membership benefits include timely Action Alerts about pending decisions on Capitol Hill, electronic delivery of the Alliance's *Policy*

Monitor, and electronic delivery of the Alliance's late-breaking update information service, *NEWS NEWS NEWS.*

American Association for the Advancement of Slavic Studies (AAASS)

8 Story Street
Cambridge, MA 02138
Telephone: 617-495-0677
Fax: 617-495-0680
Website: www.fas.harvard.edu/~aaass

The American Association for the Advancement of Slavic Studies, founded in 1938, is a nonprofit, nonpolitical, scholarly society and a leading private organization dedicated to the advancement of knowledge regarding the former Soviet Union (including Eurasia) and Eastern and Central Europe. AAASS represents American scholarship in the post–Soviet/East Central European field nationally and internationally. The national office of AAASS is affiliated with the Davis Center for Russian and Eurasian Studies at Harvard University. Most AAASS members work in the academic community, as well as government and business, but membership is worldwide and open to all.

Membership: Dues are scaled according to income levels. Members receive the *Slavic Review,* the association's quarterly journal, and *News-Net,* the AAASS newsletter. Members may also participate in the AAASS National Convention at a discounted registration fee, have the opportunity to subscribe to several affiliated journals at a significantly discounted rate, and can view the most recent job listings, announcements of funding and grant opportunities, and other valuable information through the "Members Only" site.

American Association of Collegiate Registrars and Admissions Officers (AACRAO)

1 Dupont Circle, NW, Suite 520
Washington, DC 20036
Telephone: 202-293-9161
Fax: 202-872-8857
Website: www.aacrao.org

The American Association of Collegiate Registrars and Admissions Officers was established in 1910 as a nonprofit, voluntary, professional association committed to supporting higher education and providing professional development opportunities. It comprises more than ten thousand higher education admissions and registration professionals who represent approximately 2,500 institutions in more than thirty countries. AACRAO provides professional development services including national meetings and training events, grant and award opportunities, access to relevant publications and survey results, consulting services, online workshops, and a searchable job bank.

Membership: A limited number of individual memberships are available for students, retired AACRAO members, high school personnel, personnel from international secondary and postsecondary institutions, and voting members of AACRAO who are seeking employment.

American Bar Association (ABA): Section of International Law
ABA Section of International Law
740 15th Street, NW
Washington, DC 20005
Telephone: 202-662-1660
Fax: 202-662-1669
Website: www.abanet.org/intlaw

This section of the American Bar Association works to educate lawyers on current developments in international law and practice, as well as to promote interest, activity, and research in international and comparative law and related areas. The Section of International Law, founded in 1933, is committed to the development of policy in the international arena and the promotion of the rule of law on an international scale. It offers workshops and briefings on new issues in international law and is separated into divisions and subcommittees so that members may join according to individual interests. Categories include the Business Law Division, Public International Law Division, Comparative Law Division, and General Division.

Membership: Cost is $55 per year for the Section on International Law. Membership includes subscriptions to *The International Lawyer,* the quarterly law journal on international practice, and the *International Law News,* a quarterly section newsletter, as well as discounts on other publications, access to annual meetings, and career advice and international summer internship opportunities. Membership in the ABA is a prerequisite.

American Council on Education (ACE): Center for International Initiatives
1 Dupont Circle, NW
Washington, DC 20036
Telephone: 202-939-9300
Fax: 202-785-8056
Website: www.acenet.edu/programs/international

ACE is the major coordinating body for higher education institutions in the United States. Since 1918 it has provided leadership on higher education issues and influenced public policy through advocacy, research, and program initiatives. Through its Center for International Initiatives, ACE offers programs and services that support and enhance the internationalization of U.S. campuses and works with international partners on higher education issues that have a global impact. The Commission for International Initiatives, an advisory body of ACE member presidents, guides ACE on its work in this area.

Membership: Membership in ACE is restricted to organizations and universities. However, both ACE and the Center of International Initiatives offer a number of services to the general public, including advocacy opportunities, publications, conferences and forums, and other networking opportunities.

American Foreign Service Association (AFSA)
2101 E Street, NW
Washington, DC 20037
Telephone: 800-704-AFSA (within the United States) or 202-338-4045
Fax: 202-338-6820
Website: www.afsa.org

AFSA was founded in 1924 as the professional association of the U.S. Foreign Service. With more than thirteen thousand members, AFSA represents approximately twenty-six thousand active and retired Foreign Service employees of the U.S. Department of State and the Agency for International Development (USAID), as well as smaller groups in the Foreign Agricultural Service (FAS), U.S. and Foreign Commercial Service (FCS), and International Broadcasting Bureau (IBB). AFSA's principal goals are to enhance the effectiveness of the Foreign Service, to protect the professional interests of its members, to ensure the maintenance of high professional standards for both career diplomats and political appointees, and to promote understanding of the critical role of the Foreign Service in promoting America's national security and economic prosperity. AFSA also acts in a labor/management relations capacity as the exclusive bargaining agent for Foreign Service employees.

Membership: Full membership is reserved for active and retired Foreign Service officers. Others who wish to be involved may become associate members for $92.80 per year or $1,000 for lifetime membership. Benefits include a subscription to the monthly *Foreign Service Journal,* use of the Foreign Service Club in Washington, D.C., and access to the AFSA online member area. Students may subscribe to the *Foreign Service Journal* for $20 per year. AFSA also provides merit-based scholarships for students who are dependents of Foreign Service employees.

American Political Science Association (APSA)
1527 New Hampshire Avenue, NW
Washington, DC 20036
Telephone: 202-483-2512
Fax: 202-483-2657
Website: www.apsanet.org

The American Political Science Association (APSA), founded in 1903, is a professional organization dedicated to the study of political science, including a range of international activities, and serves more than fifteen thousand members in eighty-plus countries. The majority of APSA members are scholars; however, the membership also includes government officials, researchers, consultants, and academics from around the world. APSA provides members with services that facilitate research, teaching, and professional development and supports special projects to increase public understanding of political science. APSA also assists with searches for employment, namely through its online job bank, *eJobs.* Association publications list employment opportunities, grants and studies, annual meetings, and publishing opportunities.

Membership: Dues are prorated according to annual income—$82 to $202 for individual membership and $39 for student membership. Members receive access to the print and online versions of three publications, including the *American Political Science Review,* as well as discounts on subscriptions to other publications, discounted registration for the APSA Annual Meeting, a directory of APSA members, and access to MyAPSA, a members-only resource bank.

American Society for Training and Development (ASTD)
1640 King Street, Box 1443
Alexandria, VA 22313
Telephone: 703-683-8100
Fax: 703-683-8103
Website: www.astd.org

Since 1944 the American Society for Training and Development has served professionals interested in the field of human resources and is dedicated to advancing workplace learning. ASTD's members live in more than one hundred countries and connect locally in 140 U.S. chapters and twenty-four global networks. Members work in government as independent consultants, trainers, and suppliers, and in thousands of organizations of all sizes. ASTD's website features a career center, which offers among its resources a job bank, an ongoing education certificate program, career coaching and development publications, and a salary calculator.

Membership: Costs $180 for one year, $90 for one year for seniors; $59 for one year for students. Group and chapter memberships are also available. Benefits of membership include regular newsletters and invitations to meetings focused on current developments in professional practice and training techniques. ASTD members have access to a member information exchange, a position referral service, an information center, and conferences and regional workshops. In addition, ASTD publishes an annual catalog and a "Who's Who in Training and Development," which are free to all members.

American Studies Association (ASA)
1120 19th Street, NW, Suite 301
Washington DC 20036
Telephone: 202-467-4783
Fax: 202-467-4786
Website: www.theasa.net

The American Studies Association is open to all persons who "have in common the desire to view America as a whole rather than from the perspective of a single discipline." Founded in 1951, ASA currently has more than five thousand members, representing a diverse cross section of fields such as history, literature, religion, art, philosophy, music, science, folklore, ethnic studies, government, communications, education, library science, studies, popular culture, and many others. On an international level, ASA encourages the exchange of students and faculty members, promotes the establishment of American Studies departments and associations abroad, and provides a communication forum for leaders of American Studies associations from around the world.

Membership: Cost is $55 to $99 for individual membership—dues are prorated according to annual income. $20 for student membership. Members have access to ASA publications, including quarterlies, newsletters, and a guide to internships of interest to students of American studies, as well as discounts on subscriptions and conference and event registration.

ASAE and the Center for Association Leadership
ASAE and the Center Building
1575 I Street, NW
Washington, DC 20005
Telephone: 202-371-0940 or 888-950-2723
Fax: 202-371-8315
Website: www.asaecenter.org

ASAE is the membership organization representing the association profession. Founded in 1920, ASAE now has more than twenty-two thousand association CEOs, staff professionals, industry partners, and consultant members. The Center for Association Leadership is a provider of learning and knowledge for the association community. The center was founded in 2001. ASAE and the center together serve approximately ten thousand associations that represent more than 287 million people and organizations worldwide. ASAE hosts an extensive job bank and career center for the association profession, located at www.careerhq.org.

Membership: Dues are $265 for professional membership; $295 for chief executive membership; $100 for young professional membership; $30 for student membership. Several other membership categories also exist for industry partners. Membership benefits include access to "learning experience" programs, subscriptions to ASAE publications, including *Associations Now,* discounts on more than three hundred publications, and access to ASAE's members-only knowledge resources and professional interests section, which allows one to network online with fellow association professionals.

Asia Foundation
465 California Street, 9th Floor
San Francisco, CA 94104
Telephone: 415-982-4640
Fax: 415-392-8863
Website: www.asiafoundation.org

The Asia Foundation is a nonprofit, nongovernmental organization that, since 1954, has worked to develop a peaceful, prosperous, just, and open Asia-Pacific region. The foundation supports programs in Asia in such areas as governance, law, civil society, women's empowerment, economic reform and development, and international relations. The foundation collaborates with private and public partners to support leadership and institutional development, exchanges, and policy research. In 2006 the foundation provided more than $53 million in program support and distributed 920,000 books and educational materials valued at $30 million throughout Asia.

Membership: Not available. However, the foundation does offer a variety of free resources on its website, including a quarterly newsletter, country and project reports, and an up-to-date listing of all job and internship opportunities at its offices in San Francisco, in Washington, D.C., and throughout Asia.

Asia Society
725 Park Avenue at 70th Street
New York, NY 10021
Telephone: 212-288-6400
Fax: 212-517-8315
Website: www.asiasociety.org

The Asia Society, founded in 1956, is a national nonprofit and nonpartisan educational organization dedicated to fostering understanding of Asia. The Asia Society also works to open communication between Americans and the peoples of Asia and the Pacific region. Through art exhibitions and performances, films, lectures, conferences, seminars, and programs for both students and teachers, the Asia Society provides a forum for presenting the uniqueness and diversity of Asia to the American people. The Asia Society is headquartered in New York. Regional centers are located in Washington, D.C.; Houston; Los Angeles; Hong Kong; and Melbourne.

Membership: Membership fees vary by location. At the New York headquarters, $65 for individual membership; $40 for students, associations, and senior citizens. Members receive unlimited free admission for one to the Asia Society Galleries, two invitations to Members Only exhibition previews and receptions, and discounts for one on tickets to performances, films, and lectures, and discounts on most Asia Society Gallery bookstore and gift shop purchases. Other benefits for members include the newsletter *Asia,* advance notice of upcoming Asia Society programs, and discounts at selected Asian restaurants in New York City.

Coalition for American Leadership Abroad (COLEAD)
American Foreign Service Association (AFSA) Building
2101 E Street, NW
Washington, DC 20037
Telephone: 202-944-5519
Fax: 202-338-6820
Website: www.colead.org

Established in 1995, COLEAD is a broad-based, nonpartisan coalition comprising more than fifty nonprofit foreign affairs organizations. These organizations promote effective American engagement in world affairs and strive to encourage well-informed public debate on international issues affecting U.S. interests. COLEAD provides for its members a forum to discuss mutual concerns, a basis for building partnerships among national and grass-roots organizations, a conduit for local and regional educational campaigns, and opportunities to advocate for U.S. diplomatic efforts.

Membership: COLEAD is a coalition of organizational members. However, associate memberships for individuals are also available for $20 per year. Associate members are sent regular updates about foreign affairs and the current status of funding for international programs, as well as invitations to meetings in and around their area of interest. COLEAD also puts associate members in contact with its organizational member groups.

Council on Foreign Relations (CFR)
The Harold Pratt House
58 East 68th Street
New York, NY 10065
Telephone: 212-434-9400
Fax: 212-434-9800
Website: www.cfr.org

The Council on Foreign Relations is a nonprofit, nonpartisan membership organization that aims to improve the understanding of U.S. foreign policy and international affairs. Founded in 1921, CFR is home to a think tank dedicated to the continuous study of U.S. foreign policy for the benefit of its members, as well as world audiences. By mobilizing resident senior staff, members, and other experts in dialogue, study, and publications programs, the Council serves as a forum for scholarship and policy analysis. The Council on Foreign Relations Press publishes *Foreign Affairs,* a leading journal of global politics, books, and occasional policy reports on a broad range of issues, and also produces "America and the World," a weekly radio series aired on National Public Radio.

Membership: Members must be nominated by a current member of the Council. However, the Council does offer the general public a number of services free of charge via its website, including an e-mail newsletter which includes the "Daily Brief," the "World This Week," and a number of monthly and bimonthly foreign affairs updates.

The Development Executive Group
1341 Connecticut Avenue, NW
Washington, DC 20036
Telephone: 202-249-9222
Fax: 202-318-2456
Website: http://developmentex.com

The Development Executive Group is a membership organization working to bring greater efficiency to international development by improving the accessibility and analysis of information about employment, business practices, and current trends and initiatives in the development sector. Serving donor agencies, firms, nonprofit corporations, and individual professionals working in the international development industry, this organization attempts to keep development-focused organizations connected and organized.

More than fifty-five thousand individuals are registered with the organization, and more than two hundred of the world's leading development consultancies and NGOs are executive members, including organizations found in this book such as the Academy for Educational Development, AMIDEAST, Catholic Relief Services, the Asia Foundation, and World Learning. More than twenty-five thousand reports of development projects are posted on the website, and a sixty-person team provides daily coverage of projects and news in the international development industry. The DevelopmentEx online job board is a comprehensive listing of more than a thousand international development jobs.

Membership: Costs $15 per month for individual membership. Executive and small business membership is also available. Membership benefits include contact information for firms that win contracts, information on individual consulting opportunities with development agencies, individual webpage on the DevelopmentEx.com website, contact information for other international development professionals around the world, and a subscription to The Newswire, the daily e-mail listing of international development news.

Foreign Policy Association (FPA)
470 Park Avenue South
New York, NY 10016
Telephone: 212-481-8100
Fax: 212-481-9275
Website: www.fpa.org

The mission of the Foreign Policy Association, a nonprofit educational organization, is to inspire the American public to learn more about the world. FPA was originally founded in 1918 as the League of Free Nations Association to support President Woodrow Wilson's efforts to achieve just peace. In order to achieve its mission, FPA organizes numerous events on diverse topics in international affairs, publishes and distributes books and other publications, including the annual *Great Decisions,* produces several free on-line newsletters, and hosts a resource library and a job bank on its website, both of which are searchable and available to the general public.

Membership: Costs are $250 for associate membership; $75 for national associate membership (outside New York City metro area); $50 for student membership ($25 for students outside New York City metro area). Membership benefits include advanced notification and free admission to events, access to FPA publications and FPA's National Opinion Ballot Report, and discounts on other publications.

Fulbright Association
666 11th Street, NW, Suite 525
Washington, DC 20001
Telephone: 202-347-5543
Fax: 202-347-6540
Website: www.fulbright.org

The Fulbright Association is a nonprofit membership organization of Fulbright alumni and supporters committed to fostering international awareness and understanding. The Association's central focus is to mobilize alumni and other supporters of exchange on behalf of this seminal program created by the late Sen. J. William Fulbright. The Association is involved in advocacy on behalf of the Fulbright Program, informing members of congressional and executive branch actions affecting the program, and provides mechanisms to take organized action on behalf of the program. The Fulbright Association collaborates with other organizations dedicated to maintaining U.S. support for foreign affairs programs.

Membership: Fees are $40 for individual membership; $40 for associate members; $25 for students and retired persons. Special rates are available for couples, institutions, and individuals interested in lifetime membership. Members have access to such features as a quarterly newsletter, an alumni directory, career center, chat and message boards, and alumni notes. Members also receive reduced registration rates at international, national, and chapter programs.

InterAction

1400 16th Street, NW, Suite 210
Washington, DC 20036
Telephone: 202-667-8227
Fax: 202-667-8236
Website: www.interaction.org

InterAction, founded in 1984, is an alliance of U.S.-based international development and humanitarian nongovernmental organizations. With a coalition of more 150 PVOs (private and voluntary organizations) working in 165 countries worldwide, InterAction works to overcome poverty, exclusion, and suffering by advancing social justice and basic dignity for all peoples. InterAction deals with a broad array of programs and issues, including advocacy, development, disaster response, refugee, gender and diversity, and media.

InterAction's monthly newsletter, *Monday Developments,* is devoted to covering a wide-range of issues in international development and includes an extensive listing of international employment opportunities (see chapter 5 in this volume). In addition, InterAction offers a weekly e-mail listing of extensive employment and internship opportunities in the international development and assistance field. Subscribing will enable you to receive approximately twenty-five to thirty job announcements each week from U.S.-based humanitarian and development organizations with positions available in the United States and overseas.

Membership: Membership is designed for international development organizations.

International Association of Students in Economic and Commercial Sciences (AIESEC)
127 West 26th Street, 10th Floor
New York, NY 10001
Telephone: 212-757-3774
Fax: 212-757-4062
Website: www.aiesecus.org

Since its founding in 1948, AIESEC has grown into the world's largest student-based organization, spanning more than ninety countries and seven hundred universities. The mission of AIESEC—a French acronym that stands for *l'Association Internationale des Etudiants en Sciences Economiques et Commerciales,* or International Association of Students in Economic and Commercial Sciences—is to contribute to the development of countries and their people with a strong commitment to furthering international understanding and cooperation. AIESEC works to "develop individuals, communities, and cooperation through global exchange" by facilitating work exchanges among its member countries. AIESEC provides opportunities for students to gain professional and cultural experience and build a global network, through events and activities throughout the United States and work exchange programs such as the International Traineeship Exchange Program.

Membership: Students in the United States may join AIESEC through a local sponsoring university. Check http://recruitment.aiesecng .com to find a sponsoring university in your area.

International Communication Association (ICA)
1500 21st Street, NW
Washington DC 20036
Telephone: 202-955-1444
Fax: 202-955-1448
Website: www.icahdq.org

Since 1950 the International Communication Association has been dedicated to advancing the study of human and mediated communication. The overall purposes of this academic association are to advance the scholarly study of human communication and to facilitate the implementation of such research findings. Members may join one of the Association's divisions or interest groups, which include interpersonal communication, organizational communication, intercultural/development communication, political communication, communication and technology, language and social interaction, journalism studies, and intergroup communication.

Membership: Membership dues are based on country of residence. For United States residents, $130 for regular membership; $60 for students. Members receive Association publications, including the ICA newsletter and the *Journal of Communication,* invitations to conferences, networking opportunities with colleagues around the world, purchasing discounts on certain books and journals, and access to the members only section of the ICA website.

International Council on Education for Teaching (ICET)
National-Louis University
1000 Capitol Drive
Wheeling, IL 60090
Telephone: 847-465-0191
Fax: 847-465-5629
Website: http://myclass.nl.edu/icet

ICET is an international association of educational organizations, institutions, and individuals working toward the improvement of teacher education and all forms of education and training related to national development. ICET promotes the cooperation of higher education and government institutions with the private sector to develop a worldwide network of international development resources. Their programs and services provide members with access to a worldwide resource base of organizations, personnel programs, research, and training opportunities. ICET is a member of UNESCO.

Membership: Cost is $50 for one year, $90 for two years, $130 for three years, $400 lifetime. Institutional memberships are also available. All members receive reduced rates to the ICET world conference, subscriptions to the ICET newsletter and International Yearbook on Teacher Education, information on low-cost educational travel programs, and announcements of special programs and activities in international education and regional and national conferences on education.

International Studies Association (ISA)
University of Arizona
324 Social Sciences
Tucson, AZ 85721
Telephone: 520-621-7715
Fax: 520-621-5780
Website: www.isanet.org

The International Studies Association, founded in 1959, promotes research and education in international affairs and strives to foster thoughtful discussion and systematic understanding of international issues. ISA cooperates with fifty-seven international studies organizations in more than thirty countries, is a member of the International Social Science Council, and has nongovernmental consultative status with the United Nations. The association has more than four thousand members worldwide. Regional subdivisions provide opportunities to exchange ideas and research with local colleagues. Over twenty special interest groups, called sections, offer additional contact among members interested in specific areas within the field of international studies. ISA also sponsors an annual convention where papers, issues, and panel discussions are presented.

Membership: Dues are prorated according to income, from $40 to $120 per year. Student membership costs either $25 (e-journals only) or $35 (hard copy journals). Small additional fees are required for regional membership and sectional membership in specific areas of interest. Benefits of ISA membership include free subscriptions to ISA's four journals (*International Studies Quarterly, International Studies Review, International Studies Perspectives,* and *Foreign Policy Analysis*), discounts on registration for ISA conventions and international conferences, access to ISA's career services, eligibility for grants program (workshop grants and travel grants), and use of the ISA subscriber e-mail list.

Middle East Institute (MEI)
1761 N Street, NW
Washington, DC 20036
Telephone: 202-785-1141
Fax: 202-331-8861
Website: www.mideasti.org

The mission of MEI is to increase knowledge of the Middle East among American citizens and to promote understanding between the peoples of the Middle East and the United States. In order to accomplish this mission, MEI facilitates discussion among academics, government officials, businessmen, and media representatives, supports research, writing, and public speaking on the Middle East, and hosts international scholars in Washington, D.C. MEI also publishes the *Middle East Journal,* and offers courses in Arabic, Hebrew, Persian, and Turkish as well as seminars highlighting the history, literature, and culture of the Middle East. In addition, the Middle East Institute houses the largest English-language library on the Middle East outside of the Library of Congress. MEI also sponsors conferences and offers internships to both undergraduate and graduate students.

Membership: Costs $100 for full membership; $50 for associate membership. Other reduced rates are also available. Membership benefits include the quarterly *Middle East Journal,* free access to George Camp Keiser Library, and discounts on language and regional studies courses and conference registration.

NAFSA: Association of International Educators
1307 New York Avenue, NW, 8th Floor
Washington, DC 20005
Telephone: 202-737-3699
Fax: 202-737-3657
Website: www.nafsa.org

Established in 1948, NAFSA is a member organization promoting international education and providing professional development opportunities to the field in the form of training, information, and other educational services. The organization is comprised of foreign student advisers, study abroad specialists, English as a Second Language (ESL) program administrators, and international admissions officers employed at more than two thousand U.S. university campuses. NAFSA offers new ideas, practical resources, relevant training and events, and the latest news in several specific professional areas: study abroad, international education leadership, international student and scholar services, recruitment, admissions, and preparations, and teaching, learning, and scholarship. The NAFSA website features a searchable job registry that is available to the general public.

Membership: Dues are $325 per year for regular membership; $108 for student or associate membership. Membership benefits include the bimonthly magazine *International Educator,* a weekly e-mail newsletter, discounts on conference registration, and access to a number of networking opportunities, as well as discounts and other benefits from partnering organizations.

National Peace Corps Association (NPCA)
1900 L Street, NW, Suite 205
Washington, DC 20036
Telephone: 202-293-7728
Fax: 202-293-7554
Website: www.rpcv.org

The National Peace Corps Association, a nonprofit organization of nearly twelve thousand members and 147 affiliated groups, is the national association for the people who have served as staff members and volunteers in the Peace Corps. It is not part of the U.S. Peace Corps, which is a federal agency; the mission of the NPCA is to lead the Peace Corps community and others to foster peace by working together in service, education, and advocacy. The NPCA is dedicated to supporting and implementing meaningful education programs, service projects, and advocacy initiatives. It aims to educate the American public about other countries, promote policies consistent with the Peace Corps experience, ensure the continued success of the Peace Corps, and encourage Peace Corps alumni and alumni groups to engage in community and international service. The NPCA website hosts an online career center, available to the general public, which features a searchable job bank and career advice from returned Peace Corps Volunteers.

Membership: Costs $50 per year for individual membership. Membership benefits include a subscription to the quarterly *WorldView* magazine, the monthly NPCANews e-mail newsletter, opportunities to participate in national and regional conferences and advocacy activities, and discounts on car rentals, car insurance, and Princeton Review Prep Courses.

Pact
1200 18th Street, NW, Suite 350
Washington, DC 20036
Telephone: 202-466-5666
Fax: 202-466-5669
Website: www.pactworld.org

Pact is a global network of organizations working to build the capacity of local leaders and organizations in order to meet pressing social needs in dozens of countries around the world. The goal of ending poverty and injustice is the driving force behind the work of Pact; its mission is to help build strong communities globally that provide people with an opportunity to earn a dignified living, raise healthy families, and participate in democratic life. Pact achieves this goal by strengthening the capacity of grassroots organizations, coalitions, and networks and by forging linkages among the government, business, and citizen sectors to achieve social, economic, and environmental justice.

Membership: No membership opportunities are available with Pact.

Society for Intercultural Education, Training, and Research in the United States of America (SIETAR-USA)

603 Stewart Street, Suite 610
Seattle, WA 98101
Telephone: 206-859-4351
Fax: 206-626-0392
Website: www.sietarusa.org

SIETAR-USA promotes and facilitates intercultural education, training, and research through professional interchange. The society is composed of interdisciplinary professional and service organizations that work to implement and promote cooperative interaction and effective communication among diverse peoples. Members represent more than sixty countries and come from a diverse array of fields: business and industry, consulting, training, K–12 and higher education, counseling, and all aspects of the media and arts. SIETAR-USA is a UN- and Council of Europe–affiliated nonprofit organization.

Membership: Costs $125 for full membership; $70 for student membership. Membership benefits include voting, eligibility for SIETAR-USA offices, membership directories, discounts on program fees and conferences sponsored by all members of the SIETAR global network, and subscriptions to SIETAR-USA publications and the SIETAR journal.

Society for International Development (SID), Washington, D.C., Chapter

1875 Connecticut Avenue, NW, Suite 720
Washington, DC 20009
Telephone: 202-884-8590
Fax: 202-884-8499
Website: www.sidw.org

The Society for International Development–Washington connects a diverse global constituency of international development practitioners, serving as a "knowledge broker" for ideas and best practices since 1957. SID–Washington is a membership organization that is connected with the global SID–International, based in Rome (www.sidint.org). SID–Washington provides a space for dialogue and connects a dynamic community of individuals and institutions working in foreign assistance.

Membership: Costs $75 for regular membership; $45 for young professionals (twenty-one to twenty-seven years old); $35 for students. Membership benefits include participation in Washington, D.C., chapter events, access to a network of development professionals, e-mail and newsletter updates of ongoing SID–Washington events and development issues, and discounts on the SID–Washington Annual Dinner, Annual Conference, and Career Conference.

Teachers of English to Speakers of Other Languages (TESOL)
700 South Washington Street, Suite 200
Alexandria, VA 22314
Telephone: 703-836-0774 or 888-547-3369 (toll free in U.S.)
Fax: 703-836-7864 or 703-836-6447
Website: www.tesol.org

Founded in 1966, TESOL is an international education association whose mission is to strengthen the effective teaching and learning of English. TESOL concentrates on teaching language and culture, not on English-language literature. TESOL promotes scholarships, disseminates information, and advocates credentialed instruction and quality programming. The organization publishes three serial publications and hosts an annual convention. TESOL also offers online and on-site professional development opportunities, as well as an online career center and searchable job bank.

Membership: Costs $75 for individual membership; $30 for student membership. Other membership categories available. Membership benefits include *Essential Teacher,* the association's quarterly magazine, access to interest sections and caucuses, the option to subscribe to *TESOL Quarterly,* the profession's scholarly research journal. Members receive a substantial discount on registrations for TESOL professional development events and TESOL publications.

Transatlantic Studies Association
Institute for Transatlantic, European, and American Studies
University of Dundee
Nethergate, Dundee DD1 4HN
Scotland, UK
Telephone: +44-1382-345-465
Fax: +44-1382-344-802
Website: www.dundee.ac.uk/iteas/association.htm

The Transatlantic Studies Association provides an interdisciplinary forum for scholars from all over the world to maintain an active and open dialogue about issues in transatlantic relations. Founded within the last five years, the organization primarily focuses on research coordination and dissemination. Their semi-annual publication, the *Journal of Transatlantic Studies,* publishes scholarly research from a range of social sciences, including comparative constitutionalism, environmental planning, geography, security studies, and international relations.

Membership: Costs $55 for individuals; $90 for institutions. Subscribers to the *Journal of Transatlantic Studies* automatically become members of the Transatlantic Studies Association, and vice versa.

SELECTED RESOURCES

Print

Encyclopedia of Associations: International Organizations
Thomson Gale, 2007 (www.galegroup.com)

This publication, now in its forty-fifth edition, contains more than thirty-two thousand associations located in 212 countries and is published in three parts. Parts I and II, *Descriptive Listings,* provide contact information and descriptions for these organizations, including U.S.-based organizations with binational or multinational memberships. Part III, *Indexes,* contains geographic, executive, and name and keyword indexes to all of the associations listed in the first two parts.

Encyclopedia of Associations: National Organizations of the U.S.
Thomson Gale, 2006 (www.galegroup.com)

This publication, also in its forty-fifth edition, is a comprehensive source for detailed information on nonprofit American membership organizations of national scope. Every entry offers a wealth of data, typically including the organization's complete name, address, phone number, fax number, founding date, purpose, activities, and dues, national and international conferences, together with the name and title of the organization's primary official. Also featured is an alphabetical name and keyword index so you can quickly locate the name and address of the organization you need to contact without ever having to consult the main entry.

National Trade and Professional Associations of the United States
Columbia Books, Inc., 2006 (www.associationexecs.com)

This forty-first edition of this publication lists more than eight thousand national trade associations, professional societies, and labor unions. Five indexes will enable you to look up associations by subject, budget, geographic area, acronym, and executive director. Other features include contact information, serial publications, upcoming convention schedules, membership and staff size, budget figures, and background information.

Web

Marketing Source
www.marketingsource.com/associations

The Concept Marketing Group offers a Directory of Associations that includes the full contact information for more than thirty-two thousand professional, business, and trade associations, 501(c)(3) nonprofit organizations, and other charity and community institutions. Online access to the directory can be purchased in one-month or one-year packages, both of which include daily updates.

Weddle's
www.weddles.com

Weddle's is a well-known name in the area of career development (*see chapter 5 in this volume*). This website, among many other features, offers a free online association directory. The directory, organized by general professional category, includes only links to the website of each association.

PROFILE
Belinda Chiu
Doctoral Student, The Teacher's College, Columbia University
Special Assistant to the President, The Phelps Stokes Fund

Career Trajectory

Doctoral Student, The Teacher's College, Columbia University, New York, New York, 2006–present

Special Assistant to the President, The Phelps Stokes Fund, New York, New York, 2006–present

Program Officer, The Phelps Stokes Fund, Washington, D.C., 2004–6

Research Analyst, Equals Three Communications, Inc., Bethesda, Maryland, 2004

Project Consultant, Center for Applied Research, Cambridge, MA/Philadelphia, Pennsylvania, 2003–4

Assistant Director, Dartmouth College Office of Admissions, Hanover, New Hampshire, 2000–2

Senior Research Analyst, Dove Consulting Group Inc., Boston, MA, 1998–2000

Academic Background

Doctoral Student in Education (Concentration in International Education Development), Teacher's College, Columbia University; Degree expected 2010

Democracy and Diversity Institute, Transregional Center for Democratic Studies, The New School, Cape Town, South Africa, January 2007

MALD (Master of Arts in Law and Diplomacy), The Fletcher School, Tufts University, 2004

AB, Government, Dartmouth College, 1998

What awards and honors have meant the most to you?

An honor that really meant a lot to me was being named a Truman Scholar National Finalist in 1997. This scholarship funds three years of grad school for those working on public policy. Going through the exercise of applying was very rewarding, and being selected as a finalist was truly an honor. It showed me that maybe I do have some potential to contribute to society.

I was also quite honored to receive the 1998 Morrell Goldberg Memorial Prize at Dartmouth, which is a senior class day award given for administrative talent and service. It was wonderful because I think I really understood my role as someone who can get people together and make things happen. This honor was great because I knew my work was having an impact.

Are you involved in community service?

Consultant, Management Leadership for Tomorrow (a nonprofit
organization committed to increasing the number of qualified leaders
of color in business)

Cofounder and Cochair, Fletcher Alumni of Color Association

Member, Dartmouth Alumni Council

Board Member, Dartmouth Asian-Pacific American Alumni Association

District Enrollment Director, New York City, Dartmouth College
Admissions

Member, Ambassador's Club International

Member, Comparative and International Education Society

Member, National Council for International Visitors

Founding President, International Regional Ambassador Club, New
York City

Executive Planning Committee, Tibetan Community Center, New
York City

Associate Member, Association of Black Admissions and Financial Aid
Officers in the Ivy League and Sister Schools

How do you define your cause?

There are two driving forces behind my career choices. First, I have been
very fortunate in my education and personal and community life, so what
drives me are these questions: "How do you give everybody the same awareness of opportunities, and access to those opportunities, so that they can do
what they want to do and be what they want to be?" "How do you create
those opportunities and that awareness?" I truly believe that when people are
fulfilled, when they are pursuing those things which they are most passionate about, that's when change—real social change—begins.

Second, I've always looked for things I am passionate and excited about.
If I'm not excited to get up in the morning and go to work, I won't do it
anymore. It's totally selfish, but I've had positions where I couldn't wait for
the clock to stop. I feel like I always need to learn . . . if I'm not learning, I start to fall asleep. Interest and passion have always driven me much
more than money. I figure money will follow when you're doing what you
love.

What drew you to this cause and your field?

I don't know if there's one single thing I can point to. My mom is an ed-
ucator, so I'm sure she had a lot of influence on me. I wasn't born in the
United States (I was born in Hong Kong), so as a young kid, even though
I'm American, I didn't always feel like I was truly American. Overseas, I was

never truly Chinese. I've always been aware that I straddle a couple of different identities. Even though I was very lucky in my education, I know what it's like to not fit in, to be on the outside. There are many little things that make me aware that I am not always "a part" of society—that I am fighting to fit in.

I think I became very sensitive to the people who stand on the margins of society, whether it's due to their socioeconomic situations or the color of their skin or their sexual orientation. The question of "How do you include everybody?" became a driving one for me. Having awareness, confidence, and the support of others around us is so important and providing these things for all people is my cause.

Do you have a mentor? How has he or she affected your life and career?

I have many. My first real mentor's name is Ed Dailey, an attorney and a Dartmouth alum. He became, and still is, someone I respect very much. He consistently opposes things he believes unethical. To have the guts to do this . . . even to this day, I wouldn't mind being fired as long as I know I'm standing up for something I believe in.

The first lady of Dartmouth, Susan DeBevoise Wright, has had a great influence on me. Having her as a mentor was really important. She encouraged me, told me about the Truman Scholarship, and pushed me to look beyond my self-imposed boundaries, to pursue what I loved.

Badi Foster, the president of the Phelps Stokes Fund, is someone I absolutely look up to as well. He follows this almost spiritual path to looking at issues of social justice . . . I don't think I'll ever reach where he is, but to have someone to look up to in terms of how he lives his life and the way he lets his ideals guide his work, it is amazing. . . .. Badi is a major reason why I have worked with Phelps Stokes.

Do you consider yourself a mentor to others?

I hope not! [*laughs*] When I was in my midtwenties, I always thought people in their thirties knew *exactly* what they were doing. Now that I'm thirty myself, it scares me when people ask for advice.

Yet I love being there for younger people as much as I can. For example, the whole reason I became involved with the Fletcher Alumni of Color Association is to provide mentors to younger people. I've actually given a couple of talks and been on some panels that were career-focused. It was really nice to see these nineteen- and twenty-year-olds who are so idealistic . . . but at the same time, they're a bit scared because of the expectations put on them and because they *don't* yet know what they're going to do. Sometimes they're so stressed out about college or jobs . . . I want to help them find the fun in it, to help them find something they're passionate about.

What is your best advice for developing effective networking skills?

I have to tell you, I HATE networking. I don't like networking events. I don't like schmoozing. People get so uptight and nervous in those situations about getting that job or getting that contact that they forget the most important part is making a connection with a person.

I think my best advice for networking is to meet and connect with people as people. If you connect with someone because you find something interesting about them, or they find something interesting about you, then you automatically develop a bond. Get to know people for who they are, not what they do. Some people shut down when they discover that you don't do what they want to do. You can tell when people turn off.

Always keep your eyes open and talk to people even if you're not sure why you're doing it. You never know when you might connect with the person sitting next to you.

People think that just because they're shy or not good in crowds, then they're not good networkers. But that's not true. You don't have to be someone who reaches out in a crowd and shakes everyone's hand. If you're at an event and you're shy, talk to the person alone at the cheese table—one person, that's all you need, and from that one person, who knows how many people you might get to know.

What lessons have you learned as your career has evolved?

Learn who you are. It's so easy to get caught up in what other people say—your parents, your friends, your teachers. They all have an idea of who you are and what you should do. You can get caught up in this and forget what you really want to do. You should listen to others because they do give you perspective, but at the end of the day, your gut tells you what's right for you.

Take risks. I don't think I've taken as many risks as I could have. I think one of the things I've learned as I've gotten older is to ask myself, "If I don't take this chance, am I going to regret it?" I don't want to be fifty years old, look back, and say, "Damn, I should have done it." If something doesn't work out, so be it. But I'm not going to regret missing an opportunity.

Even if you do things that are stupid, even if you do things that are not the brightest in the world, it doesn't matter. You can't regret it. I truly believe people come into your life for a reason and every experience you have happens for a reason. I probably wouldn't have said this with so much conviction four years ago. Everyone goes through hurt and everyone goes through pain, but there's always something else out there. Everything is impermanent in this life. I have to remind myself of that too.

Any final advice?

Tell your story. Find themes in your résumé and your experiences. I want to say to a lot of younger people, "I know you're smart, I know you're capable, I know you're talented, but so are a lot of people. So what is *your* story?" It's important to tell that story. This not only sets you apart from others, but this also helps you find your focus.

Stay young. I always look at things as a child would. I know it sounds immature, but it makes everything so much more fun.

Chapter 7
Internship Opportunities

Internships are building blocks of a career. In many cases they have become an implicit prerequisite for an entry-level job. Internships are the source of much practical training and office experience that employers seek. Employers want to be sure that potential hires understand the demands of the contemporary workplace and are not under the impression that the sometimes more relaxed deadlines of academic life apply in work situations.

Researching internships should be approached as seriously as searching for a relatively permanent position. You will be trading a precious commodity—your time—for valuable training in return for either no remuneration or (if you are lucky) a modest stipend. You want to make sure you choose to work in an environment where your supervisors truly care about your growth and professional development.

EXPLOITATION? NO, A CHANCE TO LEARN AND GROW

Internships can provide skills training and other valuable learning that one cannot acquire in the classroom. Actual work situations in the fields of international education, exchange, and development may be quite different from what you imagine, and the introduction an internship can provide to the daily tasks involved in a given job or organization is invaluable.

Certain career websites that we have come across warn students that some internships are arranged only "for the benefit of the employer" and may not offer any useful or pertinent experiences. One such website goes so far as to say that unless an internship provides a valuable learning experience, such as skills training or exposure to a specific business culture, the experience might be "little more than exploitation." This seems to be overstating the case.

It is true that most internships in the field of international affairs pay little to no money—few internships are actually a source of income. It is also true that most organizations, especially small ones, greatly benefit from the presence of interns. We know from experience that the National Council for International Visitors (NCIV), the Institute of International Education (IIE), and many other international education, exchange, and development organizations could not function as they do without the talent and contributions of their interns. But this certainly is not tantamount to exploitation.

Many organizations that recruit and utilize interns greatly appreciate the sacrifices interns make in order to work in their chosen fields for no salary and attempt to repay them with quality experiences that include a great deal of substantive work and opportunities to participate in events out of the office. In addition to the generous stipend it provides for its interns, NCIV emphasizes that they are not cheap labor, brought in to do the menial tasks that no one else wants to do; rather, they are an integral part of the staff. While NCIV intern supervisors make certain that every intern knows some grunt work will be required—indeed, in a small office, *everyone* is required to do some grunt work—it also strives to ensure that 75 to 80 percent of their tasks are substantive projects and research aligned with their interests. It is true that organizations want to benefit from their interns, but they typically want to see their interns flourish as well. Wise managers know that satisfied, well-trained interns are a valuable pool of future employees. They treat their interns accordingly.

A Good Internship Depends on You

Surely there are a few organizations and supervisors out there who are uninterested in the development of their interns. They may pile on mindless tasks, and an intern might find himself or herself spending a semester wasting away in front of the photocopier. The first way to avoid such an internship is to ask questions. An internship posting can tell you only so much about the tasks you will be performing. A website reveals only so much about a particular organization. Remember that an interview for an internship is just as much about you judging a potential employer as it is about them assessing you. Come prepared with a list of questions and try to glean from your interviewers exactly what tasks you will be asked to perform. Try to get a feel for the working environment of the office. What can you expect to learn in your time as an intern? Talk to current interns, if possible. Don't be shy making it clear that, while you are excited to help the organization in any way you can, you are also looking for an experience that is both substantive and meaningful.

We always advise anyone going to an office for an internship or job interview to arrive early. This builds in a margin for delays so that you are sure to arrive on time, thus demonstrating the fact that you are dependable. However, if you arrive early, you also will have time to observe while you are waiting. Are people racing around? Do they have time to offer a newcomer a smile and friendly hello? Is the receptionist polite and helpful? If the answer is yes, chances are your supervisor will be as well. An organization's culture inevitably reflects the example set by those in charge.

Once you have accepted an intern position, it is also up to you to get the maximum benefit possible in exchange for your effort. A meaningful internship experience often comes not only from the tasks you are doing but from the people you meet as well. Extend your network as much as possible. Push yourself to meet others working in your specific field of interest. It is through contacts gained in such situations that many interns find the most benefit. For example, two recent NCIV interns, Jessica Heller and Monya Hudsick, both secured full-time positions with the Meridian International Center through the contacts they gained while at NCIV. While we hope that Monya and Jess would agree the work they did as interns was both substantive and interesting, we are also sure that one of the greatest benefits of their time at NCIV was meeting the people who led them to full-time jobs.

Not Just for Students

Internships are not solely for undergraduate students or recent graduates. While these demographics may make up the majority of intern applicants, professionals further along in their careers also find internships valuable. Many of these professionals are either looking to change fields or have returned to graduate school and are using an internship for experience or academic credit. In the last several years NCIV internship supervisors have interviewed a number of internship applicants who have fifteen years or more of professional experience in fields completely unrelated to international exchange. Another of NCIV's recent interns, Mory Pagel, had more than five years of experience in the field of international exchange before applying to NCIV. He had recently returned to graduate school to study international communication and sought an internship to provide him with a different professional experience as well as academic credit. It is important, however, for "nontraditional" internship seekers to read the fine print of internship postings and make inquiries when necessary: some internship programs accept only current students and recent graduates.

Finding an Internship

Just as you would in a regular job search, cast the net wide when searching for internships. By exploring the full range of internship possibilities, you will know what to look for in terms of intern tasks, what to settle for in terms of intern compensation, and be able to better weed out the duds from the true, substantive opportunities. Apply early and often. Application deadlines can often be fluid, so if you see a posting on a database or website such as Idealist.org, be sure to check with the specific organization to make sure the details and deadlines have not changed. Tailor your cover letter and résumé to match each specific internship application. If you are applying for a government internship, remember that many positions require a security clearance, which may take anywhere from eight months to a year. Start your search and application process early.

Just as there are a plethora of job websites and search engines that have bloomed on the web, many websites devoted to helping you find an internship—at home or abroad—have also sprouted, such as Internships.com and Internabroad.com. Many job websites also contain internship listings and will allow you to refine your search to single them out. But, are these broad, more generic internship sites the best resources for helping you find your ideal internship in international education, exchange, and development?

In much the same manner as your job search, these search engines are a great tool for seeing what is out there. They will help you to get a handle on the great breadth of internship opportunities that exist. They will also allow you to search using several different terms or a combination of terms, or, if you have the patience, to scan *everything* that is listed to make sure you don't miss anything. As mentioned in chapter 5, Google is also another useful resource for such broad searching.

In most cases, however, websites and search engines more closely aligned with your specific internship interests will yield better, more efficient, results. For example, if you are interested in an internship with an international nonprofit organization, use the search engine available at Idealist.org. For those interested in international education, the NAFSA.org job and internship board is an essential resource. If internships in foreign policy or on Capitol Hill are your primary focus, try the Foreign Policy Association's job board or look on HillZoo.com. InterAction's publication *Monday Developments* is a must in the field of international development. Your undergraduate or graduate university e-mail lists or career center job boards are invaluable sources of internship information.

Of course, direct contact with specific organizations that interest you is irreplaceable. Most organizations list internship opportunities as well as application procedures on their own websites. If an organization with a mission that attracts you does not have internships available, contact them anyway; they may be able to direct you to similar organizations in the field that do.

SELECTED RESOURCES

Print

Hello Real World! A Student's Approach to Great Internships, Co-Ops, and Entry Level Positions
Jengyee Liang
BookSurge Publishing, 146 pages, 2006 (www.booksurge.com)

This book bills itself as an insider's guide to getting and succeeding in internships (with some tips for post-graduation job also in the mix). *Hello Real World!* provides the college student's perspective on how to land an internship or first job and then excel at it, as well as tips to employers on how to structure an effective internship or entry-level program for students who are new to the real world.

The Intern Files: How to Get, Keep, and Make the Most of Your Internship
Jamie Fedorko
Simon Spotlight Entertainment, 208 pages, 2006 (www.simonsays.com)

A straightforward guide for college students, this book leads you through the process of landing an internship, and then helps you to make the most of the experience once it begins.

The Internship Advantage: Get Real-World Job Experience to Launch Your Career
Dario Bravo and Carol Whiteley
Prentice-Hall, 176 pages, 2005 (www.prenticehall.com)
Designed to help you select and secure an internship in a competitive market, this book offers guidance in all phases of your internship experience: how and where to find an internship right for you, how to benefits most from your time in an internship, and how to capitalize on your experience for future career growth.

National Internships Guide
www.internships.com
This guide groups its list of internships into seven geographic regions in the United States—the Midwest, Middle Atlantic, New England, Rockies-Plains, Southeast, Southwest, and West. The organization sponsoring the internship is briefly described, the number and type (paid or unpaid, full- or part-time, summer or academic year) of positions available are provided, the duties envisioned for the intern are explained, and a key point of contact and address are given.

Vault Guide to Top Internships
Samer Hamadeh and Mark Oldman
Vault, Inc., 608 pages, 2007 (www.vault.com)
Written by the founders of the career information website Vault.com (see chapter 5), the third edition of the *Vault Guide* provides details on more than seven hundred internships. Each internship entry provides information on qualifications, pay, length of internship, and contact information, as well as background information on the company or organization.

Web

Developmentex
See chapter 5 in this volume.

Foreign Policy Association
See chapter 5 in this volume.

Idealist
See chapter 9 in this volume.

InternAbroad.Com
www.internabroad.com

As a member of the GoAbroad.com family, this site is part of a one-stop shopping opportunity for students wishing to travel internationally for many different reasons. InternAbroad.com specializes in providing resources that specifically pertain to internships.

See GoAbroad.com in chapter 5 in this volume.

InternshipPrograms.Com
www.internshipprograms.com

The internship search engine for WetFeet.com (see chapter 5), this website allows you to create a free user profile and search a database of available internships, read internships reviews, create your own "real-intern profile," and research companies and careers.

Internships.Com
www.internships.com

This site requires the purchase of an individual student membership in order to access its internship listings. It also sells its National Internships Guide (see above), as well as multiple regional guides to internships around the United States.

NAFSA: Association of International Educators
See chapter 5 in this volume.

Rising Star Internships
www.rsinternships.com

On this free site, you will find listings of internships categorized by specific field (including international affairs, international relations, nonprofit organizations, and public policy). The site also lists a limited number of entry-level positions intended for recent graduates, as well as a résumé posting service that will make your qualifications accessible to employers who search the site.

The Washington Center
www.twc.edu

The Washington Center's programs combine semester-long internships in Washington, D.C., with academic seminars. Positions for all fields of study, including international education, exchange, and development, are available; employers include the federal government, nonprofit organizations, news media, and international business. The internships are typically unpaid, although successful interns can receive academic credit.

PROFILE
Max Stewart
Executive Director, International Council of Central Florida

Career Trajectory
> Executive Director, International Council of Central Florida, Orlando, Florida
> 2004–present
> Director, International Council of Central Florida, Orlando, Florida 2004
> Programmer/Senior Programmer, International Council of Central Florida,
> Orlando, Florida 2002–4

Academic Background
> BA, Political Science, University of Central Florida, 2005

What awards and honors have meant the most to you?

My military background has meant a lot to me. I received the Presidential Scholar Award for the Air Force for ROTC—I could choose any university and go there on a ROTC scholarship. It's the highest honor from the military for incoming college students. That's how I got my college education. That's my biggest honor so far but, hey, I'm still young.

Are you involved in community service?

I'm involved with Junior Achievement. JA enables a business leader in the community or a college grad to go into high schools and talk to students about what they're going to do with their futures. Also, given my background in athletics, I taught beginner's swimming at a local YMCA. I really enjoy getting out into the community and working with families, teaching life safety classes for infants and things like that.

How do you define your cause?

Right now, my cause is wrapped up in what I do for the International Visitor Leadership Program (IVLP) with the International Council of Central Florida (ICCF). I guess the way to define my cause is that I want to give people a better understanding of the United States and, in order to help that along, give them a better understanding of who I am.

I think you get attached to different missions when you're with different organizations, and as you actually branch out to different career fields, your causes change. But the whole motivation behind what I do is that I want to better the world's understanding of the United States. My current job is a perfect fit for what caught my attention back in college.

Your cause can have many sides to it. It's not flat—there are many things that can then branch out from your primary cause. I think I've pretty much found my niche, what I want to do for the rest of my life in some capacity . . . but as you move to different organizations, your causes change. I think, especially for me, once you find the heart of what you want to do, there are many side projects that you can pursue. But you always bring everything back to that main cause that you are driven to support.

What drew you to this cause and your field?

What drew me to the field is a very interesting story, and it's relatively short [*laughs*]. Starting college, my major was aerospace engineering. I wanted to work for NASA. I had chosen this path and thought, "Man, this is it. This is my career field."

But, for whatever reason, I quickly lost interest in it and actually transferred universities [from Auburn University to the University of Central Florida]. At UCF, I took a political science class with Dr. Houman Sadri, who became my mentor in this field. The first day in the class, I wasn't all that interested. But the second time and the third time, I started answering and asking questions and I thought, "Hey, I really like this. What are some more classes that I can take?"

Through Dr. Sadri's tutoring and coaching, I switched from aerospace engineering, which is very technical, to a political science major, which is very different, very analytical. That international political economy class was probably the first time I ever thought about the international relations field, international diplomacy, and that whole array of career opportunities.

Do you have a mentor? How has he or she affected your life and career?

Dr. Sadri is someone who drew me to this cause and this field more than anyone or anything else. He is very engaging, and that was something, I think, that was lacking in my aerospace engineering major—engaging personalities. International relations is more theoretical and communicative in nature, and I found that fit me much better. Once I realized that, Dr. Sadri began to question me and push me in the right directions, show me different ways to be involved. He is on the board of ICCF and said, "You look like you're really interested in this. I'm going to set you up with an internship."

I started interning for the organization one fall, and the next spring, I was working as a programmer. The next fall I became the director of all programs, took over directing the office, and became executive director in 2004. It was so fast paced, a whirlwind, but Dr. Sadri always encouraged me. He said, "You're ready for this. If you ever need any help, just ask. But you're ready."

In this way, he shaped my whole career focus. If you can find your niche in college like this, and find someone to help guide you as Dr. Sadri did for me, it's an amazing thing. You can get a leg up on everyone else.

Do you consider yourself a mentor to others?

I don't categorize myself as a mentor. I think of myself more as an "older brother." "Mentor" to me means that you have years and years of experience—a mentor is almost like a father or mother figure. But I'm still young—I've still got many years to go before I can call myself a mentor to other people.

I still know what it's like to be a college student or a high school senior. I still remember those years. I know what young people are going through and how they're going to feel in certain situations. So I am able to say to them, when they come up against a certain situation that I've experienced, "Hey, I know what it's like. I just handled that situation in this way. What do you think? How do you think you will handle it?" Until I don't know what's going on with eighteen- and nineteen-year olds, I'll consider myself a brother. But when I start *not* knowing what's going on with them, then maybe I'll consider myself more of a mentor . . . and that day will be horrible. I think that's when my midlife crisis will begin [*laughs*].

What is your best advice for developing effective networking skills?

The best way to develop networking skills is to go to as many events as you possibly can. I go to an event and listen to what those around me are saying. I see what others are doing to meet new people, determine what *they* are doing effectively.

I always try to bring someone along with me to events. When I go to events for my job, I try to bring another staff member or a board member. That way, I'm not alone in the room, and my board and staff become connected with the same groups as well. I also usually call or e-mail the president or membership director of whatever event I'm going to in advance and say, "Hey I'll be coming. Who's on the guest list? Who are the people coming to this event? What do they do? Why are they interested?" Then I'll do some research and figure out topics that will be of interest to them.

Always have a good business card and business card holder. I carry a business card holder that's not flashy but nice, so when you give out your card, you have to open this holder first. That gives a professional touch in what you do. It looks a little better than pulling it out of your wallet or pocket all crumpled up. And if you put a business card of someone you met in there, you're bound to look at it again, instead of just putting it in your coat pocket and sending it to the dry cleaners.

Write on the back of their business card where you met the person and what you discussed. That way, one or two days later, you can send them an e-mail—or even a handwritten letter—saying that you loved talking about such and such a topic and you'd like to get together again in the future. And usually you get a response because they know that you're genuinely interested in them.

What lessons have you learned as your career has evolved?

Having worked for nonprofit organizations, I've learned that you never have everything that you want—you always have to work double to get half.

Appearance is everything for an organization, especially for a nonprofit. If you appear professional, your events are professional, and your work is professional, then people will take you seriously. But if you drop the ball even once, word gets around. And that can be very stressful at times, especially leading an organization. Being as young as I am and leading an organization, I don't know all of the pitfalls yet.

I stress again that appearance is everything. If you walk into an interview and mumble away or are sloppily dressed, then you will make a poor impression. You may have a stellar résumé but if you can't speak in front of people, you may have a tough time getting a job. You should also tailor your résumé to whatever industry you happen to be applying for jobs in—have some of your stronger points noted on the top. Never show a funny or quirky personal e-mail address on your résumé. I've had many potential interns send me résumés with e-mail addresses like "hotlips29@yahoo.com" or something like that [*laughs*] and that's just not going to cut it. Make sure your résumé is simple, not flashy with stars and hearts all over it, which I've seen before.

One final, big lesson I've learned is this: not everybody is going to be happy. No matter what you do, no matter how well a job or task is done, somebody's going to find fault with it. You just have to take the good with the bad.

Any final advice?

My best advice is to intern during college in as many different fields as you can, if you have the time, ability, and patience. I would also suggest, instead of the four-year college plan, take five years—though I'm sure whoever is paying would wholeheartedly disagree with this advice [*laughs*]. But take some time to find what you are interested in; take some time to intern during the summers for different companies. The average college student changes their major four to six times before they graduate . . . that's an average. Before you get out in the real world, have a whole bunch of experience in a couple of different fields. That'll help you most in deciding what you want to do.

Chapter 8
Volunteer Opportunities

In her late twenties and newly married, Sherry spent some time at the University of Rhode Island with her husband, a faculty member at that time. In addition to finishing her dissertation and teaching a few courses, she also engaged in several international volunteer activities at the university. She served as the president of a volunteer organization that matched international students with American host families. She also coordinated orientation and cross-cultural training sessions for international students.

Directly after graduating from college, Mark moved to the city of Yanji, in the Jilin province of China, as a volunteer with the Salesian Lay Missioners. His primary duty for his year in Yanji was to act as a teacher of English conversation at a technical high school run by Catholic priests. He organized after-school activities for his students (such as "extra English" and guitar groups), chaperoned weekend field trips for students, and taught English in several additional venues across the city.

As we discussed in the introduction to the book, idealism is typically a driving force for those interested in a career in international education, exchange, or development. Coupled with this idealism is a desire to serve. Volunteer opportunities, such as our own mentioned above, give professionals the chance to feed this desire while simultaneously gaining international experience. Sherry did international volunteer work in the United States, while Mark did international volunteer work abroad. We both gained rich experience and new perspectives from these activities, all while meeting our desire to serve.

It is certainly true that not all people are in the position to take a year or two off from the real world in order to volunteer abroad for no pay. Certainly the decision to become an international volunteer requires much discernment on your part to determine whether or not the experience will be both beneficial to your career and feasible within the confines of your life situation (i.e., paying back student loans, taking care of bills, or family obligations). Yet as Sherry's experience demonstrates, you do not have to go abroad to volunteer. Certainly your career in international relations will benefit immensely if you do indeed go abroad at some point (Sherry later worked as a paid English teacher in Brazil for a year). Yet if your situation mandates that you remain in the United States, there are still myriad opportunities for valuable international volunteer experience. Such experiences, whether in the United States or beyond, will help you to acquire solid experience in the field, increase your foreign language proficiency, gain further regional expertise, and equip you for future success in multinational and cross-cultural settings.

SAMPLE VOLUNTEER ORGANIZATIONS

AIESEC-United States
127 West 26th Street, 10th Floor
New York, NY 10001
Telephone: 212-757-3774
Fax: 212-757-4062
Website: www.aiesecus.org

AIESEC offers internship and trainee opportunities in international business for U.S. and international students. Students who are members of affiliated schools may participate. Annually, AIESEC sends approximately four hundred participants abroad and brings an equal number to the United States.

American Refugee Committee
430 Oak Grove Street, Suite 204
Minneapolis, MN 55403
Telephone: 612-872-7060 and 800-875-7060 (toll free in U.S.)
Fax: 612-607-6499
Website: www.archq.org

The American Refugee Committee is a nonprofit organization that provides health care and health care training to displaced peoples in developing nations worldwide including Liberia, Pakistan, Rwanda, Sierra Leone, Sri Lanka, Sudan, Thailand, and Uganda. Volunteer positions are categorized by country; position descriptions include job qualifications and responsibilities and time and financial commitments necessary from the volunteer.

Amigos de las Americas

5618 Star Lane
Houston, TX 77057
Telephone: 713-782-5290 or 800-231-7796 (toll free in U.S.)
Fax: 713-782-9267
Website: www.amigoslink.org

Amigos de las Americas is an international nonprofit organization providing volunteer experiences in Latin America for high school and college students interested in public health service and leadership development. Participants work with one or two other volunteers in a small community and live with host families. Participants must have some knowledge of Spanish or Portuguese.

Catholic Medical Mission Board (CMMB)

10 West 17th Street
New York, NY 10011
Telephone: 212-242-7757 and 800-678-5659 (toll free in U.S.)
Fax: 212-807-9161
Website: www.cmmb.org

Catholic Medical Mission Board is a U.S.-based Catholic charity focused exclusively on global health care. CMMB sends nearly three hundred volunteer licensed health care professionals to developing nations in Africa, Latin America, and the Caribbean each year (medical students and other students are not eligible to participate in CMMB programs). Some short-term placements are available, but one-year commitments are preferred.

Catholic Relief Services (CRS)

228 W. Lexington Street
Baltimore, MD 21201
Telephone: 410-625-2220
Website: www.catholicrelief.org

Catholic Relief Services is the official international relief and development organization of the U.S. Catholic community and works through local churches, governments, and community groups to offer development assistance. Volunteers make a full-time, two-year commitment. They serve for twelve months overseas and twelve months in the United States.

Concern Worldwide
104 East 40th Street, Suite 903
New York, NY 10016
Telephone: 212-557-8000
Fax: 212-557-8004
Website: www.concernusa.org

Concern Worldwide recruits approximately 150 volunteers per year to work in twenty-nine countries throughout Africa, Asia, Central America, and Eastern Europe in fields such as health, education, sanitation, natural resources, and emergency services, providing emergency relief and long-term assistance.

Council on International Educational Exchange (CIEE)
300 Fore Street
Portland, ME 04101
Telephone: 207-553-7600 and 800-40-STUDY (toll free in U.S.)
Fax: 207-553-7699
Website: www.ciee.org

The Council on International Educational Exchange offers short-term summer programs for volunteers interested in projects dealing with the environment, disabled persons, housing, and other issues.

See also chapter 9 in this volume.

Direct Relief International
27 South La Patera Lane
Santa Barbara, CA 93117
Telephone: 805-964-4767
Fax: 805-681-4838
Website: www.directrelief.org

Direct Relief International is a nonprofit medical commodities donor that sends medicine and medical equipment to developing nations worldwide. Some volunteers may be placed outside the United States.

Institute for International Cooperation and Development (IICD)
1117 Hancock Road
Williamstown, MA 01267
Telephone: 413-458-9466
Fax: 413-458-3323
Website: www.iicd-volunteer.org

The Institute for International Cooperation and Development offers work and study programs in Africa, Brazil, and Central America. The programs require a minimum one-year commitment, including training and orientation in the United States, group work on a development project, and development education upon return to the United States. Approximately one hundred volunteers participate in IICD programs each year.

InterAction
See chapter 6 in this volume.

International Executive Service Corps (IESC)
1900 M Street, NW, Suite 500
Washington, DC 20036
Telephone: 202-589-2600
Fax: 202-326-0289
Website: www.iesc.org

The International Executive Service Corps recruits highly skilled executives, administrators, and technical advisers (or recent retirees) to work on one of a thousand IESC projects, and to share their years of experience and expertise with people in developing nations. Volunteer experts (VEs) register in IESC's Skills Bank and are called upon to provide assistance on projects in more than 130 countries. Paid professional consultancy positions are also available.

The International Partnership for Service-Learning and Leadership (IPSL)
815 2nd Avenue
New York, NY 10017
Telephone: 212-986-0989
Fax: 212-986-5039
Website: www.ipsl.org

IPSL is a consortium of colleges, universities, service organizations, and other related organizations that have united to foster and develop programs linking community service and academic study. It sends approximately one hundred college or university students abroad each year to combine studies with community service.

International Rescue Committee (IRC)
122 East 42nd Street
New York, NY 10168
Telephone: 212-551-3000
Fax: 272-551-3179
Website: www.theirc.org

The International Rescue Committee is a refugee relief agency that sends approximately three hundred health care workers to developing countries each year for short- and long-term assignments. People with previous experience in relief activities overseas are preferred. IRC offers both paid and unpaid positions.

See also chapter 9 in this volume.

Jesuit Volunteer Corps (JVC)
P.O. Box 3756
Washington, DC 20027
Telephone: 202-687-1132
Fax: 202-687-5082
Website: www.jesuitvolunteers.org

The Jesuit Volunteer Corps, advocating the values of the Jesuits, a Catholic order of priests, offers volunteer positions both in the United States and abroad. Jesuit Volunteers International offers two-year positions in teaching, community organizing, and ministry in Africa, Central and South America, and the Pacific. Voluntary service is based on living simply, keeping faith, doing justice, and building communities. JVC provides insurance for volunteers, covers travel expenses and room and board, and provides a small stipend.

Methodist Global Ministries
The United Methodist Church
475 Riverside Drive
New York, New York 10115
Telephone: 212-870-3816 and 800-862-4246 (800-UMC-GBGM, toll free in U.S.)
Fax: 212-870-3624
Website: http://new.gbgm-umc.org

Methodist Global Ministries, officially known as the General Board of Global Ministries, is the international missions agency of the United

Methodist Church. The organization coordinates the work of 135,000 volunteers in seventy countries and forty-eight U.S. states. Methodist Global Ministries administers the Global Justice Volunteers Program, in which young adults (eighteen to twenty-five years old) live, work, and learn in the midst of foreign communities where justice support programs are under way. The United Methodist Committee on Relief (UMCOR) works in more than eighty countries. UMCOR and Muslim Aid (see below) recently established a formal partnership, embarking on joint projects such as tsunami recovery and refugee relief in Sri Lanka.

Muslim Aid
P.O. Box 3
London, E1 1WP
England
Telephone: +44-0-20-7377-4200
Fax: +44-0-20-7377-4201
Website: http://ramadan.muslimaid.org

Muslim Aid, founded in 1985 "to alleviate the suffering of the victims of poverty, war, and natural disaster," is a volunteer-reliant collaboration of twenty-three British Muslim organizations. Through their offices in Bangladesh, Bosnia, Cambodia, Indonesia, Iraq, Pakistan, Somalia, Sri Lanka, Sudan, and the United Kingdom, Muslim Aid works in partnership with local governmental and nongovernmental organizations to conduct initiatives in emergency relief, education, health care, orphan care, and economic empowerment. The organization focuses its projects on long-term sustainable development.

Partners of the Americas
1424 K Street, NW, Suite 700
Washington, DC 20005
Telephone: 202-628-3300
Fax: 202-628-3306
Website: www.partners.net

Partners of the Americas pairs a U.S. state or area with a region or country in Latin America or the Caribbean (or both). Partnership committees are community based and are composed of volunteers who work with their counterparts to assess needs, access resources, jointly plan, and carry out development projects in health, education, rehabilitation, and other areas. Partners of the Americas offers approximately one hundred partnerships each year.

See the profile of Malcolm Butler for more information. Malcolm served as president and CEO of Partners of the Americas until 2007.

Peace Corps of the United States
See chapter 10 in this volume.

Project HOPE
International Headquarters
255 Carter Hall Lane
Millwood, VA 22646
Telephone: 540-837-2100 and 800-544-4673 (toll free in U.S.)
Fax: 540-837-1813
Website: www.projecthope.org

Project HOPE began practicing "medical diplomacy" with its founding in 1958, developing relationships with peoples of different cultures and nations by sharing medical knowledge and treating patients alongside local health professional counterparts. The program sends doctors, nurses, and other health care professionals and educators to developing countries. These volunteers work to improve the skills of local health care professionals and train other educators and practitioners.

Rotary International
1 Rotary Center
1560 Sherman Avenue
Evanston, IL 60201
Telephone: 847-866-3000
Fax: 847-328-8554
Website: www.rotary.org

Rotary International is an organization of professionals worldwide who provide humanitarian service, encourage high ethical standards in all vocations, and help build goodwill and peace in the world. Rotary coordinates youth exchange programs for high school students and provides programs such as the Ambassadorial Scholarship, which offers three- or six-month assignments as well as one-year or multiyear scholarships or grants for university teachers, World Community Service, and Group Study Exchanges. Each year Rotary places approximately 1,700 participants. *See the profile of Arjun Desai for more information. Arjun served as a Rotary Ambassadorial Scholar of Goodwill in Singapore.*

Salesian Lay Missioners
P.O. Box 30
2 Lefevre Lane
New Rochelle, NY 10802
Telephone: 914-633-8344
Website: www.salesians.org/slm/index.htm

Salesian Lay Missioners is a Catholic association that sends volunteer lay missionaries to Bolivia, China, India, Mexico, Papua New Guinea, and Sierra Leone, as well as to communities in the United States. The Salesians (SDB) are a Catholic society of priests and brothers founded to reach out to poor and needy youth. The order has approximately seventeen thousand members working in one hundred countries. Volunteer missioners work in Salesian communities in their respective countries, focusing on education and human development among youth.

Mark worked as a volunteer Salesian Lay Missioner in Yanji, China, serving as an English teacher at a technical high school.

United Nations Volunteers (UNV)
UN Campus
Langer Eugen
Hermann-Ehlers-Str. 10
53113 Bonn
Germany
Telephone: +49-228-815-2000
Fax: +49-228-815-2001
Website: www.unv.org

UNV works to promote and harness volunteerism for effective development. It places participants in developing countries to work with human rights monitoring, nonmilitary peacekeeping, humanitarian, and refugee work. UNV places volunteers in more than 160 countries for a variety of time periods and assignments.

Volunteers for Peace, Inc. (VFP)
1034 Tiffany Road
Belmont, VT 05730
Telephone: 802-259-2759
Fax: 802-259-2922
Website: www.vfp.org

VFP is a nonprofit organization that promotes participation in International Voluntary Service (IVS) projects, historically known as International Workcamps. VFP offers placement in more than 3,400 IVS projects in more than one hundred countries each year, including more than forty in the United States. Volunteers come from diverse backgrounds, and each project typically has participants from four or more countries. Most projects are short term (two to three weeks) and do not require any specific professional or language training. The IVP website features a searchable International Workcamp Directory, a large repository of volunteer projects around the world.

SELECTED RESOURCES

Print
Alternatives to the Peace Corps: A Guide of Global Volunteer Opportunities
Paul Backhurst, ed.
Food First, 144 pages, 2005

Alternatives to the Peace Corps, now in its eleventh edition, is a resource for finding community-based volunteer work. The book includes listings for more than one hundred national and international organizations, guidelines for researching and evaluating volunteer organizations, budgeting and fundraising tips, and a resource section full of books, websites, and organizations for further reading and research.

Transitions Abroad: The Guide to Learning, Living, Working, and Volunteering Overseas
See chapter 5 in this volume.

Volunteer Vacations: Short-Term Adventures That Will Benefit You and Others
Doug Cutchins, Anne Geissinger, and Bill McMillon
Chicago Review Press, 216 pages, 2006 (www.chicagoreviewpress.com)

This sourcebook details thousands of opportunities for those who wish to spend short periods abroad on service-oriented programs. Volunteer organizations are listed, along with the type of volunteer work to be performed and skills required. The book also contains numerous brief volunteer journals that paint a picture of the impact of volunteer service abroad, both on the recipients of the service and on the volunteers.

*World Volunteers: The World Guide to Humanitarian and
Development Volunteering*
Fabio Ausenda and Erin McCloskey, eds.
Universe, 256 pages, 2006

This third edition of *World Volunteers* is designed as a resource for those looking to get involved in humanitarian aid projects throughout the world. Both long-term and short-term projects are listed. In addition, as a resource for those without previous volunteer experience abroad, the book presents many organizations offering workcamps, which can help familiarize volunteers with humanitarian and development work.

Web

Idealist
www.idealist.org/volunteer/travel.html

Idealist.org, in addition to its many other functions, offers an extensive list (with brief descriptions and hyperlinks) of organizations offering volunteer positions abroad in all parts of the world.

See also chapter 9 in this volume.

Volunteer Abroad.Com
www.volunteerabroad.com

A member of the GoAbroad.com family, this site is part of a one-stop shop for students wishing to travel internationally for different reasons and in different capacities, including volunteer work.

See also chapter 5 in this volume.

Volunteer International.Org
www.volunteerinternational.org

The International Volunteer Programs Association (IVPA) is an alliance of nonprofit, nongovernmental organizations involved in international volunteer and internship exchanges. Its homepage is equipped with a detailed search function that allows you to search for specific volunteer opportunities abroad. Tips on the why's and how's of volunteering abroad are presented, and the IVPA member list provides names, descriptions, and hyperlinks for more than thirty international voluntary organizations.

PROFILE
Malcolm Butler
Former President and CEO, Partners of the Americas

Career Trajectory
President and CEO, Partners of the Americas, Washington, D.C., 2001–7
President, Pax World Service, Washington, D.C., 2000
International Economic Consultant, Washington, D.C., 1995–2000
Program Director, North Carolina Outward Bound School, Ashville, North
   Carolina, 1994
U.S. Agency for International Development (USAID)
   Mission Director in: Bolivia 1977–79, Peru 1980, Lebanon 1981, and the
      Philippines 1988–91
   Executive Secretary, 1982–83
Staff Member for International Economic Affairs, National Security Council,
   White House, 1975–77
Examiner for International Affairs, Office of Management and Budget,
   Executive Office of the President, 1972–74
Foreign Service Officer, U.S. Department of State
   Mexico, 1966–69
   Iran, 1969–71

Academic Background
Graduate Studies, Economics, Oxford University, 1963–64
BA, History, Rice University, 1963

What awards and honors have meant the most to you?
I received two presidential citations while in the Foreign Service. I felt
particularly good about those because I felt like I had truly earned them. They
recognized some very significant things that I had done with USAID.

Are you involved in community service?
Board Member, U.S. Center for Citizen Diplomacy
Board Member, Volunteers for Economic Growth Alliance
Board Member, Old Dominion Soccer League
Board Member, Federation of Latino Agencies for Greater Washington
Board Member, McClean Community Citizens Association

I really enjoy serving on founding boards. I like start-ups—it's a particular challenge for me. I believe that we should make time to volunteer and
be part of our communities. I feel strongly about that. I try to not only convince those around me of that, but I try to live it as well.

How do you define your cause?

I'm not sure there's a single answer to this. I went into Foreign Service because I was interested in foreign affairs. I subsequently became very interested in the challenges of managing resources and people. I was pretty good at it, which is why, I think, I moved into some of the mission director positions and bureau management positions in the public sector. Then I made a decision that, rather than knowing less and less about more and more, I wanted to start learning more and more about less and less.

When you manage five hundred people in an entire bureau, you can't really know a whole lot about all of the details. Your job really is to know less and less about more and more. I got to the point where I really felt like I wanted to flip that. Instead, I wanted to learn more and more about a much smaller piece of the world. That led me in my business to focus on transactions. I have enjoyed more recently focusing on a much smaller group of people, in one region of the world, as well as focusing on certain types of activities.

I've always wanted to be doing something that I felt made a difference. And I'm very lucky because I don't think I've ever found myself in a situation where I didn't feel like I was making a difference. I've been very fortunate.

What drew you to this cause and your field?

I think there were three phases of my life. First, I consciously wanted to excel in international affairs and the public sector. I then decided I didn't want to live my entire professional life in the public sector, and I wanted to see if I could succeed in business. Then the nonprofit world stumbled on me, or I stumbled on them, through "happy circumstances." Though I had been on the boards of nonprofits, nonprofit work in my career was something I had never done.

There's not a unifying theme to my career decisions. I haven't had a master plan. My best advice is to keep your learning curve steep. If you have a career choice to make, always take the one that's going to give you a steeper learning curve. Always do what's going to challenge you most.

Do you have a mentor? How has he or she affected your life and career?

Oh, yes. Because I've moved around a lot in my career, I've had different mentors, from undergraduate school to graduate school to various stages of the Foreign Service and on to this stage of my career.

There are always mentors around, but I think you create your own mentors, really. There are a lot of people who are potential mentors and some will come to you, but most of them won't. It's not as if you have to recruit them, or say, "Will you be my mentor?" and sign a contract. I don't think I've ever sat across the table from someone and acknowledged that I was in a mentor relationship. You just find yourself in a mentor relationship with someone you respect and admire. You want to learn from them.

Do you consider yourself a mentor to others?

Gosh, I hope so. I can probably name four or five people who may consider that they're in a mentoring relationship with me. I make a conscious effort to be a mentor to those around me.

I'm very aware that what I do in my job is at least as important as what I say. I really do try to model my behavior in a way that I think will help people advance their careers. I very consciously make space for these people to grow. Sometimes it's not comfortable for them. But sometimes the most valuable thing I can do in my job is decide not to get involved with the decisions that are being made. That's part of a mentoring relationship.

I try to spend a third of my time running things; a third of my time outside, gaining new business, projecting our image, etc.; and a third of my time working on the people who work here.

What is your best advice for developing effective networking skills?

Show genuine interest and curiosity. You really want to know what the other person does and why and how they think about it and who they are. Constantly be in a learning, curious, information-gathering mode. People love to talk about themselves and what they do.

Establish a solid relationship before you start loading that relationship. You usually don't want to ask people for something the first time you meet them. But on the other hand, people shouldn't hold back from asking for something either. . . . Maybe I should put it in another way:

There are a lot of relationships that are valuable to establish even if you don't know why at the moment. You don't have to have an agenda at any given point when establishing a relationship.

What lessons have you learned as your career has evolved?

Well, I'm an economist by training, and the first thing I learned is that you can't have politics without economics, or economics without politics. You can't really pull them apart.

The second thing I've learned is that you cannot be scared by numbers. Don't be scared when someone puts a balance sheet in front of you. Resource management is about people and numbers, and you can't back away from the numbers. A lot of people say, "Oh, that's not for me, let the accountants do that," but you've got to be prepared to sit down with the numbers.

Third, as an economist, I've learned about the limitations of economics. This is where I am right now in my career: I think that the structure, organization, and dynamics of civil society is one of the most important issues out there. If you look at successful development stories, they are as much about bringing people together to accomplish things as they are about getting the price right. Having the right macropolicy is important, but it's no more important than making sure people in the community are organized, working together, and understand what they are trying to do. The organization of civil society, from farmers' co-ops to PTAs to labor unions to chambers of commerce to boards of directors . . . that level of involvement is terribly important. Serving on a PTA board is very, very important, to your kids, to the kids in the community . . . that's what I mean by civil society.

Any final advice?

I think it's useful to have varied experience. It's been very useful for me—having worked in the public, private, and nonprofit sectors has helped me grow tremendously. It makes me more valuable, and it has been satisfying for me professionally. I think personal growth is really what it's all about. Varied experience means you bring more to a problem or an effort, and it also means you grow more.

Keep your learning curve steep, keep growing, and the rest of it falls into place . . . well, maybe not quite . . . like I said, I never had a master plan. But if you do your job well and stay creative and positive, opportunities will come.

PROFILE
Arjun M. Desai
MD Candidate, Miller School of Medicine, University of Miami

Career Trajectory
MD Candidate, Miller School of Medicine, University of Miami, Florida, 2004–present
Ambassadorial Scholar of Goodwill, Rotary International, Singapore, 2004–5
Intern, Gibson Dunn & Crutcher LLP, Irvine/Los Angeles, California, 2004
Intern, Office of Congressman Christopher Cox, House Policy Committee, U.S. House of Representatives, Washington, D.C., 2002

Academic Background
MD Candidate, University of Miami Miller School of Medicine, 2008
BS, Economics, University of Oklahoma, 2003

What awards and honors have meant the most to you?
The first activity that ever really got me into the national arena was work with a community organization I was involved with in high school called Drug Use Is Life Abuse (DUILA). It was a community grassroots organization focused on preventative education towards teenage substance abuse. Among other projects, DUILA organized the nationwide red-ribbon week that unified students against substance abuse through wearing red ribbons and wristbands. We went to a conference with then President Clinton and the drug czar at that time, General Barry McCaffrey, and were awarded a distinguished honor from the President at the Coalition of Anti-Drug Communities of America (CADCA) meeting in Washington, D.C., for our efforts in the drug abuse arena. To be recognized by an office as high as the president's was a great honor and was really motivational to me.

Are you involved in community service?
Cofounder and CEO, Universal Children's Medical Fund, 2005–present

The idea for the Universal Children's Medical Fund was one that I got in my first year of medical school. It started off with a trip I took to India— I went with several doctors on this trip, and I was the only student. The Miami med school sponsors several international trips, to Nicaragua and some other places, so I thought, "Why don't we take a trip to India?" It's such a unique place, both culturally and medically. So we organized a group of about thirty students and six or seven doctors and took a trip over there for two weeks. The experience was about 50 percent cultural immersion and 50 percent medical training and experience.

That trip spawned the nonprofit organization called the Universal Children's Medical Fund. Now I'm working with one of the doctors who went on that initial trip and who is a facial plastic surgeon out in Los Angeles. We're creating a fund that will allow us to pay for more of these international trips for medical students. But the main focus of the new organization is also to identify children from around the world who have very complex diseases and pay for and provide all surgical and medical care here in the United States, where we have the facilities to handle the major surgeries, treatments, and recovery. For example, there are children who have major facial deformities and are identified by their societies as being inherently possessed by evil spirits, or call it what you will. We will be able to fix these facial deformities and then integrate the children into their societies and educate their communities on their previous medical problem, to hopefully decrease the chance of future stigmas.

How do you define your cause?

My defining cause, if I were to call it that, is to help provide perspective to my peers. It stems from the fact that I was fortunate enough at a young age to travel a lot and that impacted my decision, one, to go into medicine and, two, to want to do something that both involves my community and recognizes the extenuating factors *outside* of my community. To me, that means recognizing how underprivileged much of the world is compared to the United States. That traveling and exposure, both before and after my Rotary experience in Singapore, shaped my desire to want to go into medicine, as well as to help expose my fellow med students who *haven't* had a chance to travel to the outside world. Thus, my involvement with the Universal Children's Medical Fund and organizing international trips for students. While they're still young, I want to help impress upon them that they can do *a lot* with their degrees in medicine and affect a lot more people than they ever thought they could. I want to be able to show people who have never traveled before, or who have never seen any of the conditions that exist in other countries, that a world outside of our borders does exist.

What drew you to this cause and your field?

I would definitely say that my father, who came to the United States from India when he was twenty years old, helped to draw me to this cause. When he arrived, he didn't speak English, he had $200 in his pocket and two suitcases to his name. Growing up here and making a successful life for himself and his family, he has always taken it upon himself to show his children all of the aspects that led to his development, which involved traveling a lot, traveling to areas that were underdeveloped or underserved. That played the biggest role in the development of my international experience and mind-set.

Do you have a mentor? How has he or she affected your life and career?

Dr. Rajendra Desai, who is actually the first Fulbrighter to the United States from India (he trained at New England Medical Center [now Tufts Medical Center] in Boston as a Fulbright Scholar), is a mentor of mine in California. He is a Rotarian and has actually started a project called Project Deaf India, aimed at helping India's deaf population. It is a collaboration between the Rotary Club of Newport Balboa, California, and the Rotary Club of Pune, India. We've had something of an ongoing mentor relationship. We have these great sessions when I'm back in California in which I go to his house and we sit around for hours talking about everything that is going on in my life and his life.

He's very inspirational because he came to the United States in much the same way as my father, and is now this widely published, highly respected oncologist who has given me a lot of life lessons and shown me that medicine is such an impressive field to work in. He would never ever want to do anything else because he has had the chance to help so many people. He has been a constant influence in my life.

Do you consider yourself a mentor to others?

I consider myself an avid proponent of my peers. I work in and around everyone that I want to impact with my work. If I am a mentor, it is in the way that I live and conduct myself in order to show my friends, family, and peers what I value as important. I try to teach college students who are confused with what medicine means to them through leadership camps and preparatory classes. Locally I mentor handicapped individuals with sailing lessons to develop independent activities and responsibilities through nonprofit organizations.

Although I consider myself a bit too young to effectively mentor future careers, I do hope to be a mentor throughout my entire career. I love to teach and want use that interaction with other doctors, students, and anyone who is interested, to mentor.

What is your best advice for developing effective networking skills?

Taking the time to learn about people on a personal level. Really, the best advice I ever received on this subject was when I worked for Congressman

Cox. He told me that the most imperative things in networking are to remember someone's first name and talk to them like they're one of your best friends. Make sure they know you are interested in maintaining a relationship and working on that personal level. That advice has really stuck with me in the networking I have done throughout high school, college, and now graduate school. It's maintaining that personal quality time with a person; don't think of them as a business card, but as a person.

Follow-up is also important, establishing a line of communication that goes beyond, "Hey, my name is Arjun and it was great to meet you. I hope to pursue something with you." Rather, learn more about them, about their children, about their career path. Correlate your personal experiences with those people. This takes your networking beyond just "basic networking" and makes your relationships with a person a much more tangible, personal experience. Make sure your networking is from the heart.

What lessons have you learned as your career has evolved?

You hear a lot about our generation being the "on-demand generation." I think too many of my peers have shortsighted views about everything from health to career ambitions. I've learned that you need to develop and work towards a long-term goal set in order to truly make an impact in whatever realm of society you work in. It is easy to get caught up in success and even more so in failure. Just because your business is not profiting threefold in the first quarter, or you don't get every accolade imaginable in medical school, does not mean you are not on the road towards success. It is the small strides that must stay in line with long-term visions in order to truly make progress, either personally or socially.

The second lesson I live by is to always stay busy. I know it sounds a bit masochistic, but the overall message is one of less stress and more enjoyable free time. By "staying busy," I mean you should get your day to an early and efficient start. Get your workout in before school or work, multitask your day. In my case, I use my time between classes or clinic duties to complete an ongoing checklist of extracurricular activities. This includes finishing research projects, scheduling meetings, working on my nonprofit organization, organizing trips with friends. . . . By utilizing the dead time, those fifteen-minute intervals throughout the day, I can sit back when I get home and enjoy the evening, having already completed my tasks for the day. This is in contrast to the scenario where you burn those breaks with idle time and spend your evenings with computer on lap, watching TV, talking with friends, and never fully committing to any task—therefore, never completing one to the fullest or with as much efficiency as you could throughout the day. It is analogous to collecting your change from your pocket at the end of the day into a jar—the same jar that one day opens your savings account, buys a car, or mortgages your first home.

Any final advice?

Mind, body, and soul. You cannot neglect one and expect to fulfill the others. Treat your body as a temple, always educate your mind, and keep your friends, family, and personal philosophies close to your heart.

Chapter 9
Nonprofit Organizations

The NonProfit Times, a business publication focusing on nonprofit management, reported that the United States has more than 1.5 million nonprofit organizations.[1] Dr. Lester Salamon, a professor at Johns Hopkins University, conducts seminal research on nonprofit proliferation abroad, studying what he defines as the "global associational revolution." Yet despite this explosion of nonprofit activity, confusion still sometimes exists about what a nonprofit actually is and does.

Part of the confusion stems from nomenclature. Nonprofit organizations are also called not-for-profits, or NPOs. There does not seem to be any definitive preference or consensus as to which of these terms is correct; thus, all are used. However, the terms *NPO, nonprofit,* and *nongovernmental organization* (NGO) are not always interchangeable. While nonprofits are invariably NGOs, not all NGOs are nonprofits with 501(c)(3) status. The designation 501(c) is a subsection of the U.S. Internal Revenue Code, which lists provisions granting exemption from federal income tax to various charitable, nonprofit, religious, and educational organizations.

Peter Hero, president of the Community Foundation Silicon Valley, in an op-ed titled "Language Matters: It Is Time to Change Our Name" asserts that using the term *nonprofit* to describe an entire sector of organizations that work to support issues of public interest for noncommercial purposes is misleading. "What other sector of our society defines itself by what it is not?" he asks.[2]

Because of this misnomer, Hero contends, many who work outside of the nonprofit sector view it not as the vibrant, well-managed, and vitally important part of society that it generally is, but rather as a group of "well-meaning but marginal and haphazardly managed organizations." For Hero, referring to the nonprofit sector by a name that better affirms its value and the benefits it provides to the public would go a long way in changing these perceptions. He suggests "public benefit corporations" or "public benefit sector."

Others have suggested various different designations. Management guru Peter Drucker refers to nonprofit organization as the "social sector." A coalition of nonprofits has adopted the term "independent sector" to describe themselves. Regardless of perceptions or names, nonprofit organizations are actually run much more like businesses or for-profit organizations than most people realize. The February–March 2006 issue of *Nonprofit Agendas* notes that the basic tasks of running both nonprofit organizations and businesses are quite similar: preparing a budget, producing timely monthly financial statements for the board of directors, approving all cash disbursements, generating invoices for receivables, and, of course, ensuring that the organization's mission is met.

What largely distinguishes nonprofits from corporations or for-profit businesses is that nonprofits exist for the "public good." They have missions that are meant to improve society in some way. They also do not—and cannot, because of legal and ethical restrictions—distribute profits to owners or shareholders. Therefore, while nonprofits can accept, hold, and disburse money and strive to make a surplus (in fact, they *must* do so in order to remain in operation), they have no shareholders. Nonprofits are usually funded by government grants or cooperative agreements, foundation grants, or private donations—or some combination thereof. Employees of nonprofit organizations are paid a salary, although it is true that the salaries in this sector are generally lower than the salaries in for-profit businesses or corporations.

It is possible to pursue a career in the nonprofit sector that has absolutely nothing to do with international education, exchange, or development. Nonprofit organizations may be involved in any number of areas of public interest, including the arts, education, politics, public health, religion, research, and sports. International affairs, however, is also a growing and extremely dynamic area of nonprofit activity. As noted in the introduction to part II, a large number of the organizations that appear throughout this book, especially in chapter 6, are nonprofits. This chapter includes a list of selected nonprofit organizations in international exchange, education, and development. These organizations may be of interest to you as potential places of employment, or simply as examples of the types of nonprofits that exist. The list of sample organizations is

followed by selected print and web resources that can help you appreciate the full range of possibilities and guide you to nonprofits with international missions not listed in this book.

SAMPLE NONPROFIT ORGANIZATIONS

Academy for Educational Development (AED)
1825 Connecticut Avenue, NW
Washington, DC 20009
Telephone: 202-884-8000
Fax: 202-884-8400
Website: www.aed.org

Recognizing the interconnected nature of international development
and universal education, AED has worked in the nonprofit sector since
1961. AED's holistic approach to educational development encompasses
such issues as health, economic empowerment, environmental sustainabil-
ity, and good governance. With programs for disadvantaged regions both
within the United States and abroad, AED conducts student and professional exchanges, policy initiatives, and support for the programs of nongovernmental organizations located throughout the developing world.
The organization also makes available hundreds of electronic documents
on topics in international education and development, which are accessible free on the AED website.

AFS Intercultural Programs
71 West 23rd Street, 17th Floor
New York, NY 10010
Telephone: 212-807-8686
Fax: 212-807-1001
Website: www.afs.org

Created in 1914 as the American Field Service, AFS has expanded far
beyond its initial mandate of assisting wounded World War I soldiers.
Now the organization maintains international exchange programs in
more than fifty countries through a network of independent member
organizations coordinated from the AFS headquarters in New York City.
The goal of these exchanges is "to help people develop the knowledge,
skills, and understanding needed to create a more just and peaceful
world." AFS has regional service centers in Baltimore, Maryland; St. Paul,
Minnesota; and Portland, Oregon. American citizens have the opportu-

nity to host international visitors through AFS international exchange programs. The AFS website contains categorized exchange-oriented resources targeted toward educators, volunteers, young adults, and international visitors.

AIESEC/United States
See chapter 6 in this volume.

Alliance for International Educational and Cultural Exchange
See chapter 6 in this volume.

Alliance for Peacebuilding (AfP)
11 Dupont Circle, NW, Suite 200
Washington, DC 20036
Telephone: 202-822-6135
Fax: 202-822-6068
Website: www.allianceforpeacebuilding.org

The Alliance for Peacebuilding is a network of organizations working in the fields of conflict prevention and resolution. Members from nongovernmental, governmental, and intergovernmental organizations collaborate to maintain sustainable peace and security internationally. Founded in 2003, the coalition provides negotiation and mediation services, develops professional and organization capabilities, and seeks nonviolent solutions to problems and pressures of domestic and international relations. AfP builds the understanding of and support for peacebuilding policies in a variety of sectors, including government philanthropy, media, business, and religion.

America-Mideast Educational and Training Services, Inc. (AMIDEAST)
1730 M Street, NW, Suite 1100
Washington, DC 20036
Telephone: 202-776-9600
Fax: 202-776-7000
Website: www.amideast.org

AMIDEAST was founded in 1951 to focus on providing educational advising, English language training, professional training, and cultural exchanges between the United States and the countries of the Middle East. Striving to strengthen Western–Islamic relations, AMIDEAST maintains offices in twelve countries, including Egypt, Iraq, Jordan, Oman, Morocco, and Tunisia, as well as in the West Bank. The organization offers positions in all these locations. Vacancies are posted on the AMIDEAST website along with related news and an electronic newsletter.

Association of International Practical Training (AIPT)

10400 Little Patuxent Parkway, Suite 250
Columbia, MD 21044
Telephone: 410-997-2200
Fax: 410-992-3924
Website: www.aipt.org

Established in 1950, the Association for International Practical Training organizes cultural, educational, and professional exchanges for foreign nationals and U.S. citizens. AIPT serves thousands of students, trainees, and professionals annually by helping Americans interested in international careers access work opportunities abroad and by assisting companies find and train non-U.S. citizens as employees. In this capacity, AIPT is authorized by the U.S. Department of State to issue the forms required for acquisition of the J-1 work/study visa. IAESTE United States—a longstanding AIPT program initiative—provides opportunities for American scientific and technical students to develop the skills to work in today's global context.

Council for International Exchange of Scholars (CIES)

Council for International Exchange of Scholars
3007 Tilden Street, NW, Suite 5L
Washington, DC 20008
Telephone: 202-686-4000
Website: www.cies.org

Now a part of the Institute of International Education, the Council for International Exchange of Scholars was founded in 1947 to assist in administering the Fulbright Scholar Program. Working with both U.S. and foreign colleges and universities, as well as international Fulbright Commissions in more than fifty countries, CIES has approximately 2,200 on-campus representatives, as well as sixty program officers and staff at its headquarters in Washington, D.C. The Fulbright Program is one of the nation's flagship programs in international exchange. Since its founding nearly three hundred thousand participants have traveled as Fulbrighters.

Council on International Educational Exchange (CIEE)
300 Fore Street
Portland, ME 04101
Telephone: 207-553-7600 and 800-40-STUDY (toll free in U.S.)
Fax: 207-553-7699
Website: www.ciee.org

The Council on International Educational Exchange, founded in 1947, provides its members—American institutions of higher learning—with international education programs designed for students, faculty, and administrators. As part of their mandate "to help people gain understanding, acquire knowledge, and develop skills for living in a globally interdependent and culturally diverse world," CIEE hosts an Annual Conference on International Educational Exchange and is a co-sponsor of the scholarly *Journal of Studies in International Education Exchange.* This organization advocates at the state and federal level on behalf of the educational exchange community and also facilitates professional training and exchange.

Friendship Force International (FFI)
233 Peachtree Street, Suite 2250
Atlanta, GA 30303
Telephone: 404-522-9490
Fax: 404-688-6148
Website: www.thefriendshipforce.org

With 367 clubs around the world, Friendship Force International involves more than twenty-two thousand people on six continents in exchanges that feature home stays each year. FFI was founded in 1977 as a nonprofit organization dedicated to providing the opportunity for participants to connect with peoples of other cultures; the organization has provided cultural exchanges to and organized cultural programs for more than half a million individuals. Nominated for a Nobel Peace Prize in 1992, FFI coordinates an international network of local, volunteer-run clubs.

Sherry serves on the board of directors of Friendship Force International.

The German Marshall Fund (GMF) of the United States
1744 R Street, NW
Washington, DC 20009
Telephone: 202-745-3950
Fax: 202-265-1662
Website: www.gmfus.org

The German Marshall Fund is an organization that works to better relations and improve cooperation between Europe and the United States. Founded 1972 through a gift from Germany as a permanent memorial to Marshall Plan assistance, the GMF has provided coordination, resources, and scholarships to individuals and organizations working in the field of trans-Atlantic relations. Programs of the German Marshall Fund include the Brussels Forum, a summit of high-level business, academic, and political leaders from Europe and America, and the Balkan Trust for Democracy, a ten-year, $30 million grant initiative supporting good governance in Southeastern Europe. Further information about fellowships, partnerships, and grant-making opportunities are available on the GMF website.

Institute of International Education (IIE)
809 United Nations Plaza
New York, NY 10017
Telephone: 212-883-8200
Fax: 212-984-5452
Website: www.iie.org

Founded in 1919, IIE is a nonprofit organization committed to "promoting closer educational relations between the people of the United States and those of other countries, strengthening and linking institutions of higher learning globally, advancing academic freedom, and building leadership skills and enhancing the capacity of individuals and organizations to address local and global challenges." The most well-known IIE work is administering the Fulbright Program on behalf of the U.S. Department of State. The Fulbright Program has provided state-sponsored financial support for individuals engaged in international scholarship since 1946. IIE provides a wide range of services to and manages or administers programs for many corporations, foundations, government agencies, and international agencies. The organization's highly respected annual publication, *Open Doors,* reports statistics on the number of international students in the United States, as well as the number of Americans studying overseas. IIE also produces a wide array of publications on study and training abroad and financial resources. In addition to its New York City headquarters, IIE has two offices in Washington, D.C., four regional centers within the United States, and offices in thirteen international locations.

InterAction
See chapter 6 in this volume.

International Rescue Committee (IRC)
122 East 42nd Street
New York, NY 10168
Telephone: 212-551-3000
Fax: 212-551-3179
Website: www.theirc.org

Founded to bring relief to victims of both human conflicts and natural disasters, the International Rescue Committee is composed of a number of units focusing on different issues. From trafficking to water sanitation, IRC works to increase awareness and to pressure organizations into taking action to tackle some of the major problems of today's world. Established in 1933 and now present in twenty-five countries, IRC is a leader in humanitarian relief and advocacy.

International Research and Exchanges Board (IREX)
2121 K Street, NW, Suite 700
Washington, DC 20037
Telephone: 202-628-8188
Fax: 202-628-8189
Website: www.irex.org

Founded in 1968 IREX specializes in international education, media independence, social development, and the free flow of digital information. IREX is present in more than fifty countries, promoting education at all levels, advancing independent media management, and developing civil society through professional training, grant initiatives, scholarly research, and exchange programs.

Meridian International Center
1630 Crescent Place, NW
Washington, DC 20009
Telephone: 202-667-6800
Fax: 202-667-1475
Website: www.meridian.org

Meridian International Center promotes international understanding through the exchange of people, ideas, and the arts. Established in 1960, Meridian designs and implements exchange, technical assistance, and training programs for people from more than 140 nations. For example, Meridian is the largest program agency implementing the U.S. Department of State's International Visitor Leadership Program. Meridian also works to promote a free exchange of ideas and the arts, through efforts such as the International Classroom, which exposes more than six thousand K–12 students a year to foreign ideas and cultures.

See the profile of Ambassador Kenton Keith for more information. Ambassador Keith is the senior vice president of Meridian International Center.

NAFSA: Association of International Educators
See chapter 6 in this volume.

National Council for International Visitors (NCIV)
1420 K Street, NW, Suite 800
Washington, DC 20005
Telephone: 202-842-1414
Fax: 202-289-4625
Website: www.nciv.org

The mission of the National Council for International Visitors is to promote excellence in citizen diplomacy. NCIV, founded in 1961, is a national network of individual members, private program agencies located in Washington, D.C., and more than ninety community-based organizations throughout the United States. A full list of and contact information for NCIV member organizations can be found in the membership section of the NCIV website. Organizational members design and implement professional programs and cultural programs, and provide home hospitality opportunities for foreign leaders, specialists, and students. NCIV members provide services to foreign leaders participating in the U.S. Department of State's International Visitor Leadership Program and other international exchange programs. NCIV provides leadership development and nonprofit management training while developing its members' capabilities to work with foreign delegations.

Sherry is the president of NCIV, and Mark is a former program associate, communications, with the organization. Max Stewart is the executive director of the International Council of Central Florida, an NCIV organizational member located in Orlando, Florida. For more information, see the profile of Max in this volume.

Oxfam America
226 Causeway Street, 5th Floor
Boston, MA 02114
Telephone: 617-482-1211 and 800-776-9326 (toll free in U.S.)
Fax: 617-728-2594
Website: www.oxfamamerica.org

Oxfam is a nonprofit organization affiliated with Oxfam International that works to end global poverty by saving lives, strengthening communities, and campaigning for change. Working in twenty-six countries in Africa, East Asia, and Central and South America, Oxfam takes both an "on the scene" approach to development work, with employees working on the ground in regional offices abroad, as well as a broader policy role with employees working in advocacy and public education in the United States.

Phelps Stokes Fund
1400 Eye Street, NW, Suite 750
Washington, DC 20005
Telephone: 202-371-9544
Fax: 202-371-9522
Website: www.psfdc.org

Focusing on the needs of African Americans, Native Americans, Africans, and the rural and urban poor, the Phelps Stokes Fund is dedicated to improving life through education. Established in 1911, the Phelps Stokes Fund has produced a number of organizations with similar goals through its efforts. One core Phelps Stokes initiative is the Liberian Education Trust, intended to restore basic education in a postwar Liberia. Cultural and educational exchange programs are also offered; Phelps Stokes is a program agency for the U.S. Department of State's International Visitor Leadership Program.

See the profiles of Jennifer Strauss and Belinda Chiu for more information. Jennifer currently serves as the director of International Exchange Programs at the Phelps Stokes Fund. Belinda is a special assistant to the president of the Phelps Stokes Fund.

Save the Children Federation, Inc.
54 Wilton Road
Westport, CT 06880
Telephone: 203-221-4030 and 800-728-3843 (toll free in U.S.)
Website: www.savethechildren.org

An alliance of more than twenty-eight organizations working in approximately 110 countries, Save the Children is committed to creating lasting, positive change in the lives of children in the United States and around the world. Established in 1932, Save the Children reaches out to all people—parents, community members, local organizations, and government agencies—in order to improve the lives of more than 33 million children worldwide.

See the profile of Charlie MacCormack for more information. Charlie is the president and CEO of Save the Children.

Sister Cities International (SCI)
1301 Pennsylvania Avenue, NW, Suite 850
Washington, DC 20004
Telephone: 202-347-8630
Fax: 202-393-6524
Website: www.sister-cities.org

Representing 694 communities in the United States and 1,749 communities in 134 nations, Sister Cities International is a large network devoted to citizen diplomacy. Since its founding in 1956, SCI has created ties between U.S. and partner communities abroad, Sister Cities generates international collaboration that is mutually beneficial for all participants. Sister Cities International supports its local organizations from Washington, D.C., and hosts a number of events and programs meant to assist in its goal of building international bridges between communities.

U.S. Institute of Peace (USIP)
1200 17th Street, NW
Washington, DC 20036
Telephone: 202-457-1700
Fax: 202-429-6063
Website: www.usip.org

Established and funded by Congress, the U.S. Institute of Peace is dedicated to the peaceful resolution of conflicts worldwide. By teaching others and through its own efforts, USIP provides support in zones of conflict such as Afghanistan, the Balkans, Iraq, and Sudan. Officially established in 1986, USIP sponsors programs to promote peace through training, nonviolent conflict resolution, developing educational programs and training, and building institutions that support civil society throughout the world.

World Affairs Councils of America (WACA)
1800 K Street, NW, Suite 1014
Washington, DC 20006
Telephone: 202-833-4557
Fax: 202-833-4555
Website: www.worldaffairscouncils.org

The World Affairs Councils of America was founded in 1918 in conjunction with the Foreign Policy Association. It currently comprises approximately 484,000 members participating in the activities of eighty-four councils and twenty-six affiliates throughout the United States. The World Affairs Councils system operates a speakers program that includes more than 2,500 events per year. Councils also run international exchange programs, schools programs, teachers' workshops, model UN programs, foreign policy discussions, national opinion polls, travel programs, young professionals' programs, conferences, and corporate programs. The system has five flagship programs: World in Transition; Great Decisions; the NPR radio program *It's Your World;* Academic WorldQuest; and Travel the World.

World Learning

Kipling Road, P.O. Box 676
Brattleboro, VT 05302
Telephone: 802-257-7751 and 800-257-7751 (toll free in U.S.)
Fax: 802-258-3248
Website: www.worldlearning.org

Originally founded in 1932 by Donald Watt as the Experiment in International Living, World Learning promotes international and intercultural understanding, social justice, and economic development through education, training, and field projects around the world. The organization has four main components: The Experiment in International Living, School for International Training (SIT) Study Abroad, SIT Graduate Institute, and international development programs. World Learning offers exchanges for high school students to twenty-six countries and for college/university students to more than fifty countries, as well as other academic programs through SIT. With almost 1,700 staff in the United States and abroad, World Learning also manages various international development projects. The Visitor Exchange Program of World Learning works on the U.S Department of State's International Visitor Leadership Program, as well on other professional and citizen exchange programs.

Sherry participated in a World Learning Experiment in International Living (EIL) program to Germany in 1963, then led an EIL program to the former Soviet Union in 1969 (see chapter 1 in this volume). She currently serves on the World Learning board of trustees. See the profiles of Carol Bellamy and Charlie MacCormack for additional information. Carol has served as the president and CEO of World Learning since 2005, while Charlie held this same position from 1977 until 1992.

SELECTED RESOURCES

Print

Advisory List of International Educational Travel and Exchange Programs
Council on Standards for International Educational Travel, 2007
(www.csiet.org)

Produced since 1984 by the Council on Standards for International Educational Travel (CSIET), the Advisory List provides valuable information on many of the quality international exchange programs available to young people. This information includes countries served by participating exchange programs, as well as organizational contact information, background, and operational details. These programs are ranked according to their compliance with CSIET standards, with ratings of "full listing," "provisional listing," and "conditional listing." This classification offers potential students and employment seekers a comparative perspective on the key organizations in the field of international exchange.

The Chronicle of Philanthropy
www.philanthropy.com

The Chronicle of Philanthropy is a biweekly publication for the nonprofit industry. It is widely used by fundraisers, grant makers, managers of nonprofit groups and other people involved in philanthropy projects. Included in the publication are listings of upcoming events, workshops, and seminars, a directory of services, and job listings. The newspaper is useful for information gathering and will give greater insight into the trends in philanthropy and grant making.

From Making a Profit to Making a Difference: How to Launch Your Career in Nonprofits
Richard M. King
Planning/Communications, 178 pages, 2000
(www.planningcommunications.com)

This guidebook is designed to be a resource for those seeking to transition from the for-profit arena to the nonprofit world. It provides insights into how nonprofit organization leaders think, work, and hire. This guide is useful for business professionals or new college grads thinking of embarking on a career in the nonprofit world.

Global Work
www.interaction.org/pub/index.html

Global Work provides a list of volunteer, fellowship, and internship opportunities offered by ninety-nine organizations in more than 120 countries, including the United States. Readers with specific interests will find the geographic and program index guides helpful. This publication is available only from the international development organization Inter-Action.

National Directory of Nonprofit Organizations
Taft Group, 2007 (www.gale.com/taft.htm)

Now in its twentieth edition, this directory provides the names, contact information, and annual budget of approximately 260,000 organizations—180,134 of which have incomes in excess of $100,000. Entries in both volumes of this publication cover all twenty-two of the U.S. Internal Revenue Service 501(c) subsections, as well as IRS sections 501(e), 501(k), and 4947(a)(2).

Nonprofits Job Finder: Where the Jobs Are in Charities and Nonprofits
Daniel Lauber and Deborah Verlench
Planning/Communications, 240 pages, 2006
(www.planningcommunications.com)

Published once every two years, the *Nonprofits Job Finder* contains more than two thousand online and print job resources for charities and nonprofits. These job sources, along with a catalog of newsletters and journals, are grouped by career field and state for easy reference.

Search: Winning Strategies to Get Your Next Job in the Nonprofit World
Larry H. Slesinger
Piemonte Press, 104 pages, 2004 (www.slesingermanagement.com)

This book has been described as "essential" for any person wanting to get a foot in the door of the nonprofit world. Slesinger, founder of an executive search firm specializing in nonprofit recruitment, shares his job staffing expertise in *Search*. He offers strategies for those seeking a job in the nonprofit sector and provides advice on how to draft a résumé, prepare for an interview, and follow up after interviews.

Web

Charity Channel
www.charitychannel.com

As part of its mission "to create a place where nonprofit professionals can connect, learn from each other, share information, and work together to advance the cause of philanthropy," Charity Channel provides a wide array of resources designed to benefit the entire nonprofit community. These resources are made available by experienced professionals in the field who volunteer their time and efforts. The website features forum discussions, nonprofit-specific news feeds (including one dedicated to international issues), electronic newsletters, book reviews, interviews with experts in the field, and limited job listings. While the site does ask subscribers to pay a few dollars to support maintenance and resource costs, the $2 or $3 monthly fee is not mandatory; Charity Channel "will not turn away any individual without the means to pay."

Developmentex
http://developmentex.com
See chapter 5 in this volume.

Idealist
www.idealist.org

The most well-known and popular site for nonprofit job seekers (international and otherwise), Idealist is an international consortium of more than sixty-seven thousand nonprofit organizations. Approximately seven thousand jobs in the nonprofit sector are posted at any given time, so refine your search criteria as much as possible and be patient and ready to sift through long lists of organizations and open positions. In addition to posting job and internship openings, organizations on Idealist also present information about their mission and their work, upcoming programs, events, and campaigns, as well as downloadable materials. The remainder of the Idealist website is full of articles about activism, the nonprofit sector, and other related issues.

NAFSA: Association of International Educators
www.nafsa.org
See chapter 5 in this volume.

Nonprofit Oyster

www.nonprofitoyster.com

This nonprofit-specific employment site allows users to conduct state, topic, and position-specific searches of organizational vacancies free of charge. Résumé writing and posting services are also available, as the site assists you in creating an anonymous career profile that subscribing employers can search and vet. These services, along with e-mail job alerts that automatically notify you of available positions that match your declared interests, are available for a membership fee.

Opportunity Knocks

www.opportunityknocks.org

Opportunity Knocks is similar to Nonprofit Oyster, but its free nonprofit job search engine allows for much more specificity, including searches targeted according to keyword, company name, topic area, position, employment type, salary, and location. Registered users can also save searches for future reference. Electronic résumé posting and editing, automatic job notification, and application organization services are also available. The site is maintained by fees charged to nonprofit employers in exchange for job posting and evaluation services.

Philanthropy.com

http://philanthropy.com/jobs

Provided as an online service of *The Chronicle of Philanthropy,* philanthropy.com contains nonprofit-specific resources that are useful to job seekers, young professionals, and chief executives alike. This fact is reflected in the site's range of free services, which include a nonprofit question hotline, a collection of research and overviews of developments in the field, and a diverse collection of articles—updated weekly—covering topics from "getting the right degree for an overseas career" to "how charities cope when their boards need a makeover." Electronic synopses of articles from *The Chronicle of Philanthropy* are also available at Philanthropy.com, with full articles from the print edition accessible only to paid subscribers.

Notes

1. Todd Cohen, "Each 501(c)(3) Is Now," *NonProfit Times,* May 1, 2005.

2. Peter Hero, "Language Matters: It Is Time to Change Our Name," October 2001. This article originally appeared in the Association of Fundraising Professionals October 2001 newsletter and can now be accessed in the articles archives at www.kirschfoundation.org.

PROFILE
Charlie MacCormack
President and CEO, Save the Children Federation, Inc.

Career Trajectory

President and CEO, Save the Children Federation, Inc., Westport, Connecticut, 1992–present

President, World Learning, Brattleboro, Vermont, 1977–92

Vice President for Programs, Save the Children Federation, Inc., Westport, Connecticut, 1974–77

Director, Master's Degree Program in International Management, School for International Training, Brattleboro, Vermont, 1970–74

Research Fellow in Foreign Policy Studies, The Brookings Institution, Washington, D.C., 1969–70

Assistant to the Dean of the International Fellows Program, Columbia University, 1967–68

Instructor, Latin American Politics, University of New Hampshire, 1967

Staff Associate, First National City Bank International Division, Caracas, Venezuela, 1964

Academic Background

Leadership of Global Nonprofit Organizations, Harvard Business School, 2002–4

MA, PhD, Comparative Politics, Columbia University, 1974

National Science Foundation Fellow, Universidad Nacionál Autonoma de Mexico, 1968–69

Fulbright Fellow, Universidad Central de Venezuela, 1965–66

BA, Middlebury College, 1963

What awards and honors have meant the most to you?

If you don't recognize the intrinsic rewards of the goals you're achieving first and foremost, then you're probably not going to stay the course. I would say that the tens of thousands of young people who have come to love other cultures and languages, and the tens of millions of children who have health and education as a result of programs I've worked on over my career is the single greatest reward and honor that I could look back on.

Having said that, I've been lucky enough to receive honorary degrees from Middlebury and Clark universities. It's nice to get that kind of reinforcement that what you're doing matters. I've recently been elected chair of the board of InterAction, and prior to that, I was chair of the Alliance for International Educational and Cultural Exchange. Those are more work than honor, but it's always nice to know your peers believe you can provide the direction that they want to see.

Are you involved in community service?

If one has a vocation for international understanding and development, I suspect that's going to lead to a broad commitment to those kinds of causes—not just to your own employer, but also to other organizations that are working on similar kinds of issues, both locally and globally. That has certainly happened in my case. I have been on ten or twenty different boards, most of which have had to do with international development or international education.

Additionally, I think that kind of involvement sheds new perspectives and useful perspectives on one's own immediate tasks. It is a way of making sure your scope and vision are broad and that you're taking a lot of different perspectives into account when you're making your decisions. It's also another way, a specific way, of networking to help achieve larger goals.

How do you define your cause?

I think my cause has consistently been improving global understanding and well-being. That's a broad phrase, but that, at the most general level, has been my driving force.

What drew you to this cause and your field?

I was an undergraduate at Middlebury College in the early 1960s. That was a time when John F. Kennedy was president and the Peace Corps was founded. Most countries in the south were in the process of achieving their independence from colonialism. It was a time of eye-opening excitement about the larger world and its potential and, I think, a lot of optimism in general.

During my junior year, we had a visiting professor at Middlebury named Eduardo Mondlane, who was the head of the Mozambique Liberation Front [which eventually helped Mozambique gain its independence from Portugal]. He was kind of the Nelson Mandela of Mozambique. He gave a weeklong immersion seminar on African politics, focusing on the point that international affairs was going to be *the* great issue of the '60s, '70s, '80s, '90s, and beyond. He told us we would all be smart to think about getting involved because international engagement would be important, worthwhile, and meaningful.

This sentiment really resonated with me. At Middlebury, there was a lot of interest in international relations and studying languages. I pretty much decided then and there that I *did* want to pursue a career in the international arena. I can certainly say now, after having done international education and development work for four decades, Mondlane's advice was the best advice I ever got.

Do you have a mentor? How has he or she affected your life and career?

I wouldn't single out any one or two particular individuals. I think it is essential that we get help and support from others more experienced than us, and I think we can get that through direct advice, as well as through watching from a distance. I think there are also people you see at a long distance that become indirect mentors. Certainly in my formative years, President Kennedy was one; Martin Luther King Jr. was another; and Nelson Mandela has taken on that kind of role in past decades. Jim Grant, the head of UNICEF in the early 1990s, was really impressive in terms of how he made large-scale global change happen.

I think that you seize on people who say things and do things that make a lot of sense to you. These are people that I didn't necessarily know, but observed and thought about, and they have helped me make decisions in life.

Do you consider yourself a mentor to others?

I certainly make sure I spend lots of time talking with young people interested in international work. I feel that it's not just an obligation, but also a pleasure. I've been at it a long time, so some of the things I've learned, I'm happy to pass on. I probably talk at twenty colleges and universities every year about international careers, international work, and international issues. Also, when people get in touch and ask for a few minutes of my time, I will try to oblige.

Yet I haven't particularly noticed a trend that young people are making sure to drop by or send e-mails, to call and stay in good touch. Maybe it's not them; maybe it's me not noticing [laughs]. But I actually think some young people might be remiss in *not* calling, e-mailing, or dropping by more. Not just with me, but with anyone who might be able to act as a mentor or help with their career.

Perhaps this is not so much mentoring as networking. I made sure when I was in my twenties and thirties to put myself in touch with and in front of people who would be able to help me with my career and my decision making. I wanted to make sure I wasn't lost in the shuffle.

What is your best advice for developing effective networking skills?

You've got to get out and about and, quite consciously, make sure you're at some kind of gathering as often as possible. In international exchange, development, and education, in Washington or New York or Boston, almost every day there is a convention, there's a conference, there's a workshop, there's a seminar, there's a reception. There are invitation lists for these events that come out from InterAction or the State Department or the Brookings Institution or wherever. Get yourself on those lists and go. Don't just find the people whom you know; work the crowd a little bit. Introduce yourself to people.

Also, get on panels, write papers, get articles out, and all of those kinds of things. Many are called and few are chosen for real advancement in these fields. If you look at someone like Sherry Mueller or others like her, they have absolutely done the things necessary to build their careers.

What lessons have you learned as your career has evolved?

Look outward and not inward. Be sure that you are networking all of the time because that's what produces results—not just career results, but mission results.

As you move along, be sure you know and involve highly talented people in whatever you're doing because you'll never ever produce significant results solo. In addition, if you're not part of a group that's really talented, you'll spend your time compensating for those people who are not pulling their weight. That leads to a corollary lesson, which is, don't ever do someone else's job. When you're a supervisor, your job is to get the right person in the position, not to compensate for someone who is not able to do it.

More broadly, be sure you step back and ensure that what you're putting your time and energy into is *really* your calling. We get so caught up in the mechanics of getting a job, earning a salary, finding an apartment, paying the rent, on and on and on . . . that either we don't think about what we are really called to do, or we can't disengage ourselves from what is bogging us down and *do* what we really want to do.

The external world has a way of putting you on a train without ever asking you if the ultimate destination is the one you want to go to. You take the required courses in high school and college and you go get a professional degree and then you get a job. Typically, along the way, you get a spouse and a family and a mortgage. Each one of these, in terms of the parable, is a stop along the railroad track. You're happy to see each of those stops, but you're not necessarily asking yourself, "Where is this train going to go in the end?"

We're lucky in the United States that we actually do have choices. We're lucky enough to have good education and opportunities, so it makes a lot of sense to take advantage of them. A lot of people in the rest of the world never get to have any real choice about what they're going to do.

PROFILE
Jennifer Strauss
Director, International Exchange Programs,
The Phelps Stokes Fund

Career Trajectory
  Director, International Exchange Programs, The Phelps Stokes Fund,
      Washington, D.C., 2004–present
  Independent Consultant, Program Design and Management, Washington, D.C.,
      1996–2004
  Program Officer, Professional Exchange Programs, Institute of International
      Education, Washington, D.C., 1986–96
  Peace Corps Volunteer, Togo, 1981–83

Academic Background
  Certificate of Nonprofit Management, Georgetown University, 2006
  Graduate coursework, International Education, American University, 1983–86
  BA, Political Science, University of Michigan, 1980

What awards and honors have meant the most to you?
I really am struggling with this question because I don't know that I've ever received any awards in the traditional sense. I remember once when I was a program officer at the Institute of International Education (IIE), someone at the National Council for International Visitors (NCIV) told me that I had been nominated for Program Officer of the Year. I was just thrilled to know that I had even made it into the nomination process because, as far as I'm concerned, that was the pinnacle of success for me. I didn't win, but that was fine. It truly was just an honor to have been nominated.

Are you involved in community service?
I'm not on any boards. The one board that I have been asked to join is at my synagogue, where I have been very active. I teach parenting classes, which I started during what I've always referred to as "my time off for good behavior," when I was really raising kids full-time. I took some parenting classes and then was asked to become involved in leading them. So I took some leadership training programs and became a Certified Parent Educator.

Also, during that same hiatus from my professional life, I became a certified facilitator in Interest-Based Conflict Management (basically a conflict resolution trainer). So not working in an office, actually, does have its advantages [*laughs*].

I've continued to teach classes, including one I'll be doing for parents who have soon-to-be-driving teenagers. I've also written for a community newsletter in my old neighborhood, managed soccer teams . . . you know, the stuff that parents do on the side to help their children develop.

How do you define your cause?

I am a firm believer in citizen diplomacy. It's not a phrase I would have used prior to becoming involved in it, but international educational exchange has always been my passion.

What you don't know from my résumé is the fact that, when I was in high school, I was on a domestic short-term exchange program through American Field Service (AFS) Intercultural Programs. I went from the suburbs of New York City to Concord, Tennessee, and stayed with a host family for a week. The family was also hosting a young woman from Colombia who was participating in a yearlong AFS program.

Kristi [the Colombian woman] came back with me for two weeks to my home in New York and my mother, my father, and I all fell in love with her. After this experience, I asked if we could apply to be a host family, to host someone from another country for the year.

During my senior year of high school, we hosted a young woman from Madrid. She stayed with us for a year and during the course of that year, I applied for an AFS scholarship to study abroad for a year, to take a year off between high school and college. My mother questioned me. She said, "I don't understand why you're doing this now. I don't understand why you don't do this when you're a junior in college." I said, "Nope, this is something I want to do now." And eventually, when I was finally about to walk onto a plane to go to Denmark for the year, she said to me, "You know what? You are making the right decision. This is the right time for you to go." I spent thirteen months in Denmark as an AFS exchange student.

The experience abroad taught me so much about myself, and I'm still involved in international educational exchange. I feel that once you are bitten by this bug, once you realize that you are a citizen of the world and want to see the world beyond your front door, you can't help but keep going.

After college, when I was thinking about what's next, I thought, "I need to have a third-world experience." So I asked myself, "What about Peace Corps?" In order to make myself more attractive to Peace Corps, I volunteered in the Ann Arbor [Michigan] Public Schools as a teacher of English as a Second Language. I wound up going to Togo as a Peace Corps volunteer and teaching English as a second language and health.

My ideal job, when I returned to the United States, was going to be working for IIE in New York. I really wanted to work in international educational exchange. When I returned, I landed a job interview with an exchange organization in New York City . . . great job, great opportunity. But I also realized that, at the time, I wasn't ready to exchange my jungle of West Africa for the jungle of New York. And my boyfriend-now-husband was here in Washington. We had already been separated for two years, and I knew that, if we were really going to try to make it work, we'd probably be better off living not just on the same seaboard, but in the same city.

I called Sherry Mueller [when she was at IIE], following up on a letter I had written her. I came down to D.C. for one of the career roundtables she was facilitating at the time. I had, at that point, been scouring for jobs. I spoke with Sherry and, to make a very long story only slightly longer, it was the end of the fiscal year and she had fall-out funds. So she hired me on at IIE to clean out files. And that's how I got started in international educational exchange, stripping paper files and figuring out what needed to stay and what needed to be thrown out.

So you asked me what my mission is. Past is prologue, I guess. I feel that having that experience of living abroad, even hosting someone, forces you to see the world differently. It forces you to see the world far more expansively. It's a lot harder to keep your blinders on to everything else that is going on around you. If we are citizens of this world—which we are; Americans are far too self-isolated—then we need to make more of an effort to learn more about what else is there.

To finally come around to it, that's my cause: doing everything in my power to provide every opportunity for other people to grow their global knowledge.

What drew you to this cause and your field?

It never occurred to me that I would do anything else. I already knew in high school, once I started having these international experiences, that I wanted to be involved in international educational exchange. And it's funny . . . I often marvel at how strategic my son is in his thinking about his life plans, yet I realize that I was the same way. Totally single-minded. I never considered anything else.

Do you have a mentor? How has he or she affected your life and career?

Yes, absolutely. Sherry. There's no question about it. Sherry has been with me from that first moment when she hired me to strip those files to where I am now. I really appreciate everything she has ever done for me. I remember walking into her office and saying, "A mind is a terrible thing to waste." She said, "You're bored. Let's find you more to do." She enabled me to take on a program assistant position, which led to a program officer position, which eventually led me to where I am today.

When Sherry left IIE to go to NCIV, I was one of her references. For her to ask someone *under* her to speak as her reference, it's incredible. I've learned so much from her about management. I think Sherry is an incredibly astute manager. She is compassionate and takes time to look at all sides. She does not have a knee-jerk reaction to many things. She's a very, very good listener and asks cogent questions which help people to assess or reassess what their own needs are and how to articulate them. And she's taught me, in terms of how I interact with my staff, to be very respectful, to value the contributions that they bring. I just can't imagine doing it any other way. I think Sherry has taught me, by example, the value of a bottom-up management style. That, coupled with the things I've learned as a parent and parent-educator, have shaped my view and style as a manager.

Do you consider yourself a mentor to others?

I don't know that I consider myself a mentor. I have been with people who have introduced me as their mentor, and I sort of looked at them in a strange way. I have learned from so many people with whom I have come in contact, so it's just strange to see myself as the person who is doing the teaching. I truly believe that I would want to help in any way possible somebody whose passion echoes my own. There's plenty of room in this field, and there's *so* much to be done.

What is your best advice for developing effective networking skills?

Go to events, eavesdrop on airplanes, eavesdrop on subways. Subscribe to newsletters. Look and see what events are taking place at other organizations and go to those events, or at least look and see who the speakers are, then call them afterwards, talk to them. I try to identify, and then find a way to contact, people that I feel will be useful to the field as a whole and bring them in somehow. I like to think of myself as a bit of a missionary.

I'm not the person who can walk into a room and shake twenty peoples' hands. It's hard for me to go to events, but I force myself to go to them. The first few are hard because you won't know anyone. But then when you go to more, you'll see people you recognize from previous ones.

If you've been involved in Peace Corps or a similar activity, find out who's on the alumni list. I look through people's biographical information to find out what touchstones we have in common. Google is amazing for finding information on people. I think about how we used to do this before the Internet—which makes me feel older than dirt—but the Internet is an invaluable tool for expanding your network, researching people and events, and constantly learning.

What lessons have you learned as your career has evolved?

One of the lessons I've learned is the importance of relationships and cultivating networks, always looking for friends. I have accosted people on subways . . . I've overheard their conversations and thought, "Wow, he or she would be an *excellent* person to meet with international visitors . . ."

Be open to different types of experiences. I've been single-minded in terms of my career trajectory, but, as I think this book is trying to show, remember that there is no "one path."

Don't be afraid. Try your best. I like to think that one of the hallmarks of the things I've done is a dedication to doing it well. Choosing the right thing, not the expedient thing, is important. It's not just the issue of the moral compass, but it's also taking the time to step back and think it all through, then do it right.

Chapter 10
U.S. Government

Some years ago, most Americans contemplating a career in international affairs envisioned working in the Foreign Service. This fact was reflected in the names of some APSIA (Association of Professional Schools of International Affairs) schools, such as Georgetown University's School of Foreign Service or the School of International Service at American University. For U.S. citizens interested in traveling abroad and pursuing an international career, the U.S. Department of State and related agencies beckoned. The Foreign Service was the ideal, and conscientious performance would propel those who survived the rigorous admissions process up a structured career ladder.

This idea does not necessarily hold true today. The proliferation of internationally focused private organizations—many of them nonprofit, all of them nongovernmental (NGO)—has created a growing arena for those interested in careers in international education, exchange, and development. The Foreign Service is now only one option among many. Ambassador Kenton Keith, senior vice president of the Meridian International Center, who spent thirty-three and a half years in the U.S. Foreign Service, agreed with this assessment. In years past, Ambassador Keith said, those interested in the international realm had the options of the Foreign Service, the Peace Corps, or the U.S. Agency for International Development (USAID). Today there are infinitely more choices for those pursuing an international career. As Ambassador Keith told us:

> I think that some of the NGOs may actually have more personally rewarding work to offer, in particular for people who have a passion in one area or another. If your passion is environmental protection, you can have an international career in that. If your passion is educational exchange, if your passion is sports . . . with the proliferation of NGOs and interest groups,

it's possible to have a job in international, nongovernmental work that is every bit as rewarding as being in the Foreign Service. And as globalization increases, there will be more and more opportunities for international work in nongovernmental organizations.

A recent survey from the Gallup Organization, "Within Reach . . . But Out of Sync," echoes Ambassador Keith's opinion, reporting that many young people between the ages of eighteen and twenty-nine think that the private sector offers more opportunity for creativity and attracts better minds than the traditional federal programs. Because of this, the government now faces "unparalleled and fierce" competition from private organizations in attracting the United States' best and brightest.[1]

CHANGES IN THE FOREIGN SERVICE EXAM

This information is not meant to imply that careers with the Foreign Service have become passé or obsolete. Nearly twenty thousand diplomatic hopefuls take the Foreign Service written exam each year, and this number may rise with the implementation of changes to the traditional Foreign Service exam. These changes, in fact, seem to be in reaction to the competition for potential employees that the government is facing from other sectors. For years, the Department of State has selected its diplomats through a two-stage test seen as a "model of merit-based rigor."[2] First, candidates take a lengthy written exam answering hundreds of questions that are legendary for their detail, complexity, and historic breadth. Familiar with the present political conditions in Lesotho? Know anything about the Etruscans, who preceded the Romans in Italy? You would need to in order to pass the traditional Foreign Service exam. Those who pass the first round of tests face a daylong, oral barrage of questions and situations from a group of current Foreign Service officers. This has always been viewed as an extremely clear-cut process: pass and you're in; fail and you need to reconsider your career options.

However, the Department of State's overhaul of its hiring process revamps this traditional approach to identifying diplomats for the Foreign Service. George Staples, director general of the Foreign Service and director of human resources for the State Department, calls this new hiring tactic the "Total Candidate Approach." The goal, Mr. Staples states, is to "improve our ability to find the best . . . compete more effectively with the private sector to attract the best, and . . . make our process faster in hiring the best."[3] In this new approach, the State Department weighs résumés, references, and intangibles such as "team-building skills" in choosing who represents the United States as a diplomat. A written exam is still part of the hiring process but no longer is the "be all and end all" of who becomes a Foreign Service officer. The Foreign Service, it seems, intends to reestablish itself, to be not just one more option among the many for an international career, but *the* option, much as it was decades ago when Ambassador Keith began his own career.

In addition to the Department of State, other federal agencies, such as the U.S. Department of Justice and the U.S. Department of Agriculture, have expanded their international activities, and more positions are available in these arenas. Change works in both directions, however; one formerly independent branch of the government that traditionally employed many Foreign Service officers, the U.S. Information Agency, was absorbed into the Department of State in 1999.

INTERNATIONAL CAREERS ON CAPITOL HILL

Capitol Hill also offers opportunities for meaningful government work that is international in scope. The oft-repeated maxim that "all politics is local" should probably be lengthened to "all politics is both local *and* global." The distinctions are increasingly blurred. For a variety of reasons, the idea that representing the American people is not simply a domestically focused job has become more pervasive on the Hill. Members of Congress are increasingly captivated by international issues and traveling abroad. They are expected to be knowledgeable about a large number of complex trouble spots overseas. Thus, representatives and senators need globally experienced people on their staff to handle their international affairs portfolios. Furthermore, Capitol Hill also offers opportunities to work directly on the staff of internationally focused groups such as the Senate Committee on Foreign Relations and House Committee on Foreign Affairs.

For example, we have a mutual friend with a passion for both international affairs and the politics of Capitol Hill. She was able to combine these interests to pursue an internationally focused career on the Hill, first as a staff member for the Senate Committee on Foreign Relations, then as a legislative aide for Representative Jim Moran (D-VA), and subsequently as a staff member on the Senate Appropriations Subcommittee for State and Foreign Operations. Currently, she works as a legislative aide for Senator James Webb (D–VA), a member of the Senate Committee on Foreign Relations. Each of these positions has allowed her to consistently have an impact on international affairs without ever having to work off the Hill.

As this case demonstrates, the U.S. government remains a source of excellent globally oriented job opportunities. Although the application process can be daunting, salaries are competitive, and benefits are excellent. For those captivated by international relations and who are comfortable working in a more structured environment, pursuing a career in the federal government can be worth the elaborate application procedures and security clearances that are an inherent part of the hiring process.

SAMPLE GOVERNMENT DEPARTMENTS AND AGENCIES

Peace Corps of the United States
Paul D. Coverdell Peace Corps Headquarters
1111 20th Street, NW
Washington, DC 20526
Telephone: 800-424-8580
Website: www.peacecorps.gov

The Peace Corps offers approximately eight thousand volunteer positions in developing countries, in project areas such as education, business development, health care (HIV/AIDS awareness), and information technology. Every assignment is a twenty-seven-month commitment, including accrued vacation; no short-term assignments are available. The Peace Corps attempts to match country placement with volunteer requests, but placement in the country of your choice is not guaranteed. Most assignments require a bachelor's degree and additional experience; knowledge of a foreign language is not required, and language training is provided. The minimum age for becoming a Peace Corps volunteer is eighteen—there is no maximum age. All expenses are paid during service, including complete medical and dental care and a variety of other benefits. Recruitment begins at the regional level.

The Peace Corps offers a number of services for returned volunteers, including *Hotline,* a free semimonthly electronic bulletin of employment and educational opportunities. The organization also provides a variety of career resources, including job hunting tips and techniques, a guide to graduate school programs that give special consideration to returned Peace Corps volunteers, and a list of job links highlighting government agencies that seem most appealing to and most interested in hiring returned Peace Corps volunteers. These resources are available for download on the Peace Corps Returned Volunteers Services website, www.peacecorps.gov/index.cfm?shell=resources.former.

See the profiles of Carol Bellamy and Jennifer Strauss for more information. Carol served as a Peace Corps volunteer in Guatemala from 1963 to 1965, then served as the organization's director from 1993 to 1995. She became the first former volunteer to serve as director. Jennifer was a Peace Corps volunteer in Togo from 1981 to 1983.

U.S. Agency for International Development (USAID)
Ronald Reagan Building and International Trade Center
1300 Pennsylvania Avenue, NW
Washington, DC 20523
Telephone: 202-712-0000
Fax: 202-216-3524
Website: www.usaid.gov

USAID is an independent federal government agency that advances U.S. foreign policy objectives by supporting and implementing economic growth, agriculture and trade, global health, and democracy; conflict prevention; and humanitarian assistance. The organization receives its overall foreign policy guidance from the secretary of state. For young professionals, USAID offers a Junior Officer training program that gives entry-level candidates the opportunity to become tenured employees. The USAID website careers page lists position vacancies in several different areas, including the civil and foreign services, and describes opportunities in USAID's various fellowship and internship programs.

See the profile of Malcolm Butler for more information. Malcolm served as a mission director and executive secretary for USAID.

U.S. Department of Agriculture (USDA)
Foreign Agricultural Service (FAS)
1400 Independence Avenue, SW
Washington, DC 20250
Telephone: 202-401-0089
Fax: 202-205-9004
Website: www.fas.usda.gov

The Foreign Agricultural Service of the U.S. Department of Agriculture works to improve foreign market access for U.S. products, build new markets, improve the competitive position of U.S. agriculture in the global marketplace, and provide food aid and technical assistance to foreign countries. FAS has the primary responsibility for USDA's international activities—market development, trade agreements and negotiations, and the collection and analysis of related statistics and market information. With approximately one thousand employees stationed in more than ninety countries, the organization describes itself as a relatively small agency by U.S. government standards. The FAS website provides various career services, including international development-related position openings in FAS, in the USDA as a whole, and in various international organizations concerned with agricultural trade.

U.S. Department of Labor
Bureau of International Labor Affairs (ILAB)
200 Constitution Avenue, NW, Room C-4325
Washington, DC 20210
Telephone: 202-693-4770
Fax: 202-693-4780
Website: www.dol.gov/ilab

The Bureau of International Labor Affairs is responsible for all internationally focused activities conducted by the U.S. Department of Labor. It is a center for federal research and policy regarding global issues in trade, immigration, economic interdependence, human trafficking, and child labor. The mission of ILAB is "to create a more stable, secure, and prosperous international economic system in which all workers can achieve greater economic security, share in the benefits of increased international trade, and have safer and healthier workplaces where the basic rights of workers and children are respected and protected." All employees of the bureau are located domestically in the Washington, D.C., office; its international efforts are accomplished through liaisons, short-term travel, and grants for foreign organizations. The ILAB website contains links to employment information and opportunities throughout the Department of Labor, including the Office of Child Labor, Forced Labor, and Human Trafficking (OCFT), the Office of International Relations (OIR), and the Office of Trade and Labor Affairs (OTLA), all of which are subdivisions of ILAB.

U.S. Department of State
Bureau of Educational and Cultural Affairs (ECA)
2201 C Street, NW
Washington, DC 20521
Telephone: 202-203-5029 (academic inquiries) and 202-203-5096
(private sector inquiries)
Website: http://exchanges.state.gov

The Bureau of Educational and Cultural Affairs works to foster mutual understanding between the people of the United States and the people of other countries. It sponsors such exchange programs as the flagship International Visitor Leadership Program (IVLP) and the Fulbright Program, newer programs such as the World Sports Initiative and the National Security Language Initiative, and a host of exchange programs for students of all ages, as well as scholars, diplomats, and other professionals. Career opportunities in ECA can be accessed on the Department of State's main career page, www.state.gov/careers.

The U.S. Department of State also sponsors a number of internships, fellowships, and other programs. These opportunities provide highly qualified college or university juniors, seniors, and graduate students with the chance to gain firsthand knowledge of U.S. foreign affairs. Available programs include the Cooperative Education Program, Fascell Fellowship Program, Presidential Management Fellows (PMF) Program, Stay-in-School, Student Disability Program, Student Internships, Summer Clerical Program, and the Thomas R. Pickering Foreign Affairs/Graduate Foreign Affairs Fellowship Program. Information on these programs is available at www.careers.state.gov/student/index.html.

Foreign Service
2401 E Street, NW
SA-1, room H518
Washington, DC 20522
Telephone: 202-261-8849
Website: www.careers.state.gov

Foreign Service officers help formulate and implement the foreign policy of the United States by serving as the frontline personnel at all U.S. embassies, consulates, and diplomatic missions—nearly 265 locations worldwide, including Washington, D.C. Foreign Service officers follow one of five career tracks (Management, Consular, Political, Economic, or Public Diplomacy). The Foreign Service also employs specialists in fields such as medicine, office and information management, and human resources. In 2007 the traditional Foreign Service Exam was computerized and redesigned. This exam will be accessible several times per year in locations around the world. For more information regarding these changes and the Foreign Service application process, visit http://careers.state.gov/officer/index.html.

See the profiles of Ambassador Kenton Keith and Malcolm Butler for more information. Both Ambassador Keith and Malcolm are former Foreign Service officers.

Office of Language Services
2401 E Street, NW
SA-1, room H1400
Washington, DC 20522
Telephone: 202-261-8777
Fax: 202-261-8807
Website: www.state.gov

This division of the Department of State maintains a roster of approximately one thousand interpreters and English Language Officers, assigning them to accompany visiting foreign and American leaders on a freelance contractor basis for periods of up to a month. The office also provides interpreting services to many other government entities. Information on the qualifications necessary to become an interpreter, the types of assignments that can be applied for, and the application process is available at http://exchanges.state.gov/education/ivp/escort.htm and www.usajobs.gov/EI33.asp.

SELECTED RESOURCES

Print

Congressional Quarterly
http://public.cq.com

Congressional Quarterly is a nonpartisan publication that has reported on Congress and politics since 1945. In addition to its flagship publication, *Congressional Quarterly* also produces *CQ Weekly* newsmagazine; *CQ Today,* a legislative news-daily; and a number of specialty e-newsletters, such as *CQ Homeland Security* and the *CQ Midday Update.* These publications, along with a regularly updated list of Capitol Hill job openings, can be accessed on the Congressional Quarterly website.

Federal Résumé Guidebook: Strategies for Writing a Winning Federal Electronic Résumé, KSAs, and Essays
Kathryn Troutman
JIST Works, 368 pages, 2007 (www.resume-place.com)

The process to apply for and successfully obtain a federal job can be mind-boggling. The *Federal Résumé Guidebook* leads you through the complicated federal hiring process and gives practical tips on how to write the optimal résumé for federal positions, as well as how to best express your KSAs (knowledge, skills, and abilities). The author of this book is also the head of a company that specializes in demystifying the federal hiring employment process. Her website, The Résumé Place, is listed below.

The Hill
www.thehill.com

The Hill is a nonpartisan newspaper written for and about the U.S. Congress. It has the largest circulation of any Capitol Hill publication and, in addition to its free website, it publishes two blogs: The Hill's Congress Blog (http://blog.thehill.com) and The Hill's Pundits Blog (http://pundits.thehill.com). Its classified section contains a listing of employment opportunities on Capitol Hill and in government relations.

Hill Rag
www.capitalcommunitynews.com

The *Hill Rag* is a monthly community newspaper based on Capitol Hill that is accessible online for free. While it offers no job listings, the *Hill Rag* gives insight into the culture and community of Capitol Hill, which can be an invaluable asset to anyone interested in pursuing a career there.

IAWG Dispatch
http://iawg.newsletter.devis.com

Published by the Interagency Working Group (IAWG) on U.S. government-sponsored international exchanges and training, this quarterly electronic journal highlights topics, initiatives, and events related to the IAWG mandate: improving coordination and efficiency among federally sponsored international exchange and training programs. The dispatch provides insight into the lesser known activities of the IAWG member agencies, which include the Department of Commerce, the Department of Defense, the Department of State, the Department of Justice, NASA, USAID, the National Endowment for the Arts, the National Security Council, the Peace Corps, the Census Bureau, and many others. These insights may suggest new and unexpected career opportunities to readers interested in entering or transitioning into the field of international exchange. Subscription is free and available via the IAWG website.

Inside a U.S. Embassy: How the Foreign Service Works for America
Shawn Dorman, ed.
American Foreign Service Association, 136 pages, 2003 (www.afsa.org)

Inside a U.S. Embassy is designed to answer such questions as "Who works in an embassy?" and "What do diplomats actually do?" The book takes readers inside U.S. embassies and consulates in more than fifty countries, providing detailed descriptions of Foreign Service jobs and firsthand accounts of diplomacy in action. The book also includes profiles of diplomats and specialists around the world serving in Foreign Service positions, ranging from the ambassador to the security officer to the IT professional. Also included is a selection of "day-in-the-life" entries from seventeen different posts, each describing an actual day on the job in an embassy.

Realities of Foreign Service Life
Patricia Linderman and Melissa Brayer-Hess
Writers Club Press, 292 pages, 2002

Coauthored by a member of a Foreign Service family (Brayer-Hess), this book provides reflections and perspectives on the realities of Foreign Service life as experienced by members of the Foreign Service community around the world. The writers share their views on a wide variety of topics pertinent to anyone leaving to live abroad, but especially to those who are leaving for extended periods and plan to raise a family abroad. Challenges to Foreign Service officers and their families are discussed, including maintaining long-distance relationships, raising teens abroad, dealing with depression, coping with evacuations, readjusting to life in the United States, and many others.

Roll Call
www.rollcall.com

Roll Call reports on congressional news and information and is published Monday through Thursday while Congress is in session (Mondays only during congressional recess). *Roll Call* provides readers with up-to-date news of the legislative and political happenings on Capitol Hill. RollCall.com is the online version of the newspaper, providing not only the full content of the print edition but also breaking news stories and daily e-mail alerts. Access to the resources on RollCall.com is a free service for print subscribers and is also available on a subscription basis. A free job board is available to nonsubscribers, however, at RCJobs.com (see below).

Ten Steps to a Federal Job
Kathryn Troutman
The Résumé Place, Inc., 290 pages, 2002 (www.resume-place.com)

Anyone who has ever applied for a job in the federal government may have a familiar story: hours spent pouring over job openings on websites, many more hours spent perfecting an application for the perfect federal job, and then . . . nothing. No acknowledgment, call, or e-mail, and certainly no job interview. So how can anybody get past that seemingly impenetrable wall of the federal hiring process and obtain a federal job? *Ten Steps to a Federal Job* walks you through the process, giving an insider's perspective on the best strategies for obtaining a U.S. government job, including how to rewrite your résumé for a federal application. More information on the author and her company specializing in federal employment assistance is available on her website, www.resume-place.com.

Web

Avue Central
www.avuecentral.com

Avue Central is a free federal employment service. It offers private and secure access to a listing of thousands of federal jobs worldwide. This website will help you understand the federal hiring process, as well as navigate—or even circumvent—some of the frustrating rules and regulations that can bog down your federal job application. Avue Central also allows users to search and apply for federal jobs directly through its site.

Careers in Government
www.careersingovernment.com

Careers in Government (formerly Jobs in Government) was launched as a means for job seekers interested in public sector careers to find opportunities more readily. Careers in Government features a searchable job bank of federal openings, a list of participating government agencies, and the ability to search for government jobs by city and state.

Fed World
www.fedworld.gov

Fed World is managed by the National Technical Information Service, an agency of the U.S. Department of Commerce. It serves as a clearing-house of information disseminated by the U.S. government, including a searchable database of federal job openings. The website also enables users to conduct searches that span the websites of all federal departments and agencies.

Hill Zoo
http://hillzoo.com

Hill Zoo is a web forum for congressional staff members and the wider Capitol Hill legislative community. The site features event listings in Wash-ington, D.C., various advertisements and classifieds (including for housing in the D.C. area), and listings of position openings on and off the Hill.

Opportunities in Public Affairs
www.opajobs.com

The Opportunities in Public Affairs website publishes an eponymous newsletter containing more than two hundred job listings on Capitol Hill and in public affairs. Individuals can subscribe for a single issue or up to twenty-four issues (subscription rates vary). A limited number of posi-tion openings are posted on the website for free.

RC Jobs
www.rcjobs.com

This website hosts the job board for *Roll Call* newspaper (see above); RCJobs.org features a searchable bank of employers and job openings on Capitol Hill and in public affairs, the public sector, and related fields and organizations.

The Résumé Place
www.resume-place.com

Founded by Kathryn Troutman, author of the *Federal Résumé Guide-book* and *Ten Steps to a Federal Job* (see above), the Résumé Place specializes in writing and designing professional federal and private-sector résumés, as well as in coaching and education in the federal hiring process. Troutman is a recognized expert on federal employment; she created the format and name for the new "federal résumé" that became standard in 1995. She also created the Certified Federal Job Search Trainer program—the first federal career train-the-trainer program ever—to train career counselors and military career counselors in the federal hiring process.

USA Jobs

www.usajobs.gov

USA Jobs is the official employment site of the U.S. federal government. Users can create and store résumés on the site and can also search for open positions in any federal government agency. The site also offers federal job seeker services and information, answering such commonly asked questions as how federal jobs are filled, how to build an effective résumé, how to interview successfully for a government job, and how to best express your KSAs (knowledge, skills, and abilities).

Notes

1. *Within Reach . . . But Out of Synch: The Possibilities and Challenges of Shaping Tomorrow's Government Workforce,* a report by the Council for Excellence in Government and the Gallup Organization, December 5, 2006.

2. Elizabeth Williamson, "Foreign Service Hiring Gets a Re-exam," *Washington Post,* December 12, 2006, p. A1.

3. Ibid.

PROFILE
Ambassador Kenton Keith
Senior Vice President, Meridian International Center

Career Trajectory
> Senior Vice President, Meridian International Center, Washington, D.C.,
> 1997–present
> U.S. Ambassador to the State of Qatar, 1992–95
> U.S. Information Agency (USIA), U.S. Department of State, 1965–97
>> Washington, D.C., 1995–97, Director, Near East, North Africa, and South Asia
>> Doha, Qatar, 1992–95, Ambassador
>> Cairo, Egypt, 1988–92, Public Affairs Officer
>> Paris, France, 1985–88, Senior Cultural Affairs Officer
>> Washington, D.C., 1983–85, Deputy Director, Near East, North Africa, and
>> South Asia, USIA
>> Brasilia, Brazil, 1980–83, Deputy Public Affairs Officer
>> Washington, D.C., 1977–80, Special Assistant to Deputy Director, USIA
>> Damascus, Syria, 1974–77, Public Affairs Officer
>> Fez, Morocco, 1973–74, Branch Public Affairs Officer
>> Tangier, Morocco, 1972–73, Western Arabic Training
>> Istanbul, Turkey, 1968–72, Branch Cultural Affairs Officer
>> Jeddah, Saudi Arabia, 1967–68, Assistant Public Affairs Officer
>> Baghdad, Iraq, 1966–67, Junior Officer Training
> Officer, U.S. Navy, 1961–65

Academic Background
> Graduate work, Comparative Politics, George Washington University, 1978–79
> BA, International Relations and French (Navy ROTC), University of
> Kansas, 1961

What awards and honors have meant the most to you?

The first award that meant a lot to me was a Presidential Award I received for work I did in Egypt trying to get public and private sector cooperation in USIA programming.[1] It meant a lot to me because it was at a time when the U.S. government was spending less and less on cultural programming, and I thought it was more and more important. I was in Egypt with an extraordinary ambassador, Frank Wisner. His leadership created an environment in which the private sector—both American and Egyptian—understood that the embassy wanted and needed their cooperation at a critical juncture in our bilateral relationship. In October of 1988, the Egyptian government was opening a new opera house that was built for them by the Japanese. We saw this as a moment when American presence would be important as a gesture in support of the Egyptian economic reform policies. We wanted to see American companies in Egypt be viewed by the Egyptian population as good corporate citizens, not as exploiters.

So we raised a million and a half dollars to bring over a Houston-based opera troupe to do *Porgy and Bess* as an opening presentation at the Cairo Opera House. This was one of several things we eventually did because it created momentum for the kind of public-private partnership that had real payoff for both the private and public sector. That was seen as something of a model, and, on that basis, I received that Presidential Award.

Another honor that gave me a lot of satisfaction and a sense of pride was receiving *Chevalier* in the French Order of Arts and Letters. Basically, that was because of my work with the Fulbright Program. When I arrived in Paris as the senior cultural affairs officer, I became cochair of the Fulbright Commission in France. The other co-chair was a senior member of the French Ministry of Education, a man who eventually became a senior ambassador. The Fulbright Program had been eclipsed, at that point, by the French government's own academic exchange programs, and they only paid lip service to their membership in the Fulbright Program. Not many resources were being devoted to it. My goal was to try to breathe some life into it, which I was able to do with a lot of help from many people. We accomplished this by basically going to French companies and convincing them that it was in their interest to sponsor academic exchanges, that it would eventually benefit the field and the individual companies down the road.

Thus the Fulbright Program in France suddenly took on a different complexion. The French got on board very quickly. . . . I worked closely with Jacques Chirac and his team at the mayor's office. He was mayor of Paris at that time [Chirac held this post from 1977 to 1995]. I had very close relations with the minister of culture, the minister of education, and the university system in Paris. In fact, it was the chancellor of the universities of Paris who actually pinned on my letter as *Chevalier.*

Paris was a great canvas for me. It was open, I had resources, and I had a receptive government to deal with. I was in a place with intellectual openness . . . there were a lot of special circumstances that have rarely been combined, and I did my best to take advantage of them.

Are you involved in community service?

Board Member, AFS Intercultural Programs
Board Member, Council of International Educational Exchange (CIEE)
Board Member, Partners for Democratic Change
Advisory Board Member, University of Kansas Office of International
  Programs

Vice President, Washington Institute of Foreign Affairs
Member, American Academy of Diplomacy
President, Association of Black American Ambassadors

I've also always believed that African Americans have a perspective that is important in our international relations. It is also important that we have a voice to share our views with the government; thus my involvement with the Association of Black American Ambassadors. We have brought our own backgrounds to the enterprise, and we believe it's important for us to take our collective views and feed them back to the government and to American citizens at large who are interested.

How do you define your cause?

I am still inspired by experiences and engagement with people from different societies, in cultural and academic realms. Something very interesting and very important happens when people can meet in those circumstances. So I am particularly interested in seeing healthy exchanges at all levels, in high school, in university, and in professional life continue . . . it is critical, in a globalizing world, for Americans to know the rest of the world and for the rest of the world to know us.

But my cause didn't come all of a sudden. On a personal level, I grew up in a cold war environment, in Kansas City, Missouri, in which we actually had nuclear attack drills. I realized, even as a youngster, that our lives, the lives of people in Kansas City, were somehow connected to what happened in other parts of the world. Even as a youngster, I knew I wanted to work abroad. I don't know why, but I knew that. I had the feeling that becoming a foreign correspondent or a diplomat would be a fascinating way to lead your life.

When I went to university, I was advised by a very, very treasured mentor, a man named Cliff Ketzel, who was a political science professor. He gave shape to my understanding of both this country's relations with the outside world and the possibility of my personal involvement with that. He's the one who urged me to take the Foreign Service exam.

I went into the Foreign Service after the navy, and it wasn't until maybe when I got to Turkey that I realized cultural exchange and educational exchange are extremely powerful tools. They are powerful in the sense that they create a mutual understanding on the part of those people who came into contact with one another. Something magical happened when people engaged at that person-to-person level—something magical and almost totally separate from government-to-government relations. That realization has been an engine for my career and what I have tried to accomplish in government and after.

What drew you to this cause and your field?

Very simple things. I remember once at my church being introduced to an international visitor from Indonesia. I was in junior high school, probably, when that took place. Mind you, I grew up in an inner-city school situation in Kansas City, and we didn't have that many international visitors. But that interaction with this intelligent and interesting man who came in and tried to get to know us, I thought, was a pretty interesting thing.

I began to think about foreign countries. There was a neighbor who had been in the war and showed pictures of Southeast Asia, and that piqued my interest as well.

Then television came. Television brought with it these black and white series of foreign intrigue, and I was fascinated with the fast cars and beautiful women, with living overseas. In high school, I began to take French. A high school teacher who had spent some time in France came back talking about a different lifestyle and different attitude. All of that went into the mix. My parents certainly did not discourage me and my two siblings from pursuing any career we wished. They had a lot of confidence that we would do just fine. They knew that whatever our career paths were, we wouldn't be in Kansas City.

Do you have a mentor? How has he or she affected your life and career?

Cliff Ketzel . . . he was an iconoclast. Ketzel had been a part of the State Department Reserve. Remember, we're talking about the cold war, and we all thought it was highly possible that a bomb could wipe out the city of Washington, D.C. There could be an emergency during which the country's internal affairs might have to be conducted from somewhere other than Washington. There needed to be a group of wise people who would get together and make decisions, and he was in that group.

My time in university was a period when not much was happening on the student front. The campus was anything but activist. So for Ketzel to be an iconoclast in that period was quite difficult. But he was somebody who was much loved. He was a good professor, a good lecturer, and he had a good approach to teaching students. He was more interested in teaching than in publishing.

One day after class, he asked me what I intended to do. I said, "Well, I have my military obligation, but I've always been interested in working abroad." So he said, "I think you ought to take the Foreign Service exam and I think you ought to take the USIA option." At that point, it all sort of snapped into place in my mind.

Do you consider yourself a mentor to others?

I hope so. Half the people who are running U.S. public diplomacy around the world, in my mind, are people I consider my protégés. People I have assigned and mentored over the years are now in senior positions of public diplomacy, and I hope that they would consider me a mentor.

If you believe in something very strongly, if you think you have an important mission and you know that you are able to influence others to support that same mission, then it's your duty to mentor. I was in a particularly privileged position to be a mentor because I could recruit, I could assign, and I could reward. I look over there [at the Department of State] and I see the body of public diplomacy officers and I am very happy to see that some of my favorite protégés are doing well.

What is your best advice for developing effective networking skills?

I'm not the best person in the world to talk about networking skills. In my Foreign Service career, I never found myself in a position where I needed to network for support to get jobs. Some people did. I always knew what I was going to be doing next; not because I asked for the job, but because somebody else asked me to move to a specific position. For example, when I finished as cultural affairs officer in Istanbul, the area director came up to me and said, "We want to send you to Morocco for a couple of years, and then we're hopeful some things will develop in the Middle East and we'll need you to be available for that."

I wouldn't know how to advise people in their networking efforts. But I would say that, more important than networking in a Foreign Service career is career planning. Knowing what you need, recognizing the gaps in your experience and bidding on jobs that will close those gaps. All of my jobs in the Middle East, in the early part of my career, were small posts. What I lacked in order to move to the next level was management experience at a large post. The opportunity came for me to go to Brazil as deputy political affairs officer, essentially in an inside management role, managing branch posts and program coordination. Although I found it frustrating in some ways, not being able to actually get out there and mix it up with my Brazilian hosts, it was a career move that was absolutely critical for me. From there I went on to larger posts and responsibilities.

I think that the implication of the word "networking" is that you are *part of a network*. Audience building is something else. When you're in Egypt, for example, you've got to have a wide circle of contacts. That's a different thing from networking for your personal growth. And I would make the distinction there because I've prided myself, in all of my posts, on knowing the people I needed to know.

For me, more important than networking per se is finding the right mentor. I can see the need for making yourself known and part of a network. But I think more important is to get solid advice from someone who has been there.

What lessons have you learned as your career has evolved?

A critical lesson I have learned is that all of our exchange programs depend on an asset that we have here, the American citizen. If we weren't sure that the "product" we have to "sell" is a good product, then our exchange programs would sink under their own weight. But in fact, the interaction with the average American is such a positive thing for foreign exchange participants. Americans come across when you meet them as open, as hospitable, as hard working, and as unprogrammed to react negatively or positively. People in the United States are remarkably unprogrammed. International visitors are often bemused that Americans can be working next to someone for over ten years and not know whether that person is a Republican or a Democrat or a Christian or a Jew, and frankly NOT CARE.

It is, on the one hand, very positive that Americans are unprogrammed. On the other hand, foreigners find it strange that Americans don't know anything about the rest of the world. If they knew more, maybe they would be more programmed. But it's not part of our DNA. That's not to say that there isn't prejudice or ethnic difficulty or racism—those things exist. But, as a set of national attitudes, we are not programmed to be against anybody. And I think that's a pretty important thing. It's a great reservoir.

On a professional level, a lesson I learned in the Navy that has served me well since then is that no matter how good your excuse is, if at the end of the day you have not achieved what you're committed to achieving, that's what's going to be remembered. You could have a perfectly legitimate excuse for why it didn't get done, but the fact will remain that it didn't get done. That will have an influence on your life and, if it becomes a pattern, an influence on your career. I have seen very talented people who essentially were not achievers. Something always seemed to come up. There was always some "reason," which often sounded quite legitimate. But at the end of the day, they had failed. People like that get left by the wayside. I tell people that if you're supposed to get something done by Friday afternoon, don't think that it's okay to work over the weekend and get it in Monday morning. That's not good enough.

Any final advice?

For people interested in foreign affairs, fifteen years ago, I would have said that it's the Foreign Service you need to be after, or Peace Corps or USAID. But now, I think that some NGOs [nongovernmental organizations] may actually have more personally rewarding work to offer, in particular for people who have a passion in one specific area or another. If your passion is environmental protection, you can have an international career in that. If your passion is educational exchange, if your passion is sports . . . it is possible now, with the proliferation of NGOs, interest groups with deep connections and multiple activities, to have a job in nongovernmental work that is every bit as rewarding as being in the Foreign Service.

My advice for young people who are looking for careers overseas is to throw the net out wide. There will be a miniscule number of people who get into the Foreign Service. At the same time, the proliferation of NGOs—human rights, children's issues, trafficking issues, advocacy in one form or another, public health—there are just many, many areas and they are proliferating. That is one of the interesting areas of inquiry that has developed over the last fifteen years, how the government interacts with NGOs.

Note

1. The U.S. Information Agency (USIA), formerly an independent branch of the government that traditionally employed many Foreign Service officers, was absorbed by the Department of State in 1999.

Chapter 11
Multinational Organizations

Employment in a multinational organization can be the highest aspiration for many international career seekers. Pursuing employment with these organizations can be intimidating, however, given their size and scope as well as the aura of mystery and intrigue that sometimes surrounds them. These concerns are not completely unfounded; it can be much more difficult to get your foot in the door at a large multinational organization than, say, a smaller nonprofit. Some multinationals have downsized their staffs or streamlined their structures in response to reduced funding; many have strict hierarchical organizational structures. Most have language and experience requirements that may seem daunting to the entry-level professional. Some have strict national employment quotas. Despite these potential obstacles, however, multinational organizations still offer exciting opportunities for anyone seeking a challenging international career with truly global scope and impact.

THE CULTURAL CONTEXT OF MULTINATIONAL ORGANIZATIONS

In our interview with him, Fayezul Choudhury, controller and vice president of strategy and resource management at the World Bank, emphasized the importance of "cultural context" when you are attempting to get a job or begin a career with a multinational organization. Of course job seekers can still use the strategies with a multinational that they might with any other organization: submit a résumé and hope it gets noticed (although Choudhury warned that this approach may be a bit of a "crapshoot" because hundreds of résumés pour in each day); find an internship and work your way up; or use a personal connection. These techniques can work with multinational organizations, but Choudhury pointed out that you must approach them in different ways than you might with an organization staffed mostly by Americans.

Networks in multinational organizations often run along ethnic and national boundaries, rather than collegiate or professional ones. Knowing people is important, just as in an American context, but it is also important to use your relationship with a person in a more subtle way. While some Americans have no problem receiving a frank and honest request from a job seeker, people of other cultures may not be accustomed to or comfortable with such direct interactions. Thus, while no single rule can guide your actions when it comes to networking at multinational organizations, you must always remember to keep cultural context in mind.

A CROWDED BAZAAR, NOT A ONE-STOP SHOP

Multinational organizations tend to list job openings and information on their own websites. There are few print and electronic clearinghouses that centralize resources and vacancies in this field. However, many universities with international programs have career resource sections that contain links and advice for employment in international organizations. Also, conducting a targeted search in a general job-listing website using the terms "multinational organization" or "international organization" should provide focused results. Applying a similar approach in general search engines such as Google will uncover an array of organizational homepages as well as websites containing lists of multinational organizations that will help broaden your research beyond the sample organizations and resources listed below.

SAMPLE MULTINATIONAL ORGANIZATIONS

Inter-American Development Bank (IDB)
1300 New York Avenue, NW
Washington, DC 20577
Telephone: 202-623-1000
Fax: 202-623-3096
Website: www.iadb.org

The Inter-American Development Bank was established to promote the economic and social development of Latin America and the

Caribbean. IDB, which has forty-seven member countries, is a major source of external public financing for member countries in Latin America. It has field offices in twenty-eight countries. Most applicants for professional positions at IDB have graduate degrees in such fields as economics, engineering, agriculture, administration, or environmental sciences and have at least eight years of relevant work experience. In addition, most positions require fluency in at least two of the four official languages of the bank (English, Spanish, French, and Portuguese). The IBD website provides details for available employment, including junior professional and internship opportunities. Approximately two hundred positions with IBD are filled each year.

International Monetary Fund (IMF)
700 19th Street, NW
Washington, DC 20431
Telephone: 202-623-7422
Fax: 202-623-7333
Website: www.imf.org

The International Monetary Fund, established in 1945, is an intergovernmental organization that maintains funds—available for use by member countries—designed to promote world trade and aid its 185 member states with balance-of-payments problems. Most of the organization's staff members are in Washington, D.C., although the IMF also maintains small offices in Paris and Geneva. The IMF has a professional staff of about eight hundred, two-thirds of whom are economists. The remainder of the professional staff includes accountants, administrators, computer systems officers, language specialists, and lawyers. Details about specific positions with the IMF—including those for experienced economists, support-level positions, and the Research Assistant Program—are available on its website.

Organization of American States (OAS)
17th Street and Constitution Avenue, NW
Washington, DC 20006
Telephone: 202-458-3000
Fax: 202-458-3967
Website: www.oas.org

The Organization of American States concerns itself with hemispheric problems ranging from regional security and the settlement of political disputes to economic, social, educational, scientific, and cultural relations among its thirty-five member states. Members are the United States, Canada, and all independent Latin American and Caribbean countries. The OAS maintains national offices in each of its active member states. The 600-person professional staff of the OAS—135 members of which are stationed in the United States—generally concentrate on fields such as economics, finance, statistics, business, education, science, and culture. Fluency in at least two of the organization's four official languages (Spanish, Portuguese, French, and English) is recommended. Job and consultancy vacancies are posted on the OAS website along with information on its internship program.

Union of International Associations (UIA)
Rue Washingtonstraat 40, B-1050
Brussels, Ixelles/Elsene
Belgium
Telephone: +32-02-640-1808
Fax: +32-02-643-6199
Website: www.uia.org

Founded in 1907 as the Central Office of International Associations, the Union of International Associations was instrumental in establishing the League of Nations. Its mandate focuses on improving research, awareness, and communication regarding "transnational associative networks," which includes both intergovernmental and international nongovernmental organizations. Its yearbook, now in its forty-third edition, catalogues and extensively profiles more than forty thousand of these organizations. This, along with much of the large amount of information compiled and organized by the UIA, is available via the organization's website. UIA membership comprises thirty-five countries, including the United States. The organization conducts annual meetings of its general assembly and maintains a small full-time staff.

United Nations Development Programme (UNDP)
1 United Nations Plaza
New York, NY 10017
Telephone: 212-906-5000
Fax: 212-906-5364
Website: www.undp.org

The United Nations Development Programme (UNDP), funded by voluntary contributions from member nations and nonmember recipient nations, administers and coordinates technical assistance programs in 166 countries. The UNDP seeks to increase economic and social development in developing states, mandated by the United Nations. The seven thousand–member UNDP staff performs a wide variety of duties usually revolving around the design, monitoring, and administration of development projects. Typical requirements include a strong postgraduate academic background with an emphasis on international development, several years of relevant experience in a developing country, fluency in at least two official UN languages, strong commitment to the ideals of the United Nations, and other relevant interpersonal and work skills. Job vacancies within the UNDP, categorized by project area and worldwide location, are posted on its website. Information on the UNDP's Leadership Development Program, Junior Professional Officers Program, and Internship Program is also available.

United Nations Educational, Scientific, and Cultural Organization (UNESCO)
7, place de Fontenoy
75352 Paris 07 SP
France
1, rue Miollis
75732 Paris Cedex 15
France
Telephone: +33-0-1-45-68-10-00
Fax: +33-0-1-45-67-16-90
Website: www.unesco.org

UNESCO is a specialized agency within the United Nations that monitors international developments and assists member states in solving critical issues. The organization's mandate is to build peace among its 192 member countries and in the world through fostering knowledge, social progress, exchange, and mutual understanding among peoples. UNESCO focuses on education, science, and technology, social and human sciences, communication, information and informatics, and culture. The UNESCO headquarters coordinates the organization's 2,500-person staff; the New York liaison office has a more modest staff of 12 to 15. Vacant posts within UNESCO, as well as information regarding internships and young professional and associate expert positions, are posted on its website.

United Nations Information Center (UNIC)
1775 K Street, NW, Suite 400
Washington, DC 20006
Telephone: 202-331-8670
Fax: 202-331-9191
Website: www.unicwash.org

The United Nations Information Center serves as a center of reference for the United Nations. Its goal is to raise awareness of the United Nations and to strengthen internal and external partnerships by enhancing public understanding of the United Nations' substantive impact. The United Nations comprises sixteen different specialized agencies throughout the world, including the UN Development Program (UNDP), the World Health Organization (WHO), and the UN Educational, Scientific, and Cultural Organization (UNESCO). The UNIC website contains multiple resources for job seekers interested in employment at the United Nations, including links to main UN job vacancies pages and information about UN fellowships and internships.

World Bank
1818 H Street, NW
Washington, DC 20433
Telephone: 202-473-1000
Fax: 202-477-6391
Website: www.worldbank.org

The World Bank was established in 1945 as an international development institution with a mandate to reduce global poverty and improve living standards around the world. Funded by membership subscriptions and by borrowing on private capital markets, the World Bank finances foreign economic development projects in developing countries in areas such as agriculture, environmental protection, education, public utilities, telecommunications, water supply, sanitation, and public health. It is made up of two unique development institutions owned by the Bank's 185 member countries—the International Bank for Reconstruction and Development (IBRD) and the International Development Association (IDA). In its hundred-plus country offices and its Washington, D.C., headquarters, the World Bank employs a staff of roughly ten thousand development professionals. The World Bank's website includes a listing of all job and consultancy vacancies, as well as details on its numerous entry programs (Young Professionals Program, Junior Young Professionals Program, and Internship Program).

The World Bank also offers summer employment to a small number of highly qualified graduate students (who have completed one year of graduate studies or have already entered a PhD program) studying economics, finance, human resource development, social sciences, environment, agriculture, private sector development, statistics, and related fields. To qualify for these salaried positions, students must be nationals of a Bank member country and must plan to attend graduate school in the following fall semester.

See the profile of Fayezul Choudhury for more information. Fayezul is the controller and vice president of strategy and resource management at the World Bank.

World Health Organization (WHO)
Avenue Appia 20
CH–1211 Geneva 27
Switzerland
Telephone: +41-22-791-2111
Fax: +41-22-791-3111
Website: www.who.int

The World Health Organization is the directing and coordinating authority for health in the UN system. It works to extend health services to underserved populations of its member countries and to control or eradicate communicable diseases. The WHO also promotes cooperation among governments to solve public health problems. Headquartered in Geneva, Switzerland, with six regional offices and 147 country offices, the WHO has a staff of more than eight thousand professionals. The WHO website offers a listing of international job vacancies, internship information, and various resources to aid those interested in applying to the organization.

SELECTED RESOURCES

Print
Worldwide Government Directory with International Organizations
CQ Staff Directories, 1,815 pages, 2007 (www.cqpress.com)

This sizable publication provides contact information (phone, fax, and e-mail) for the leadership of more than one hundred international organizations, as well as thirty-two thousand elected and appointed officials in 201 countries. Anyone interested in working or communicating with multinational organizations and foreign governments will find the publication useful. The directory is available as a paper volume or as an online resource by subscription. Free limited-time trials are available.

Yearbook of International Organizations
K. G. Saur, 1,740 pages, 2006 (www.uia.org/organizations/pub.php)

Produced under its current title since 1950 (and now in its forty-third edition), this five-volume publication of the Union of International Associations is a comprehensive directory containing profile listings for more than forty thousand intergovernmental and international nongovernmental organizations. These listings, indexed both alphabetically and topically, include the organization's name and acronym in all working languages, complete contact information, executive leadership information, membership, mandate, history, structure, finances, activities, and publications. It also contains an array of statistical data concerning participation, activity levels, issue focus, and budgets.

Web

International Civil Service Commission
http://icsc.un.org/joblinks.asp

While not a position vacancy-listing page itself, this website contains links to many multinational organization recruitment/human resource pages. The UN application form and information on how to apply for UN openings can also be found on the site.

International Organizations Employment Guide U.S. Department of State
www.state.gov/p/io/empl/11076.htm

This website from the U.S. Department of State delivers valuable information on employment opportunities and the requirements needed for professional and senior positions in the United Nations and other international organizations. It is best used for gathering information on the job types available in the international field and on topics such as expected salaries and recruitment procedures. Some information on short-term and long-term positions with the United Nations can also be found.

Northwestern University Library
www.library.northwestern.edu/govinfo/resource/internat/igo.html

The Northwestern library website houses an extensive and updated list of international government organizations. Listed links are not limited to the United Nations or UN affiliates but rather draw from a large variety of fields (economics, education, peace and security, banks, conservation and agriculture, human rights, women and children, and health).

UN Galaxy eStaffing System
https://jobs.un.org

Galaxy is the UN's official recruitment website. It contains a searchable database as well as a list of available vacancies in various occupational groups. In addition, Galaxy contains a link to the UN Peace Operations recruitment website and an extensive list of field and professional jobs.

UN Jobs
http://unjobs.org

UN Jobs lists nearly two thousand positions in approximately sixty organizations located around the world. You can search for jobs by new listings, organizations, duty stations (locations), and upcoming deadlines. Many of the job openings require advanced degrees and several years of experience. Some jobs for recent graduates or those with limited professional experience are available on this site.

PROFILE
Fayezul Choudhury
Controller and Vice President of Strategy and Resource Management, The World Bank

Career Trajectory
> The World Bank, Washington, DC
>> Controller and Vice President of Strategy and Resource Management, 2006–present
>> Vice President and Controller, 2000–6
>> Director of Accounting, 1995–2000
>> Chief, Asset and Budget Accounting, 1993–95
>> Chief, Loan Accounting, 1990–93
>> Chief Accountant, International Finance Corporation, 1987–90
>> Staff member, Organization Planning Department, 1985–87
>
> Price Waterhouse, UK
>> Manager to Managing Consultant, Price Waterhouse, London, UK, 1984–85
>> Managing Consultant, Price Waterhouse, Lagos, Nigeria, 1981–84
>> Managing Consultant, Price Waterhouse, London, UK, 1978–81
>> Public Accounting, Audit Assistant to Manager, Price Waterhouse, London, UK, 1974–78

Academic Background
> MA (Honors), Engineering and Economics, University of Oxford, 1974

My college degree was back in the early '70s when students really didn't think too much about careers. They were too focused on changing the world! I think from the 1980s onward, students became much more focused on careers.

I knew I didn't want to be an engineer, but I didn't really know what I wanted to do. My initial career choice is thus a story of random events. In the summer of 1974, just after college, there was an outpouring of stress relief, mainly involving lots of beer. One evening, a bunch of us were at the pub—it was a lovely summer's evening by the river—and most of my friends were talking about the things they were going to do. It suddenly occurred to me that "Holey moley, I've got to get a job! I'm on a student visa, and I have no idea what I'm going to do with myself."

Are you involved in community service?
Member of the Board of Trustees, World Learning

How do you define your cause?

It's very easy to subscribe to the mission of the World Bank: "to help the world's poorest." I think the important questions are, "Is that what brought you here?" or "Is that what motivates you here?" Or is it just comfortable to say that you work at an organization whose mission is to alleviate poverty rather than saying you work at a place whose mission is to launch bombs?

I'd love to be able to say that I have a passion to help the world's poor and that's the only reason why I'm here. Yet at the moment, it would be dishonest to say that's the case. The reality is, your career starts with yourself. Do you enjoy your work? Do you enjoy your environment? Do you enjoy the people you work with? Often, though not always, the answer to those questions is a function of "Are you effective in your job?"

A lot of being happy in the workplace starts with how well you do what you do. That's not the only criterion, but I think it's a necessary starting point. The purpose of the organization you work for, for some people, is what motivates them or drives them. For other people, it doesn't drive them or motivate them to the same extent, but it does give them a safe anchor. If you take the World Bank as an example, I would say many of its employees are concerned, even have moral outrage, about the extent of poverty in the world. But for the rest, it's just a job. That doesn't mean they're bad people or aren't concerned about poverty . . . but it's just human nature. It's just a job and they enjoy the work. But if they found another job somewhere else that was better . . .

For people who feel very passionately about something, they can forge a career in that area. But I think the majority of people just need to be comfortable with the mission of the organization (and certainly shouldn't be *uncomfortable* with it). You need to balance your passion with self-interest.

The question is, "Where do you derive your satisfaction?" You need to ask yourself that question very, very honestly and searchingly. I think most people derive their satisfaction from being good at what they do and feeling they are valued. A lesser number of people derive their satisfaction from the mission of the organization, from being a participant in the mission. In the end, I hope there's a *very* small number of people who just don't give a damn and will do anything for money [*laughs*].

Self-awareness is so important in so many aspects of life. It pervades. If I looked at contented people, they are typically self-aware. Once you are aware of what motivates you and why, once you know what your capacities are and where your strengths lie, I think then you circle into career opportunities that will be the right fit for you.

What drew you to this cause and your field?

I stumbled into accounting and finance. I didn't particularly have a great interest in this profession before I joined it, but with experience I have come to enjoy it. As for working in the field of development . . . in a nutshell, it is very satisfying to feel that you are contributing—no matter how indirectly—to improving people's lives.

Do you have a mentor? How has he or she affected your life and career?

Mentoring now is a much more structured thing, but the more structured it gets, I find it works less well. What I've always found is that when you work with someone more senior than you and they have confidence in you, then you become the go-to person. It's mutual interest. I certainly found this as I moved up the chain, and now, when I look at subordinates, it's the same thing. You want go-to people, people you know can deliver. I call that "implicit mentoring," I guess. More formal mentoring works less well.

Mentoring becomes effective when you get a chance to see someone close up. And I think that's when you can give much more targeted advice. So the mentoring has to go hand-and-fist with career development and developing someone. I don't think you can really separate the two out.

I have been very fortunate in having a number of people whom I have worked for who have given me opportunities to grow, who have counseled and coached me, and who have been my advocates. I guess you would call that mentoring.

Do you consider yourself a mentor to others?

Yes, I do believe I have mentored a number of people, much along the line I have been mentored.

What is your best advice for developing effective networking skills?

Networking is much more of an American concept. Of course people know people and that's just fine, but it's a more elaborate and systematic kind of networking that happens in the United States. My son is a junior at university and is looking for summer internships. They encourage him to go to the alumni website and see who's working where to identify openings. You would probably not get that in other parts of the world. If someone contacted you and said they went to the same college as you, it would probably not open too many doors. It's a very different cultural context for networking.

I think networking is . . . let me put it this way . . . maybe . . . [*long pause*] . . . I guess networking can be helpful, but it depends on the organization. For getting that foot in the door, maybe it's helpful. For most organizations, getting a foot in the door is the most difficult part. What happens at the World Bank is much more ethnic or national networks than anything. Since I'm a Bangladeshi, I'll get a lot of Bangladeshis writing to me with interest in the Bank, and if they are qualified, I will ask our HR people to see if there are any openings . . . [*pause*]

Maybe I'm just arguing against myself here! The only reason I'm being interviewed for this book is because of a network, which shows the power of it all. I think I've probably gone 180 degrees [*laughs*]. Networking *does* work, I guess. It should just be a little more subtle than the way it's often characterized. Networking is knowing people. It's knowing people and being respectful of how much you ask of them. If you meet someone at a cocktail party and ask for something unreasonable, that's probably not a great idea. But if you know someone reasonably well, then you can maybe take the liberty to ask for a little more time or attention commitment.

This whole notion of networking has to be grounded in your own cultural context. Every culture has its own version of it. Often if you're living and working in America, what's pushed is the American version of it, and that's something that people from many cultures are saying: "I just can't do that. That's not me." They probably have their own version. If you lined up ten different cultural types and said, "Here's the assignment. You're trying to get a job at the UN. How would you go about it?" you'll get ten different answers. They would all be forms of networking, but they'd take on different cultural shades.

What lessons have you learned as your career has evolved?

Nothing irks me more than the person who seeks credit. It's smart to pass the credit to your boss and subordinates.

Anticipating problems and solving problems are talents in short supply, and those who have them get noticed.

The more senior you get, influencing skills and persuading skills become more important.

Any final advice?

You spend more hours in the workplace than anywhere else. Make sure you enjoy it!

PROFILE
Carol Bellamy
President and CEO, World Learning

Career Trajectory
  President and CEO, World Learning, Brattleboro, Vermont, 2005–present
  Executive Director, UN Children's Fund (UNICEF), 1995–2005
  Director, U.S. Peace Corps, 1993–95 *(Carol is the first person to have been*
     both a volunteer for the Peace Corps and its director.)
  Managing Director, Bear Stearns & Co., 1990–93
  Principal, Morgan Stanley, 1986–90
  President, New York City Council, 1978–85
  Senator, New York State, 1973–77
  Associate, Cravath, Swaine & Moore, 1968–71
  Peace Corps Volunteer, Guatemala, 1963–65

Academic Background
  JD, New York University School of Law, 1968
  AB, Psychology, Gettysburg College, 1963
I think too many people get too strict in their majors in college today. They think that if they want to be a lawyer, then they *have* to take political science. . . . No, you don't *have* to take political science; you don't have to take anything. Maybe history would be good; maybe English lit would be good. I think undergraduates in particular ought to get a broad experience in college, including an international experience.

What awards and honors have meant the most to you?

In 2006 I received the highest Japanese government award given to non-Japanese citizens, the Grand Cordon of the Order of the Rising Sun. It was actually presented to me by the emperor. I received the award because of my work at UNICEF, but it was really because of the work of ALL of the people at UNICEF, not just me. But I was very honored, and my Japanese friends tell me this is a very important honor. I appreciate it, as the Japanese are thoughtful people around the issue of sustainable development.

Another acknowledgment that meant a lot to me was being named by *Forbes* magazine in 2004 as one of the 100 Most Powerful Women in the World. I appreciated that because, quite often, *Forbes* lists (and other lists like them) identify people—and these are good people—largely in the private sector or perhaps because of government titles. I am involved in humanitarian work and development work, which are sometimes seen (in my view totally incorrectly) as "soft issues." Sometimes they don't receive the recognition they should. I thought that including somebody representing a humanitarian and development organization on this list of globally powerful women was important.

Are you involved in community service?
American Bar Association, Rule of Law Committee
Advisory board member, Acumen Fund
Board member, Child Rights International

How do you define your cause?
I don't have a single cause or a single mission. Prior to my fifteen years of international work, I largely divided my adult career in the public and private sectors. I was a corporate lawyer and an investment banker, in both roles deeply involved in business transactions. I didn't go to law school thinking I was going to work in the private sector, but lo and behold, my favorite courses were on contracts and corporations. So I spent twelve years in business, but I also spent thirteen years as an elected public official in the city and state of New York.

So I haven't had a single, definable mission, but I'm motivated by several things. I think quality of work is a critical component. One needs to engage in ethical behavior. I think one can have a variety of vocations, but at the same time maintain a balance in life through one's *avocations*. I'm shaped from head to toe by the most important experience in my life, which was being a Peace Corps volunteer. I believe that however one engages in it, some form of community service is the most important thing one can do in one's life. In the long run, it allows you to make a small contribution to better the world out there, and you benefit as much as you contribute.

What drew you to this cause and your field?
When you lose an election, you have to go out and find a job, so that was a motivator [*laughs*]. [Carol ran for mayor of New York City in 1985.] Other than that, I've made choices because they seemed like the right thing to do. One of the things I learned in the Peace Corps is that you hope you can have an impact in whatever you do in some small way, but you also learn that you *can* fail in some things. Yet failure should never be an obstacle. If you take failure to be a learning experience, you can use it to become stronger in what you do going ahead. I say that because it allows a much broader range of choices. You're not motivated by fear and you're willing to try different things . . . I've been willing to try different things, some of which I've done well, some of which I've done less well.

Do you have a mentor? How has he or she affected your life and career?

There weren't a lot of women out there to be my mentors when I was starting my career. There have been several people throughout who have affected me, though no one person in particular. One of my first bosses was something of a mentor to me. When I got elected to office, there was another woman in public office—it was the first time they had women in the state senate—so we had to be supportive of each other.

Also, my mother was a mentor to me, though not as much when I was young. She really became something of a mentor to me later in my life.

Do you consider yourself a mentor to others?

Have I mentored? A little bit. In part in the early days, when there were so few women in politics, you'd make the rounds, encouraging more women to get involved. Actually, one of the contributions I've made is having the opportunity to encourage some of the people who were younger. I've helped support what I've always called "the greenhouse"—an opportunity to help younger women find their wings and soar and do even greater things. I suppose I've given them at least a small foundation to stand on, but then they've risen to greater heights on their own.

I always say that if others aren't trying to hire away the people you have in the institution you're running, then you have the wrong people. And I want to give young people experience and opportunities too! Some of my early bosses did this for me, and then they knew, when I was about to crash and burn, how to grab me back. I think that's a good thing to do: give young people opportunities.

What is your best advice for developing effective networking skills?

Sometimes people go at networking too intensely. They always ask, "How many networks do I have?" To me, networking can be at all different levels. It's not about how many business cards you have, but rather the impact that interacting with others has on you and where you think you can contribute. I believe networks that are two-way streets—ones in which you're contributing as well as taking—are the best kind. Informal networks are generally better than formal networks. It isn't quantity as much as quality . . . I know that sounds pretty trite, but I actually do believe it!

Never burn bridges. This doesn't mean that the relationships you've maintained with people in your life have to be maintained at their most robust level, but even dotted-line connections aren't bad things. Staying in touch isn't a bad thing to do.

What lessons have you learned as your career has evolved?

Be open to experimenting and trying. Don't be afraid to fail. There are a lot of lessons that can come out of not always being successful.

Be serious about what you do; be careful and respect quality and integrity in what you do; but never take yourself too seriously. You want to at least enjoy what you do. It doesn't mean you have to love your job every day—there will always be bad days. But if you don't get up every day and say, "You know, I kind of like doing this," then *don't do it.*

Chapter 12

International Business, Consulting, and Research

Leading up to this final chapter, we have attempted to provide the broadest possible cross section of the jobs and careers available in international education, exchange, and development. We certainly, however, have not covered *all* the possibilities.

International business, consulting, and research are rapidly growing employment sectors with many intriguing opportunities for globally oriented job seekers. You may find that one of these types of careers in international affairs is best suited to your skills and your cause: perhaps as a cross-cultural trainer for a corporation; as a consultant for a USAID for-profit contractor; as a grants officer for a foundation that funds international projects; or as a researcher for a think tank.

All of these positions fall within the realm of international education, exchange, and development. As the private sector continues to expand, as more businesses continue to take their operations international, and as a greater number of consultants with internationally specific skills are needed, the number and kinds of jobs that can be characterized as international will grow. We present this final chapter as an attempt to nick the surface and highlight a few of the possibilities that lie beyond what we have presented in the previous eleven chapters.

There are a multitude of international employment opportunities in the business sector, particularly as more and more multinational corporations become involved in training and development activities that were previously confined to the nonprofit world. As the boundaries between government, business, and the social (nonprofit) sector blur, there is an urgent need for those who can forge creative partnerships among these sectors.

In all aspects of international affairs, there is a much greater use of consultants than ever. To retain their downsized, lean, and mean structure, organizations often outsource tasks that in the past were handled by their own employees. Opportunities to join consulting firms—large and small—for work on internationally oriented projects increase by the day. One benefit to consulting is that you can often work on various topics in a variety of settings, not necessarily being relegated to just one office or a single long-term project.

As a group, think tanks (the term commonly used to describe public policy research institutes) are not inherently international in scope. Many of these organizations, though, either include international projects in their repertoire or are completely internationally focused. For example, the Brookings Institution, as a general policy research organization, may simultaneously focus on the future of the economy of the Great Lakes region and perceptions of U.S. foreign policy in East Asia. International projects are a large part of what Brookings does, but its focus also encompasses much more. The Henry L. Stimson Center, however, is focused exclusively on international peace and security. In addition, not all of these think tanks are on the east or west coast. The Stanley Foundation, headquartered in Muscatine, Iowa, sponsors significant international research studies and symposiums. If a more academic, analytical, and research-oriented approach to the fields of international education, exchange, and development sounds appealing to you, consider looking into the ever-expanding (both in size and influence) realm of think tanks.

Similar to think tanks, foundations are not necessarily international and may be focused on any number of topics. From social and religious issues to regional economic concerns, a foundation may fund any number of domestically oriented projects, depending on the interests and concerns of the family or group that runs it. However, just as the number of nonprofit organizations, businesses, and consulting firms focused on international issues is increasing, so too is the number of foundations interested in funding internationally focused projects. The Foundation Center maintains a large directory of these organizations that may provide employment opportunities or support research and program initiatives that you wish to pursue abroad.

SAMPLE BUSINESS ORGANIZATIONS

Business Council for International Understanding (BCIU)
1212 Avenue of the Americas, 10th Floor
New York, NY 10036
Telephone: 212-490-0460
Fax: 212-697-8526
Website: www.bciu.org

The Business Council for International Understanding, although a nonprofit, comprises internationally oriented companies. BCIU works to expand international business and commerce by promoting dialogue and cooperation between the business and government communities, with special attention on commercial diplomacy. BCIU operates in New York; Washington, D.C.; Houston; London; and several other major cities.

Business for Diplomatic Action (BDA)
555 Market Street, Suite 600
San Francisco, CA 94105
Phone: 415-732-3620
Fax: 415-732-3636
Website: www.businessfordiplomaticaction.org

Founded by advertising executive Keith Reinhard, Business for Diplomatic Action works to enlist the business community in actions to improve the standing of the United States in the world. BDA is committed to involving U.S. corporations in public diplomacy activities and sensitizing Americans to, and then mobilizing them in a solution for, rising anti-Americanism around the world.

National Foreign Trade Council (NFTC)
1625 K Street, NW, Suite 200
Washington, DC 20006
Telephone: 202-887-0278
Fax: 202-452-8160
2 West 45th Street, Suite 1602
New York, NY 10036
Telephone: 212-399-7128
Fax: 212-399-7144
Website: www.nftc.org

The National Foreign Trade Council is an advocacy and public policy organization that supports an open world trade system and "a rules-based world economy." NFTC and its affiliates serve more than three hundred member companies.

Organization for International Investment (OFII)
1225 19th Street, NW, Suite 501
Washington, DC 20036
Telephone: 202-659-1903
Fax: 202-659-2293
Website: www.ofii.org

The Organization for International Investment is a professional business association that represents U.S. subsidiaries of companies headquartered abroad through advocacy, lobbying, and networking services. OFII member companies range from medium-sized enterprises to some of the largest firms in the United States.

U.S. Chamber of Commerce
1615 H Street, NW
Washington, DC 20062
Telephone: 202-659-6000
Fax: 202-463-5836
Website: www.uschamber.org

The U.S. Chamber of Commerce is a business advocacy association working for the rights of businesses and the maintenance of free enterprise. It represents more than three million businesses, as well as thousands of local chambers of commerce and more than one hundred American Chambers of Commerce in ninety-one countries.

U.S. Council on International Business (USCIB)
1212 Avenue of the Americas
New York, NY 10036
Telephone: 212-354-4480
Fax: 212-391-6568
Website: www.uscib.org

The U.S. Council for International Business works to advance the international interests of American businesses while contributing to economic growth, human welfare, and the protection of the environment. USCIB is the American partner of the International Chamber of Commerce (ICC), the Business and Industry Advisory Committee (BIAC) of the Organization for Economic Co-operation and Development (OECD), and the International Organization of Employers (IOE).

SELECTED BUSINESS RESOURCES

Print

Careers in International Business
Ed Halloran
Impact Publications, 192 pages, 2003 (www.impactpublications.com)

Careers in International Business focuses on methods to help young professionals succeed as they seek and begin employment in the sectors of international finance, marketing, management, logistics, and sales. The book includes advice on researching international business organizations and corporations, preparing for and successfully handling interviews, and conducting business in a variety of foreign cultures.

Directory of American Firms Operating in Foreign Countries
Uniworld Business Publications, Inc., 6,278 pages, 2007
(www.uniworldbp.com)

The nineteenth edition of the *Directory of American Firms Operating in Foreign Countries* contains information on approximately four thousand American multinational firms with more than sixty-three thousand branches, subsidiaries, and affiliates in 191 countries.

Directory of Foreign Firms Operating in the United States
Uniworld Business Publications, 1,709 pages, 2006
(www.uniworldbp.com)

The thirteenth edition of the *Directory of Foreign Firms Operating in the United States* contains more than thirteen thousand business contact records including firms from eighty-six countries.

Principal International Businesses: The World Marketing Directory
Dun & Bradstreet, 3,385 pages, 2005 (www.dnb.com)

The 2005–6 edition of *Principal International Businesses* provides information on approximately fifty thousand companies in 133 countries worldwide. Updated annually, the guide is organized alphabetically, geographically by country, and by type of business.

Web

The Riley Guide
www.rileyguide.com/intlbus.html, www.rileyguide.com/employer.html

The Riley Guide is a free employment and job resources website. The above subpages, focusing on "International Business Resources" and

"Business and Employer Research," contain links to business directories, industry profiles, and other resources you will find useful when examining the field of international business.

SAMPLE CONSULTING ORGANIZATIONS

Large international consulting firms that provide many client services include:

Accenture
New York City Office
1345 Avenue of the Americas
New York, NY 10105
Telephone: 917-452-4400
Fax: 917-527-9915
Website: www.accenture.com

Accenture is an international management consulting, technology services, and outsourcing company working in many industries. The firm has more than 158,000 employees in approximately 150 cities in forty-nine countries.

Bearing Point
New York City Office
3 World Financial Center, 14th Floor
New York, NY 10281
Telephone: 212-896-1800
Website: www.bearingpoint.com

Bearing Point is an international management and technology consulting company working in a variety of industries. Bearing Point is not quite the behemoth that Accenture is, with "only" seventeen thousand employees in sixty countries.

Booz Allen Hamilton
Worldwide Headquarters
8283 Greensboro Drive
McLean, VA 22102
Telephone: 703-902-5000
Website: www.boozallen.com

Booz Allen Hamilton is an international strategy and technology consulting firm working with corporations, governments, and other public agencies. The firm employs more than nineteen thousand people on six continents.

Chemonics International
1717 H Street, NW
Washington, DC 20006
Telephone: 202-955-3300
Fax: 202-955-3400
Website: www.chemonics.com

Chemonics International is an international consulting firm that promotes economic growth and higher living standards in developing countries. Chemonics has more than two thousand employees working on development projects in more than 135 countries.

Deloitte and Touche
New York City Office (one of three)
Two World Financial Center
225 Liberty Street
New York, NY 10281
Telephone: 212-436-2000
Fax: 212-436-5000
Website: www.deloitte.com

Deloitte and Touche, as a part of the Swiss firm Deloitte Touche Tohmatsu, is a worldwide organization of member companies providing audit, tax, consulting, and financial advisory services. Deloitte has more than 150,000 employees located in nearly 140 countries.

Smaller consulting firms dealing more specifically with issues of international education, exchange, and development include:

Abt Associates, Inc.
Economic development and health care consulting; seven corporate offices in the United States.
www.abtassociates.com

Ard, Inc.
Economic development, agriculture, democracy consulting; based in Burlington, Vermont.
www.ardinc.com

Carana Corporation
Economic development and privatization consulting; based in Arlington, Virginia.
www.carana.com

Creative Associates International
Education and democracy, and governance consulting and project development; based in Washington, D.C.
www.caii.com

DAI
Social and economic development consulting; based in Bethesda, Maryland.
www.dai.com

DevTech
Democracy, economic development, women's rights, and education consulting; based in Arlington, Virginia.
www.devtechsys.com

DPK Consulting
Economic development and democracy consulting; based in San Francisco.
www.dpkconsulting.com

Emerging Markets Group
Economic and sustainable development consulting; U.S. office in Arlington, Virginia.
www.emergingmarketsgroup.com

John Snow International (JSI)
International health care consulting; based in Boston.
www.jsi.com

Management Systems, Inc.
Democracy and economic development and evaluation consulting; based in Washington, D.C.
www.msi-inc.com

SELECTED CONSULTING RESOURCES

Print
Consultants and Consulting Organizations Directory
Thomson Gale, 2008 (www.galegroup.com)

The thirty-first edition of this directory contains more than twenty-five thousand firms and individuals listed in subject sections arranged to encompass fourteen general fields of consulting activity.

Web

Top-consultant.com
www.top-consultant.com

This website allows you to search a database of consulting firms by name, industry, sector, location, or a combination. A long list of consulting firm "advertisements," while tedious to scroll through, provides an overview of some of the larger consulting firms and the work that is available with them.

Think Tanks and Foundations

Brookings Institution
1775 Massachusetts Avenue, NW
Washington, DC 20036
Telephone: 202-797-6000
Fax: 202-797-6004
Website: www.brookings.edu

The Brookings Institution is a nonprofit research organization providing recommendations and analysis on various public policy and international issues.

Carnegie Council for Ethics in International Affairs
Merrill House
170 East 64th Street
New York, NY 10065
Telephone: 212-838-4120
Fax: 212-752-2432
Website: www.cceia.org

The Carnegie Council, as its name suggests, promotes ethics in international affairs, including ethical leadership on issues of war, peace, religion in politics, and global social justice.

Center for Strategic and International Studies (CSIS)
1800 K Street, NW
Washington DC 20006
Telephone: 202-887-0200
Fax: 202-775-3199
Website: www.csis.org

The Center for Strategic and International Studies, a nonprofit research organization, provides insight on and policy recommendations for issues of global security and economic issues.

Council on Foreign Relations
See chapter 6 in this volume.

Foreign Policy Research Institute (FPRI)
1528 Walnut Street, Suite 610
Philadelphia, PA 19102
Telephone: 215-732-3774
Fax: 215-732-4401
Website: www.fpri.org

The Foreign Policy Research Institute conducts research on pressing international issues, long-term historical and cultural questions, and policies relevant to U.S. national interests.

The Foundation Center
Headquarters
79 5th Avenue/16th Street
New York, NY 10003
Telephone: 212-620-4230
Fax: 212-807-3677
Website: www.fdncenter.org

The Foundation Center maintains a large database of U.S. foundations and grant makers and the grants they award. The center provides research, education, and training programs regarding many topics related to philanthropy. In addition to its New York headquarters, the center has field offices and research centers in Atlanta, Cleveland, San Francisco, and Washington, D.C. Its three major publications are listed below.

The Henry L. Stimson Center
1111 19th Street, NW, 12th Floor
Washington, DC 20036
Telephone: 202-223-5956
Fax: 202-238-9604
Website: www.stimson.org

The Stimson Center is a nonprofit research institution devoted to strengthening international peace and security institutions, building regional security, and reducing the threat posed by weapons of mass destruction.

The Stanley Foundation
209 Iowa Avenue
Muscatine, IA 52761
Telephone: 563-264-1500
Fax: 563-264-0864
Website: www.stanleyfoundation.org

The Stanley Foundation is a nonpartisan nonprofit focused on researching issues of peace and security, as well as advocating principled multilateralism.

U.S. Institute of Peace (USIP)
See chapter 9 in this volume.

Woodrow Wilson International Center for Scholars
Ronald Reagan Building and International Trade Center
One Woodrow Wilson Plaza
1300 Pennsylvania Avenue, NW
Washington, DC 20004
Telephone: 202-691-4000
Website: www.wilsoncenter.org

Established by Congress as a memorial to the former president, the Wilson Center is a nonpartisan research organization working to provide sound policy analysis on public policy and international issues while bridging the gap between scholars and public officials.

SELECTED THINK TANK AND FOUNDATION RESOURCES

Print

The Foundation Directory
The Foundation Center, 2,734 pages, 2007 (http://foundationcenter.org)

Part 1 of this two-volume set gives current data on each foundation that holds assets of at least $2 million or distributes more than $100,000 in grants annually. It also provides information about recent, sizeable grants awarded by each foundation, offering insights into the priorities of particular foundations. Part 2 features midsized foundations with programs that award grants ranging from $50,000 to $200,000 annually. Subscriptions to a searchable online database of this publication's information are available on the Foundation Center's website, http://foundationcenter.org.

Foundation Grants to Individuals
The Foundation Center, 987 pages, 2006 (http://foundationcenter.org)

This publication lists all organizations that award grants to individuals in fields ranging from education and the arts to medicine. Listings include detailed information on contact names, eligibility requirements, and the specifics of the application process for certain grants.

Guide to Funding for International and Foreign Programs
The Foundation Center, 629 pages, 2006 (http://foundationcenter.org)

Similar to *The Foundation Directory,* this publication is one in a series of smaller, subject-specific guides produced by the Foundation Center. These guides are updated annually with new contact and grant information.

World Directory of Think Tanks
NIRA, 493 pages, 2005 (www.nira.go.jp)

Published by the Tokyo-based National Institute of Research Advancement (NIRA), this fifth edition of the *World Directory of Think Tanks* provides detailed information on more than three hundred research institutions in seventy-five countries. It is updated every three years.

Web

World Press
www.worldpress.org

This world news website contains an extensive, alphabetically arranged list (complete with hyperlinks) of international think tanks and research organizations.

PROFILE

Lobna "Luby" Ismail
Founder, President, and Senior Trainer, Connecting Cultures, LLC

Career Trajectory

Founder, President, and Senior Trainer, Connecting Cultures, LLC, Silver Spring, Maryland, 1990–present

Intercultural Program Specialist, American University, Washington, D.C., 1988–90

Program Director, Fulbright Grant Program, Washington, D.C., 1988

Academic Background

MA, Intercultural Relations (Specialization in Intercultural Training and International Student Exchange), Lesley College, 1988

BA, International Service (Specialization in Arabic and Cross-Cultural Communication), American University, 1984

What awards and honors have meant the most to you?

The first honor that comes to mind is the Parent of the Year award from the Multiple Sclerosis Society that I received in 1999. That's probably not what you want to hear [*laughs*] . . . but that one means a lot to me because, truthfully, the whole reason I started my own business [Connecting Cultures] is that I wanted to have a balance between my babies and my business, which are really my two passions. Children and family, but also increasing understanding across cultures.

Winning Parent of the Year from the MS Society meant a lot to me because I do have a disability, multiple sclerosis. But it also meant something to me because of my attempt to bridge my desire for a career and my desire to be a mother. When I was working at American University as an intercultural specialist, I loved the work. It was a great position, but it was also anywhere from forty to sixty hours plus a week. When you're younger, you just think about your career. But I have to say, I never thought about my career *and* my desires for a family when I was young. I urge young professionals to think not just about their immediate career goals but also think about their lives. You may get married, you may have children. . . . What's important to you? What do you anticipate? For me, I knew I hoped to have children one day, which I did. I always tell my children I'm so blessed I had them because otherwise, I don't think I would have had the courage to start my own business.

In addition, I have received a number of awards that have come from the U.S. Department of Justice, from law enforcement, from the U.S. military—from people I never thought in my entire life I would be talking to about culture and why understanding culture is important. That's what's so exciting about the field today: people are talking about culture. It's no longer considered something that's touchy-feely. It's seen as imperative, particularly in a post–September 11 United States and world.

Are you involved in community service?

One of the things that has really meant a lot to me is a program I started for preschool kids called Don't Laugh at Me. The idea came to me out of a song sung by Peter Yarrow that goes, "Don't laugh at me, I'm short, I'm tall, I'm fat, I'm thin, don't laugh at me." We have the kids take on a role and ask themselves, "How would I respond to someone who is making fun of me based on who I am?" It's so important to work with children because I find that, if we can start early, then perhaps we don't have as much work to do when they grow up. Children are so open, so resonant—I love that.

Something really small but that has also been really important to me is getting adults and children to know that Africa is a *continent,* not a country. Just recently, on NPR, they referred to "China, India, and *Africa.*" Ugh, I cannot stand that! I try to illustrate the massiveness of the continent. Africa is composed of fifty-two countries.

I've always volunteered to be engaged in cultural arts, trying to expand the perception of what culture is. Many Americans will say, "Oh but I don't really have a culture." I'll say, "Of course you do! There *is* an American culture! Let's look at that."

I was selected as a Peace Fellow in the Seeds of Peace Initiative, which brings together Israeli and Palestinian teenagers. They had selected two Arab-Americans and two American Jews from the D.C. area to participate as part of the dialogue. That was a tremendous experience for me to see the teenagers at the camp in Maine. Then we went to Jordan, Palestine, and Bosnia. It was a wonderful program that I carry with me until now.

Going to Saudi Arabia on a Malone Fellowship (offered by the National Council on U.S.–Arab Relations) was a chance for them to see Americans, but also for us to see Saudis. To learn from them, to exchange what we're doing, to show the human face. . . . And also for me, as a Muslim, so many times Americans and Muslims are separated. So for *Americans* to see an American Muslim, and also for people in countries like Saudi Arabia to see American Muslims, has been really important to me.

How do you define your cause?

Because my experience at age sixteen living outside of the United States so transformed me, I think that exchange programs and opportunities to live, visit, work, and study in a culture outside of one's own should be a requirement for life. I'm so passionate about that. If we can get behind the labels, then no longer is it "Muslim" or "American" or "Arab" or "Jew." It's Susan or Mahommed or Mehta or Ayesha or John. You see the person and the humanness and the connections.

One of the things my company has been doing is training Arab and Muslim teenagers to come to the United States on the YES Program (sponsored by the U.S. State Department) to live for one year and study at an American high school. I just recently met some of the students—when they first arrive, we do a whole day of training on American culture, studying in America, and making friends with Americans. To see them talk about how things are going for them and their observations and living with a family, and of course their enthusiasm about being here and how they'd been engaged and how it's different . . . it was very insightful to hear about another experience. I just spoke to an Afghan student who talked about the difference between interacting with girls here compared to Afghanistan and how the American students are reacting to him. I really love working with young people. In the last few years, I've been having second sessions with the students participating in the U.S. Department of State programs I've been working with, and also with American students who are going over to Arab and Muslim countries. I hope we can do more of that in the future.

What drew you to this cause and your field?

It's who I am. I grew up in a Christian community with few other Muslims, and I was essentially born connecting cultures. Being the first child of parents who came from Egypt, I was their introduction to American culture. I would say, "I want to go to a pep rally," and they would say, "What's a pep rally?" or "Why are these boys calling you?" or "What's a prom?"

And then with my friends, it was the other end of the spectrum. They would ask, "Why can't you eat the pepperoni on the pizza?" or "Why aren't you eating right now?' (of course it was during the month of Ramadan) or "Why won't your parents let you date?" I was raised connecting across cultures. I was a brown person at a time when desegregation had just begun and there was a real attempt at integration. I remember people saying that I wasn't clearly black or white—what was I? I said, "Well, I'm an Egyptian." So I've always been in a place of helping people understand differences in culture and those things outside of the "norm," whatever that is.

Do you have a mentor? How has he or she affected your life and career?

Gary Weaver at American University has been a mentor. He is the reason I really came to know about the field of cross-cultural training. Sitting in his class when I was just nineteen years old, this science of culture that I never knew, I was so fascinated and turned on to it. When I graduated and was really trying to think, "Well, what am I going to do?" I'll never forget when Gary said to me, "Just get out there. You really need to just get out there and start doing it."

I have also found mentors in women who are working independently, who have their own businesses. They have provided support, asking questions like "How are you managing?" Looking at women in business has been very, very important to me. I have always gravitated particularly to females because I'm always inspired by women's stories. We always get "his-story" but we rarely get "her-story," so I really value that. And there are so many talented women in the fields of intercultural studies and cross-cultural communications.

My biggest supporter, though, has been my husband. He has been a mentor, and I would not have been able to have my business if it wasn't for him. He believed in me and my vision, supported my decision to resign from my position at American University and have the guts to say, "Okay, let's see what I can do." He has been my counselor, adviser, mentor, and cofacilitator. It's really important to have someone you can trust who is willing to tell you, when needed, "You know what? I don't think this is the best idea."

Do you consider yourself a mentor to others?

I've always tried to let younger people know my experiences in the field: what's great about it, what's tough about it, and where you can get training and experience in intercultural communication and training, like the Portland Summer Institute. One of the things I've mentored people to do is, if they really know that they want to do cross-cultural communication and training, I recommended that a few people attend Georgetown University's nine-month training, design, and development institute. It is excellent—you really learn the science behind training, and you can tailor it to cross-cultural communication. It's very important to have a background in public speaking and training in general.

Particularly after September 11, I think there needs to be more Muslim Americans who are equipped to provide cross-cultural training. Through the Justice Department we have proposed to not only go to deliver the training to law enforcement personnel, but we would also do a "training of trainers." We would identify some Muslim Americans in the community in which we were presenting and say, "Let's train you now so you will be able to deliver the same training in your community." These are baby steps but so essential. So many young Muslim Americans don't know it can be a career. But I love it. What's the number one requirement? Passion. If you have the passion for it, then you will find a way to make it possible.

What is your best advice for developing effective networking skills?

It is really so essential to talk to everyone and anyone. People often ask me how I expanded my business. I have no marketing strategy, I'm not out there pounding the pavement. It has all been word of mouth. At the beginning, working out of my home was a detriment in this regard. I would only be "out there" when I was working on a job. I'd come back to my home office, and then I wasn't networking. Then I applied and was selected for a protégé program with Women of Washington. It was great for me because it got me out and connected with powerful, interesting women. It was a deliberate way for me to socialize. Also, I occasionally go to breakfast at my local chamber of commerce or to other lunch events at small businesses in my community.

Another great way to network is to apply to speak at conferences. I have done training sessions at conferences, and those were great networking opportunities because conferences bring people from all over the country and sometimes the world. What happens is you get this one-hour window to entice them with what you have to say and who you are. Then after you present, many people come up and say, "That was great. Can I get your card? Here's my card. We would love to have you come to our area of the country." Speaking at conferences was a great thing for networking. And conference organizers are always looking for speakers and presenters. They usually don't pay, but the conferences are so valuable as networking opportunities.

What are some lessons you have learned as your career has evolved?

Passion, passion, passion for what you do is so important. And once you've found a field that matches your passion, do your best to stay in it. I know it can be so hard to begin in a field, and it can be even harder to stay in. In the early years, I would look at the international job vacancies because I was never quite sure of the status of my business. It was either flood or famine; it was either lots of work or no work. If it wasn't for my husband and his faith in me—and honestly having someone who had a secure income to carry us through—I don't know how things would have worked out. But there came a time when I stopped looking at the Sunday classifieds, and that was a big moment for me. I had come to trust my business and my skills and myself. Still it's not easy sometimes. For example, this month, I have *no* business. I won't take in any money. Part of this is my choice due to my family obligations, but part of it is just how the consulting and training business works.

It's important for people to know this, to know that it is never simple, no matter how experienced you become.

Don't underestimate volunteering. Do an internship. These can be great opportunities for you. The organization gets a chance to see you, find out how valuable you are and how quickly you can make things happen. Suddenly they might be thinking, "You know what? Next month a position *is* going to open up. Would you be interested?" On top of that, one of the best things I ever did when I was young was informational interviews. When I would set these up, people would immediately say, "Oh, we don't have any work here." Then I would say, "Well, I would really just love to know more about you and the work that you do as I explore the field." People usually respond positively to this.

When you go down one career path and you find it's not working out, that's okay. That's how you're evolving. I started off doing international development work, and I hated it. It wasn't me. Sometimes you figure out what you want to do by learning from the things you've done that you *didn't* want to do.

Conclusion
It's Not a Small World after All

Everyone has a story that proves how small our world has become. Sherry once ran into a former colleague she worked with in Washington, D.C., and hadn't seen in years in a Moscow department store. Mark bumped into a classmate whom he hadn't seen for years from his university located in South Bend, Indiana, on the steps of Sacre-Coeur in Paris. When a chance encounter like this occurs, when we see someone who lives close to home in a place so far away, we all have a tendency to exclaim, "What a small world!"

Yet, these chance encounters aside, the reality is that it's *not* a small world after all. Rather, the world of the individual has simply grown enormously. Each of us is coping with so much more information today than ever before. Most of us encounter far more people and places than our grandparents ever dreamed about. When we are transported by the Internet, television, or cell phone to other countries and continents, we are not any closer to these places than we were before. Instead, the size of our individual world, measured by the amount of information and experiences we have access to, has grown exponentially.

The consequence of this for your job search and career development is that there are more roads than ever before that you can take. There is so much more information available to help you learn about those avenues. One of the realizations we came to during our collaboration on this book is just how huge the world of the job seeker has become, how much information is out there for you to sift through and evaluate. While editing the lists of resources contained in part II, we found ourselves amazed by the sheer volume of it all. Career websites and books, job boards and search engines, long lists of organizations, more acronyms than you could ever care to decipher—the amount of information was daunting. And we are the first to admit that the information contained in this book is only "selected"! It was staggering to realize that there is so much more beyond what we had already compiled.

The Internet not only has transformed the way a job search is performed, but it also plays host to more information about jobs and careers than any one person can possibly process. When Sherry wrote her first book on careers in 1998, using the Internet for career research was almost an afterthought. Now it is a primary tool for a job search. Even in the last several years, the job search capabilities on the Internet have been further transformed and expanded—the recent emergence of dynamic networking websites is a good example of this ongoing transformation. The major challenge then becomes, once you have logged on (or opened this book, for that matter), where do you begin? With so much information out there, how do you know what to use, what sources to trust? How do you deal with "the overwhelm"?

We wanted to give you simple answers to these twenty-first-century questions. We hoped we could conclude with a nugget of advice that would allow each and every reader to easily transcend the overwhelm and find that one career resource that will lead to his or her dream job. We found this to be an impossible task. We certainly encourage you, as we have throughout, to begin where your interests lie. Locate your cause, find what drives you, then seek out the resources listed in part II that match. Yet even this advice, we realize, is complicated. What if you are like Mark and still unsure of where your cause lies? How do you find the right resource when you are not even sure what you are looking for? While we could not come up with a single solution for these questions, we do offer some simple suggestions.

The first is acceptance. Accept that, in our information-saturated society, overwhelm is a permanent condition. Whether it is in our job searches or our actual jobs, we will forever be dealing with too much information, too many demands, and too little time. Whatever you cross off your to-do list will always be replaced with an even longer list of things yet to accomplish. By coming to terms with this fact, rather than trying to deny it or change it, you will find that you are better equipped to adapt to information overload.

Second, be patient. Especially if you are still in the midst of honing your interests and discovering your cause, give yourself time to locate the organizations and opportunities that are right for you. This may mean allowing yourself plenty of time to page through part II, as well as consider and research the many resources there. But more often than not, it will also require you to have multiple experiences, whether they be short-term volunteer projects, internships, or full-time jobs. In the end, as Luby Ismail points out in her profile, the trial, and sometimes error, of experience is often the only way we can uncover what we are truly meant to do.

And finally, take comfort in the fact that everyone else is on overwhelm too. You're not the only one whose world has grown. Others are bombarded by information and requests as well. Everyone copes with that feeling that if I can *just* get this one big project done, then everything will be okay.

So what can we do when we feel overwhelmed? We can step back from our work and our career deliberations. We can take a walk or talk to a friend. Maybe grab a beer or watch a movie. We can work out or play with a pet. We can decompress and unwind in some way and, when we feel energized again, tackle things with renewed vigor. There is no escape from the overwhelm; there are only strategies to deal with it. And sometimes the best way to deal with the stresses of your job search and career development is to just not think about them at all for awhile.

Another realization we came to during our collaboration is that writing a book is a lot like building a career. Both are continuous journeys. As we discussed in chapter 4, building your career does not end when you land that first dream job. In the same way, our roles as authors were not over when we submitted the final draft of the manuscript. Already we were considering ways to share the substance of the book—identifying distribution sources with our publisher, serving as panelists for sessions on careers at professional association meetings, and elaborating on subjects in jointly authored articles.

We have set in motion an ongoing process that has engaged us, helped us distill lessons learned, and clarified our thoughts on a wide range of topics. Just as rewarding careers are avenues of constant learning and growth, how much we learned as the book developed—from our research and from each other—amazed us. We knew we worked well together, but we were pleasantly surprised at the ease of our cooperation. We quickly agreed on tasks that needed to be done and divided them between us with little discussion. Again, this is parallel to building a career. It is not a process that can be forced but grows naturally from working with people you like and respect and embracing a cause that is meaningful.

In one of the quotations we share at the beginning of the book, Albert Schweitzer predicts that "the only ones among you who will be really happy are those who will have sought and found how to serve." As we examined our own experiences and those of the professionals we profiled, it became clear that tremendous benefits rebound to us when we help others. Sherry remembers hearing the revered management guru Peter Drucker speak at a conference in the early 1990s. In a presentation focusing on nonprofit leadership, Drucker pointed out that volunteers benefit as much from performing the services they render as do the recipients of those services. He reminded his audience that once their basic needs are met, human beings gain great satisfaction from being of service—from making a difference. Thinking of your career as the way you will be of service to those around you is the best advice we can offer.

In the end we must admit that our take on careers in the fields of international education, exchange, and development are but two in a sea of many. The resources presented are only selected—it was not our intention to provide a comprehensive list of every conceivable organization or reference that could have relevance for you. Rather, our goal was to provide a service, to *be* of service to you as you plan your career. We certainly hope that our work will act as a compass to help you map a professionally and personally rewarding career path. We wish you all the best on your continuous journey.

Index

239